W0007711

Studies in Military and Strategic History
Series Standing Order ISBN 0-333-71046-0
(outside North America only)

You can receive future titles in this series as they are published by placing a standing order. Please
contact your bookseller or, in case of difficulty, write to us at the address below with your name and
address, the title of the series and the ISBN quoted above.

Customer Services Department, Macmillan Distribution Ltd, Houndmills, Basingstoke, Hampshire
RG21 6XS, England

Studies in Military and Strategic History

General Editor: **Michael Dockrill**, Professor of Diplomatic History, King's College London

Published titles include:

Anglo-French Relations 1898–1998
From Fashoda to Jospin

Edited by

Philippe Chassaigne
Professor
Université Michel de Montaigne

Michael Dockrill
Professor of Diplomatic History
King's College, London

First published 2002 by
PALGRAVE
Houndmills, Basingstoke, Hampshire RG21 6XS and
175 Fifth Avenue, New York, N. Y. 10010
Companies and representatives throughout the world

PALGRAVE is the new global academic imprint of
St. Martin's Press LLC Scholarly and Reference Division and
Palgrave Publishers Ltd (formerly Macmillan Press Ltd).

ISBN 0-333-91261-6 hardback

A catalogue record for this book is available from the British Library.

Library of Congress Cataloging-in-Publication Data

Anglo-French relations 1898–1998: from Fashoda to Jospin / edited by Philippe Chassaigne, Michael Dockrill.

    p. cm. — (Studies in military and strategic history)
    Includes bibliographical references and index.
    ISBN 0-333-91261-6
    1. Great Britain—Foreign relations—France. 2. Great Britain—Foreign relations—20th century. 3. France—Foreign relations—Great Britain. 4. France—Foreign relations—20th century. I. Chassaigne, Philippe. II. Dockrill, M. L. (Michael L.) III. Studies in military and strategic history (New York, N. Y.)

DA47.1. A68 2002
327.41044′09′04—dc21

          2001036340

10 9 8 7 6 5 4 3 2 1
11 10 09 08 07 06 05 04 03 02

Printed and bound in Great Britain by
Antony Rowe Ltd, Chippenham, Wiltshire

Contents

List of Figures

List of Tables

Preface

Organizing a Conference is quite a difficult task, yet sooner or later every academic is bound to have to face it. It is then both a duty and a pleasure for me to acknowledge my debts to the following persons and institutions: the Maison des Sciences de l'Homme d'Aquitaine and Professor Jean Dumas, then its Director, for invaluable logistic support right from the start. The Centre d'Etudes urbaines (CESURB) of the University of Bordeaux, and its Director, Professor Josette Pontet; the Pôle européen of the University of Bordeaux and its Director, Professor Joseph Ritz; the British Consulate General, James Rawlinson; the Mollat Bookshop; the French Department of Foreign Affairs and the Conseil général de la Région Aquitaine, for their generous financial support. Sir Christopher Mallaby, formerly HM's Ambassador in Paris, for giving this Conference a touch of international class. Jean-Pierre Dormois and Peter Cain for helping me to recruit the 'Anglos'. Professor Anne-Marie Cocula, then Vice-Chancellor of the University, Professors Marc Agostino, Hubert Bonin and Bernard Lachaise who chaired the sessions. And, last but not least, Professor Michael Dockrill, a wizard at international diplomatic history, without whom the publication of this collection of papers would not have been possible.

PHILIPPE CHASSAIGNE

Acknowledgements

Unpublished Crown copyright material at the Public Record Office is reproduced by permission of the Director of the Public Record Office. The Master, Fellows and Scholars of Churchill College, Cambridge, have given us permission to quote from the papers of Sir Eric Phipps. Extracts from the Neville Chamberlain papers at the University Library, Birmingham, are reproduced with the permission of the University of Birmingham. The Bodleian Library, Oxford, and Viscountess Simon have given us permission to quote from the papers of Sir John Simon in the Bodleian Library. We are grateful to the Trustees of the National Maritime Museum for permission to quote from the Chatfield papers, and the Chef du Service Historique de l'Armée de Terre for permission to cite and quote from documents in the Archives de l'Armée de Terre, Vincennes. We would also like to thank the Directors of the Bank of England for allowing us access to the Bank of England archives and to the Ministères des Finances, Paris, for permission to quote from their archives. We apologize if we have unwittingly infringed any other copyrights.

PC and MLD

Notes on the Contributors

Elisa Boccaletti gained her first degree con Laurea at the University of Genoa; she was awarded a Master's degree in Economics from Bocconi University, Milan, and a Master's degree in Economic and Social History from the University of Oxford. She is currently Research Officer on the Leverhulme Project on Entrepreneurship in Britain and France.

Robert Boyce teaches international history at the London School of Economics and Political Science. He is the author or editor of *British Capitalism at the Crossroads, 1919–1932. A Study in Politics, Economics, and International Relations* (1987); *Paths to War. New Essays on the Origins of the Second World War* (1989); *French Foreign and Defence Policy, 1918–1940. The Decline and Fall of a Great Power* (1998); *The Communications Revolution at Work. Studies on the British and Canadian Experience*, School of Policy Papers (1998) and *The Great Crisis, 1928–1933. Watershed of the Contemporary World* (forthcoming).

Nigel Brailey has been Lecturer in History, Asian and International, at the University of Bristol since 1969, and was Visiting Professor of International History and Politics at the University of Niigata, Japan, in 1994–95. His publications include *Thailand and the Fall of Singapore* (1986) and *Two Views of Siam on the Eve of the Chakri Reformation* (1989), and he has edited E. M. Satow, *A Diplomat in Siam* (1996) and *The Satow Siam Papers* (4 volumes, publication started in 1997).

Antoine Capet is Professor of British Civilization at the University of Rouen. A specialist in Britain of the Second World War, his main publications are *Le Poids des années de guerre. Les classes dirigeantes britanniques et la réforme sociale, 1931–1951* (1987) and *Contre le nazisme ou contre l'Allemagne? Le débat sur l'anti-germanisme en Grande-Bretagne* (1998).

Philippe Chassaigne is Professor in Modern and Contemporary History at the University of Bordeaux. The author of numerous articles on nineteenth- and twentieth-century British history, his main publications are *Histoire de l'Angleterre* (1996), *Industrialisation et société en Europe occidentale (1880–1970): Royaume-Uni et Allemagne-RFA* (1997), *Démocra-*

tie et société dans l'Angleterre en guerre, 1939–1945 (1999), *Pauvreté et inégalités en Grande-Bretagne, 1942–1990* (2000).

François Crouzet is Emeritus Professor at the University of Paris-Sorbonne, where he has taught British history for 22 years. His main works in English are: *Capital Formation in the Industrial Revolution* (1972), *The Victorian Economy* (1982), *The First Industrialists* (1985) and *Britain Ascendant* (1992). He is a CBE and has been awarded honorary degrees by four British universities.

Richard Davis is Maître de conférences at the University Charles de Gaulle-Lille 3, France, where he teaches nineteenth- and twentieth-century British history. He is the author of several articles on British foreign policy in the twentieth century. He is currently working on a study of Britain, de Gaulle and the Common Market.

Michael Dockrill is Professor of Diplomatic History at King's College, London. He is the author of many books on Britain's foreign relations in the twentieth century, including *British Defence Policy since 1945* (1989), *Diplomacy and World Power: Studies in British Foreign Policy* (1996, with Brian McKercher) and, most recently, *British Establishment Perspectives on France, 1936–1940* (1999).

James Foreman-Peck is Economic Adviser at HM Treasury and Visiting Professor at Middlesex University Business School. He has been Professor of Economic History at the University of Hull, Visiting Associate Professor at the University of California, Davis, and Fellow of St Anthony's College, Oxford. His books include *A History of the World Economy. International Relations since 1850*, and *Public and Private Ownership of British Industry 1820–1990* (with Robert Millward).

Jacques Leruez was Director of Studies at the Centre Nationale de la Recherche Scientifique and is a renowned specialist in British politics; among his publications are *Economic Planning and Politics in Britain* (1975), *L'Ecosse, une nation sans Etat* (1983, new edition 2000) and *Phénomène Thatcher* (1991).

Isabelle Lescent-Giles is Lecturer in Modern Economic History at the University of Paris-Sorbonne, France. Her Ph.D. was on the iron industry in the Midlands and in South Wales in the nineteenth century, and she is currently working on Britain's economic performance in the last four decades of the twentieth century. She has written numerous articles on British economic history.

Sir Christopher Mallaby was Her Majesty's Ambassador in France from 1992 to 1995.

Peter T. Marsh is Professor of History and International Relations at Syracuse University in the United States and Honorary Professor of History at the University of Birmingham in the United Kingdom. Author of books and articles on a variety of facets of nineteenth and twentieth century British history, his most recent works are a biography of *Joseph Chamberlain, Entrepreneur in Politics* (1994) and *Bargaining on Europe. Britain and the First Common Market, 1860–1892* (1999).

François-Charles Mougel is Professor of Modern and Contemporary History at the Institute of Political Studies in Bordeaux, France. A leading specialist in British political history, his main publications are *Elites et système de pouvoir en Grande-Bretagne 1945–1979* (1987), *Histoire culturelle du Royaume-Uni de 1919 à 1959* (1989) et *Histoire du Royaume-Uni au XXe siècle* (1996).

William Philpott is Senior Lecturer in European History at London Guildhall University. He has published widely on British military policy and Anglo-French defence relations in the first half of the twentieth century, including a book, *Anglo-French Relations and Strategy on the Western Front, 1914–1918* in the Palgrave series *Studies in Military and Strategic History*. He has co-edited with Professor Martin Alexander another volume in this series, *Anglo-French Defence Relations between the Wars*. He is a Fellow of the Royal Historical Society and a member of the Board of the Army Records Society.

Pascal R. Venier is Lecturer in French History and Politics, European Studies Research Institute, University of Salford, Manchester. His research is on late nineteenth-century diplomatic history.

Introduction: *'Perfide Albion'* All the Way?

Philippe Chassaigne and Michael Dockrill

The contributions presented here are taken from an international Conference held at the Maison des Sciences de l'Homme, University of Bordeaux (France), on 6–7 November 1998. The original idea was to bring together the – relatively few – French historians working on modern and contemporary Britain. But, underpinning all our efforts at organizing the Conference, was one anguished question: whatever had happened to the French school of British studies, once of good international repute? The fact that the final product was a Franco-British Conference, with more participants coming from the other side of the Channel, is in itself revealing enough of how British history has become a *terra incognita* to an overwhelming majority of the French academic community. Paul Mantoux, Elie Halévy or André Siegfried have had very few disciples and we must praise Professor François Crouzet for not letting British history disappear altogether from the French academic scene. He has had disciples in a number large enough that we can now speak of a renewed, burgeoning school of French historians of Britain.[1]

Yet historiography was definitely not on the agenda of the Conference. The idea was to select a theme broad enough to be treated from a variety of angles, a somewhat coherent picture eventually emerging from this impressionist approach. Franco-British relations over the past century were to be that catalysing theme. The Conference opened on 6 November 1998, exactly 100 years and 2 days since Captain Marchand had to withdraw from the dilapidated fortress of Fashoda in front of a British expeditionary column. The crisis may have quickly sunk into almost total oblivion in Britain; in France, to mention the very word of 'Fashoda' has long been sufficient to unleash Anglophobia to an almost uncontrollable degree, along with the burning of Joan of Arc,

1

Napoleon's exile to St Helena or the 'treason' of Mers-el-Kebir. *'Perfide Albion'* all the way.... Was there anything beyond this story of reciprocal defiance, not to say hatred? What about the armies of the two countries fighting side by side during the Great War, or Churchill's proposal, in May 1940, to merge the two nations into one so that they would fight uninterruptedly against Nazism, even if the German army was to conquer the Continent? What about the reciprocal influences, at an economic, political, cultural level? These were some of the questions the participants to the Conference wanted to address, and I hope that some of the answers lie in the following pages.

In 1990, when concluding a remarkable and somewhat iconoclastic book on the destinies of France and Britain in the nineteenth and twentieth centuries,[2] Professor François Crouzet assessed rather gloomily the image each people had of its neighbour:

> The revival of the phobias... has continued and even accelerated. In short, on either side of the Channel, the other country has been presented as a selfish and greedy Shylock, in a hurry to obtain his pound of flesh, and has served as a scapegoat for many of the difficulties which western Europe has undergone.[3]

Yet, and this was the only ray of light, he wondered whether 'the two fallen nations who find themselves on board of the same European boat in the middle of the storm' would not be better off if they were 'rowing side by side'.[4]

It is of course quite tempting to try our hand at a new assessment. At first glance, the two countries seem to have been more or less permanently at odds with one another: we only need to mention the squabbles of the early 1980s between Margaret Thatcher and President Mitterrand over the British contribution to the European budget; the reiterated campaigns of *frog baiting* orchestrated on a grand scale by *The Sun* on every possible occasion, be it the bicentennial of the French Revolution or Jacques Delors's efforts in favour of a more integrated Europe; the tensions between French peasants and British farmers at the time of the 'mad cow crisis', which on several occasions neared the point of a commercial war between the two countries – although it is hard to believe that British customers could seriously do without *foie gras* and Bordeaux wines...; or, last but not least, the obvious lack of communication that existed, at least at the beginning of their respective premiership, between the 'archaic' Lionel Jospin and the 'modern', and 'modernizing', Tony Blair.

In 1990, an opinion poll conducted for the *Observer Magazine* showed that about one-third of the 'Brits' deemed their French neighbours to be 'stylish' and 'arrogant', one-fifth 'devious' and 'sexy', while only a tiny fraction (less than 5 per cent) would consider them as 'hard-working', 'intelligent' or 'courageous'.[5] It is not very difficult to conceive that the same poll conducted in the days of Edward VII would have given a globally similar portrait.[6]

Yet there are reasons for hope: at the time of the 1997 British general election, the greater part of the French press seemed suddenly to discover that there was, on the other side of the Channel, a country where the booming economy had led to a continuous decrease in unemployment, to the extent that it stood at half the French level; where great efforts had been made to overcome the 'institutional rigidities' that once plagued British economic structures; where the state, its frontiers 'rolled back' to more appropriate limits, was no longer antagonistic with the entrepreneurial culture. There was no better proof to this than the fact that a substantial number of French citizens had decided to cross the Channel and settle, be it in London or in the green valleys of Kent.[7]

Model or counter-model – to quote Jacques Lcruez's paper on the British attempt at economic planning – seem to have been the only two options open to Franco-British relations during (at least) the past century. By 1898, they offered the image of two countries that had long been turning their back on one another, looking in diametrically opposed directions, yet with more elements in favour of rapprochement than of estrangement. Of course, now and then, a particular attempt at conciliation could fail on relatively minor details – for instance, Sir Edward Grey's lucid commentary, as reported by Nigel Brailey in his essay. Peter Marsh shows this process of rapprochement operating as early as in the negotiation of the Cobden–Chevalier treaty in 1860. One generation later, Théophile Delcassé was still working at it when he undertook to realign dramatically French foreign policy (Pascal Venier). And the way François Crouzet describes Elie Halévy's 'conversion' from Anglophobia to Anglophilia is just another illustration of this phenomenon, this time in a field far remote from diplomatic history. Such a rapprochement was based on a community of interest between the two countries – in this case, their common antagonism towards Imperial Germany – but also on the feeling of sharing, beyond obvious, but relatively minor, differences, the same culture, of which parliamentary democracy, or a common filiation with classical Antiquity and Judaeo-Christianity, were major aspects.[8] Yet, in spite of all these encouraging elements, the history of the last 100 years of Franco-British relations is marked by difficulties such that they appeared on more than one occasion to be hardly possible to overcome.

These difficulties have been sufficiently highlighted in the 16 essays collected here. Yet it would be unfair to argue that nothing but crises happened between the nations during this past century. Is it really necessary, by the way, to repeat that the Fashoda incident in itself has been quickly forgotten by the British and that it means virtually nothing to them? With the benefit of hindsight, we can see now that most of these crises, however acute they seemed to be at the time, were in fact nothing more than gut reaction. For example the relations between Britain and France in the 1930s, as described by Michael Dockrill and William Philpott, were such that British officials displayed, to put it mildly, little admiration for their French counterparts and constantly considered them with suspicion – it is telling enough to remember Robert Vansittart's lapidary dismissal of Léon Blum as 'naive and weak'. Yet diplomats on both sides were convinced in depth that the alliance between the two countries was the ultimate solution: if not, why would Sir Eric Phipps, the British ambassador in Paris, have tried so desperately to change the course of French politics?

This period of our national history, of which we have altogether little to boast about, illustrates revealingly the impact of misconceptions and even fantasies in the making of politics. This was certainly not the first time: in the nineteenth century, every French attempt at regaining a little bit of the naval power lost during the Napoleonic Wars terrified the British with the prospect of an imminent invasion of their country – something which, needless to say, not only never happened, but was also much beyond the aims, and possibilities, of successive French governments. Throughout the interwar years, British officials' major fear was that their former ally would take the lead, that Britain would lose her freedom of action and possibly find herself engaged in a war against Germany, where only French interests would be at stake. Yet France did not want to (and could not) get herself in such a situation: how French diplomacy, after Poincaré's brief attempt at imposing the treaty of Versailles on Germany in 1922–23, placed itself in the wheel of the policy of the British Foreign Office is well known. It lasted until 1939, and the Munich Conference was the most blatant illustration of this attitude.[9] In quite a different field, the dark intentions of which the Bank of France officials were suspected at the time of the 1931 crisis, or the way Churchill considered France and the French people – such as the Anglophile feelings he thought commonplace among the population – pertain to the same process of reconstructing reality instead of

simply facing the facts. Richard Davis's account of how British authorities handled the 'de Gaulle problem' in the 1960s is yet another
example of this predilection for vain assumptions – and is it not possible
to find an ultimate illustration of this tendency in the suspicions some
French Socialists harbour about Tony Blair's 'New' Labour, and wonder
whether he did not forsake the very essence of 'socialism' to obtain an
electoral landslide.

'Model or counter-model' is probably the essential question, the one
that makes sense of the ups and downs in Anglo-French relations during
these last 100 years. To put it briefly, Britain has often been offered the
part of the 'model' – a thing, we are quite aware, that will not be great
news to any Briton with a minimum of nationalistic feeling – and France
that of the 'counter-model'. And indeed, France appears in the end as
more frequently following the British lead than taking it, the virile
declarations of successive generations of statesmen being nothing
much more than make-believe. It is a well-known fact that on two
occasions (in 1814 and 1875), the French modelled themselves on British institutions. Again, France was playing second fiddle to Britain on
the diplomatic scene – and not always harmoniously – in the 1930s, or
again in the Suez expedition of 1956. It ceased with the advent of the
Fifth Republic, which is no doubt one of the merits of its founding
father, but France was soon to surrender to the Beatles in particular
and to pop culture in general, quite probably the most successful form
of British imperialism. Of course, one must be careful not to overgener-
alize. It would be, for instance, inaccurate to think of a British model of
economic development that the French would have followed: Isabelle
Lescent-Giles, James Foreman-Peck and Elisa Boccaletti show in their
respective essays how important differences were between the two economic cultures on both side of the Channel, and it is then all the more
interesting to see that it is in this particular field that the British felt the
need to adopt a French 'recipe' – economic planning. It proved only a
very limited success, since the concept of 'planning' itself was quickly
abandoned and will quite probably never be considered ever again by a
British government. This leads us to relativize the very idea that there
could be a 'French model' in something else than in the *'art de vivre'* (yet,
100 years ago, Elie Halévy would have put even this assumption to the
test). But this is quite certainly another sign that France and Britain,
though often rivals, are in fact complementary, and comes like an echo,
60 years later and in a very much less tragic situation, to the hazardous
schemes of a full union of the two countries elaborated in the gloomy
hours of 1940.

Notes

1. The more up-to-date line-up will be found in Frédérique Lachaud, François-Joseph Ruggiu et Isabelle Lescent-Giles (eds), *Tendances récentes de l'historiographie britannique* (Paris: Presse de l'Université de Paris-Sorbonne, 2000).
2. François Crouzet, *Britain's Ascendant. Comparative Studies in Franco-British Economic History* (Cambridge: University Press, 1990).
3. Ibid., p. 425.
4. Ibid., p. 412.
5. 'Damn Foreigners! What the Brits Really Think of Europe', *Observer Magazine*, 28 October 1990. Maybe the French reader was to find some solace in the fact that the Germans stand out as very much less 'sexy' (1 per cent of answers given) and much more 'arrogant' (48 per cent) than the French....
6. See Sylvaine Marandon, *L'Image de la France dans l'Angleterre victorienne* (Paris, 1967).
7. In April 2000, the news that top model Laetitia Casta was to become a British tax resident caused quite a stir since she had just been selected as France's new 'Marianne'.
8. As underligned in Philip J. Bell, *France and Britain, 1900–1940. Entente and Estrangement* (London: Longman, 1996), p. 3.
9. On this, see Comité d'Histoire de la Seconde Guerre mondiale, *Les Relations franco-britanniques de 1935 à 1939* (Paris, 1975), and Jean-Baptiste Duroselle, *La Décadence, 1932–1939* (Paris, 1979).

1
Britain and France: Some Comments on a Complex Relationship

Sir Christopher Mallaby

Britain and France have long been involved with each other – for 1000 years at least. Passionately, creatively, disastrously, victoriously. The Norman invasion of England in 1066 was the last invasion of Britain. It brought the first real British involvement in Europe. We had, of course, been influenced heavily by the Romans but reverse British influence towards the European mainland really began when the French kings of England, following the Conquest, wished to continue to play a role in France. There were repercussions for centuries. The Hundred Years War can be seen not as an English–French war but more Franco-French, given that the English leaders were Normans.

In any case, it was the start of a long and bitter rivalry. Hume said: 'From this period we may date the commencement of that great animosity'. A more modern historian, Tout, wrote: 'the two countries entered the war as kinsfolk and neighbours, and emerged with the tradition of national enmity'. That was part of a wider process of the formation of nations in Europe: Michelet saw the Hundred Years War as the anvil upon which the French nation was forged.

Through the centuries after that, there were many reasons for hostility between Britain and France. Until 1815. The important fact about this date is that it is now almost *two* centuries ago. And the colonial rivalry between Britain and France, which did continue after Waterloo, *was* staunched by the Entente Cordiale in 1904.

Since then we have had, so far, almost a century of alliance. In two world wars and the cold war – the three great conflicts of this century – we stood together. There are many reminders of our alliance. Think of those touchingly peaceful British military cemeteries dotted about northern France. Or I think of the most moving event of my period as ambassador in France. It was the commemoration at Arromanches in June 1994 of the fiftieth anniversary of the Normandy landings. Eleven hundred British veterans marched across the beach where they had landed exactly 50 years before in similar rainy weather, some of them missing a limb or their sight since that landing. One of the mayors at a coastal village said of the forces who landed in 1944: 'Ils ne savaient pas que c'était impossible: alors, ils l'ont fait'.

The legacy of this intimately intermingled history, together with the similarities of the international standing and the population size of Britain and France today, is a sense of rivalry, a readiness to criticize, a reciprocity of *schadenfreude* where the British and the French press leap at opportunities to report the troubles of the other country. Sometimes, when discussing this subject either side of the Channel, one has the feeling that 1815 must have been *after* 1945.

Yet there is also mutual fascination and much admiration, as well as rivalry. To call it a love–hate relationship is too strong on the negative side. 'Best of enemies', the title of a good book on the subject, is not right because there are no hostilities, or even hostility, between the two countries. What we really have is co-operation and rivalry. My favourite expression is 'rival companions'.

Today, there is much similarity between the two countries, but also important differences. There is much co-operation and contact. Our economies are increasingly interdependent, through trade, investment and joint companies. Every day in 1997 goods worth almost 900 million francs crossed the Channel between us. France remains Britain's third export market and the UK is France's second. Britain is the third largest investor in France. British companies are an integral part of the French economy. For instance, Kingfisher in Britain owns Darty and now Castorama. France is also deeply involved in the British economy with investments which are greater than those of Japan. They include services essential to the everyday life of the British people, such as water supplies and buses, as well as more dramatic undertakings such as the involvement of Elf in the North Sea. The volume of trade with France today is 180 per cent higher than ten years ago, and our stock of investment in France is up 200 per cent.

There are similarities in foreign policy. Britain and France are both permanent members of the United Nations Security Council. Both are nuclear weapon states. Both want the North Atlantic Treaty Organization to continue. Both have an active, global foreign policy and the political will to send troops abroad to restore or maintain peace. That is a positive aspect of our colonial history. One positive side-effect of the awful story of Bosnia was the strong growth in defence co-operation between Britain and France, from platoon commanders on the ground to defence ministers. I had innumerable meetings about this with the Balladur and Juppé governments, co-ordinating British and French policy in a very close co-operative effort. Seeing how well we co-operated in this military operation, we consciously took steps to perpetuate that co-operation which continues now to flourish.

But there also differences between us in foreign policy. Take the example of Europe. France after the war, like Germany for different reasons, wanted a new start. Britain was proud of her achievements during the war and did not see a need for a break with the past. Today, Britain has long been a partner in Europe. Britain and France both want a *Europe des Patries*. They both want to be leaders in the European Union. The difference is that France *is* among the leaders, and Britain, though often influential, is not as much of a leader as its present government wants. In addition to our differences over trade policy and over the common agricultural policy, there is the euro. France was the great proponent of the euro and will participate from the start. Britain will not join for several years, so at first Britain will not participate in a whole range of important new interests that will now be shared by the countries of the euro.

Ten million British visitors come to France every year. Four million French people go to Britain. All those British visitors, many of them returning year after year, are the answer to those who think that the criticism of France in the British media represents public opinion. Published opinion and public opinion are not the same. And, even in the field of popular writing, the success of Peter Mayle's books about a British family living in Provence is a demonstration of affection for France. The British agree increasingly with Charles Morgan's principle that France is 'an idea necessary to civilisation'.

Cultural exchanges between Britain and France, and mutual influence in this field, have long been comprehensive and extensive. From Shakespeare to Tintin. We have strong youth and student exchanges.

We should get rid of the stupid stereotypes in each country about the other. The French are surprised to learn that there has been no fog to speak of in London since 1947; and the British would be surprised by the mist that charmingly veils Bordeaux today. The British think that the economy of France is dominated in every aspect by the state. But France is a very successful exporter and has an economy larger than Britain's. The French think that British economic policy is jungle liberalism with little social provision. But unemployment in Britain is so low *because* enterprise is encouraged, and the social provision for those not in employment is much greater than the French think. On Europe, the British think that France is idealistic but in fact the French approach is really self-interest, a means of magnifying French influence. The French think the British are anti-European but the new Labour government wants Britain to join the euro and to play a more influential role in the leadership of Europe. It has been suggested that the socialisms of Jospin and Blair are completely different and that this could be a bone of contention. But the Jospin government is in fact pragmatic in many of its decisions, notably its privatizations.

Here are some guesses about the future. Britain will join the euro, assuming that it works well for the first several years. Britain will then become more influential in Europe, but Franco-German co-operation will continue. Britain and France will both become more efficient economically, and that will be an example of convergence between them. Pride will disappear on neither side of the Channel, and may remain a stronger feature of the national character on the French side. The key point for me is that rivalry and prejudice will not disappear but co-operation and contact between Britain and France will gradually erode them. The continuing peace and alliance between the two countries will eventually manage to efface the memory of our enmity before 1815.

A great and important question for me, as ambassador, was whether anything can be done to accelerate this process of improvement in our mutual psychology. One idea I had was to found the Entente Cordiale Scholarships. The scheme is now in its third year. It brings about 20 very gifted graduate students from Britain to France and in the other direction each year. As these people advance in life, and influence important decisions, bias and ignorance in Britain towards France and in France towards Britain will be countered by people who really know the other country. That should be a help in the long-term improvement of our relationship.

2
French and British Businessmen in the Nineteenth Century*

James Foreman-Peck and Elisa Boccaletti

Differences between the French and British in 'national character', diet, culture and mores have been a continuing source of fascination and distaste to both nations. Sometimes they are even represented as determinants of foreign policy or economic performance. This essay casts a more objective light on such Franco-British contrasts where they concern businessmen. It compares the characteristics and behaviour of a substantial sample of, at least at one time, moderately or very successful entrepreneurs and managers in the two countries.

The topic matters because businessmen transformed nineteenth-century Britain and France, though whether they did so sufficiently, or excessively, remains controversial. 'Entrepreneurial failure' theses have been as popular in France as in Britain.[1] Businessmen's willingness to take calculated risks, to work hard and long, and to defer gratification, determined the supply and quality of entrepreneurship in the two countries. These propensities in turn depended upon conditioning by national societies. In Western Europe as a whole, states played an expanding role in determining the business environment, by legislation, taxation, subsidies, prohibition of some activities and encouragement of others. Their geographically adjacent 'social experiments' offered a form of 'yardstick competition' unavailable in the closed and monolithic empires of the East. European states and societies thereby learned from each others' errors and successes.[2]

We first discuss state-initiated influences upon business options in Britain and France. Opportunities also depended on natural endowments and the way in which they were exploited. We explain how the distribution of industry and enterprise in the two countries reflected these openings. National institutions shape entrepreneurship and respond to legislation and culture as well. We pay particular attention to

11

the types of firm that were the vehicles of business acumen. Informal and formal human capital may be the most vital contributors to the supply of entrepreneurship. In our assessment, we distinguish family, geographical and religious influences under the heading of informal capital, and education and training under formal human capital formation.

Entrepreneurial opportunity

In Britain during the second half of the nineteenth century, but much less in France, limited liability legislation and stock exchange quotation created business opportunities. The 1856 Joint Stock Companies Act imposed very little obligation on registering British companies; no disclosure of financial information to shareholders was necessary, though the rules of the London stock exchange did require that balance sheets be circulated to shareholders.[3] Scotland in particular provided a remarkably liberal business environment compared with France.

At the beginning of the nineteenth century Scots law already provided three major advantages of incorporation – transferability of shares, separate legal personality of the company and limited liability of shareholders.[4] In Scotland therefore businesses could develop more easily than in England before 1856, because of the different legal standing of partnerships and unincorporated companies. Though there was convergence with England in the legal environment for business in the nineteenth century, such differences as remained in the granting of general limited liability were more favourable to Scotland.[5] The unwillingness to take up limited liability in Scotland led to painful demands on unprotected shareholders, with for example the failure of the Western Bank in 1857, and the 1878 collapse of the Bank of Glasgow, which called for £2750 to be paid by each £100 shareholder. But it was arguably the absence of limited liability that maintained depositor confidence in Scottish banks.

The other side of the coin of easy British access to limited liability status with minimal reporting requirements was moral hazard. Charles Dickens's *Martin Chuzzlewit*, written between 1843 and 1844, offers a vivid portayal of the corrupt founders and operation of the 'Anglo-Bengalee Disinterested Loan and Life Assurance Company'. A generation later, in 1875, Anthony Trollope described the immigrant nouveau riche foreign railway promoter Melmotte in *The Way We Live Now*, implying that he was thoroughly dishonest. Under limited liability, debtors could only recover in total the nominal capital of the company and each shareholder might only lose the capital subscribed. In a large enterprise, small shareholders were able to exercise little control over management unwilling to disclose more information than the minimal requirements of the law. During the railway boom of the 1840s British directors awarded themselves shares which they sold at the height of the boom, overcapitalizing their companies. Ernest Terah Hooley, a late nineteenth-century company promoter, was particularly renowned for his ability to exaggerate the true value of the companies' shares he sold to the public. In more extreme cases, without fear of criminal proceedings, management could easily expropriate shareholders' capital for themselves by establishing fraudulent companies.

Of course later nineteenth-century France shared these shortcomings, if to a lesser extent, as illustrated by Émile Zola's character Aristide Saccard, the unscrupulous financier in the novel, *Money* (1891). But from 1807 to 1867 the authorization of a share-issuing limited liability company – Société Anonyme – was a very arduous process, requiring six months to a year, and was generally restricted to what the Conseil d'État judged to be large enterprises of 'public utility'. Only 642 were ever authorized and probably only 200 were trading in 1867 – with one-half listed on the Paris Bourse.[6] French legislation of 1863 and 1867 introduced more general limited liability than before but, interpreting British experience, still imposed greater reporting requirements than in Britain. The sentencing to five years' imprisonment in 1893 of the 87-year-old Ferdinand de Lesseps over matters arising from the liquidation of his Panama Canal company reflected a continuing more rigorous French company regulatory regime.

Numbers of companies registered and the size of their average nominal capital reflected this rigour. French company registrations were less than one-quarter of British at the end of the nineteenth century and nominal corporate capital was little more than one-third.[7]

Industrial distribution

Apart from the legislative framework, natural endowments also determined entrepreneurial opportunity. A coal deficiency, relative to Britain, is a continuing theme in nineteenth-century French economic history, explaining not only the smaller extractive sector but also the slower mechanization of firms and transport.[8] Perhaps independently, thanks to the land redistribution of the French Revolution, the much larger French agricultural sector was reflected in fewer big industrial companies as well. In 1907 there were 93 British companies, but only 21

French, with paid-up capital of more than £2 million.[9] Moreover, 41 of these British companies but only two French businesses were in industry. Agriculture was still a large sector in France at the beginning of the twentieth century, absorbing resources that in Britain had been transferred long ago to manufacturing and commerce.

Business leaders of the largest firms are unlikely to be typical of businessmen as a whole, so to establish their characteristics it is necessary to employ data sets in addition to those including only the largest firms. The samples here exclude the metropolitan area, where many of the largest firms were often based, in both France and in Britain, paying particular attention to distinctive regions. Both French and Scottish samples are centred on the third quarter of the nineteenth century.[10] We compare nineteenth-century Alsace and Scotland in more detail, on the grounds that these were regions of their respective national economies that were reckoned to be especially dynamic. The assessment of businessmen in Alsace is possible because of the work of Michael Hau.[11] Scotland is a useful comparison, like Alsace being more Protestant than the rest of the country, having twice as many ancient universities as England, and a reputation for 'canniness', being particularly astute or mean with money.[12] Moreover, as Edinburgh architecture suggests, frequent alliances with France against their mutual enemy, England, left a French influence in Scotland.

In 1801 Alsace held 2.67 per cent of the French population and 3.15 per cent in 1936.[13] Scotland accounted for a larger (but declining) proportion of the inhabitants of Great Britain, around 14 per cent at the mid-century, with approximately 10 per cent of income tax receipts. More than one-half of the population of Alsace were employed in agriculture, 15 per cent in industry, 14.6 per cent were artisans and 18.3 per cent worked in services at the mid-century. Scotland was far less agricultural. The 1841 census recorded just over one-fifth of the working population as agricultural labourers, farmers or graziers.

Mid-century economic growth in the two regions was comparable, but the economy of Alsace suffered in the 1880s from the separation from France. From 1850 to 1869 agricultural and industrial output rose about 60 per cent but to the 1880s the increase was only 50 per cent.[14] The implied average compound growth rates are respectively 2.5 per cent per annum and, say, 1.2 per cent per annum. Without the disruption of the change in sovereignty, tax data suggest a doubling of Scottish income over the 30 years from the mid-century, an average growth of 2.3 per cent per annum.[15]

Alsace was smaller and less diversified industrially than Scotland. There were no bankers or merchants in Alsace comparable with industrialists. The region was divided into two departments, Upper and Lower Rhine. Lower Rhine was much less industrial; for firms covered by the industrial census of 1839–45, the relationship was one to five compared with Upper Rhine for the turnover, and one to six for the assets. Table 2.1 shows the predominance of the textile industry, in the sample, with 48 cases (65 per cent). Within textiles, cotton accounted for half of all entrepreneurs: this domination was particularly pronounced in the Upper Rhine, whereas the Lower Rhine entrepreneurs were more diversified. The textile industry in Alsace employed 14 per cent of the active population in 1882, when textile employment was about 14 per cent lower than in 1869.[16]

Turning to the Scottish industrial distribution of businessmen (Table 2.2), we observe that textiles and clothing accounted for only 18 per cent of our businessmen. The country was far less specialized apparently, not only than Alsace, but than the French sample as a whole. This was an indication of the breadth of business opportunities that gave the (lowland) Scottish economy its strength.[17] Industrialization began in the late 1820s, thanks to exploitation of coal and iron ore deposits. The early coal-mining businessmen came from agricultural employment. Their industrial relations, along with those of iron and steel makers, were extremely poor. Textiles employment probably peaked a little earlier than in Alsace. The Dundee jute industry continued to flourish on very low wage labour though prospering especially in the 1850s and 1860s.[18]

Families as a source of informal human capital

The greater size of the British industrial sector is reflected in the higher proportion of British big business leaders with fathers in business than in France. Another difference between the two countries is the extent of state entrepreneurship in France providing an alternative source of

Table 2.1   Distribution of Alsatian businessmen in the sample by industrial activities (numbers)[16]

	Cotton	Wool	Silk	Mixed fabrics	Metallurgy	Others	Total
Lower Rhine	3	2	0	0	7	7	19
Upper Rhine	34	4	2	3	4	7	54
Total	37	6	2	3	11	14	73

Table 2.2   Distribution of sampled Scottish businessmen by industry sector (numbers)

Food, drink, tobacco	8	Transport, communication	8
Bricks, pottery, glass, cement	5	Extractive industries	11
Timber, furniture	1	Metals	6
Construction industry	7	Civil, mechanical, engineering	11
Paper, printing, publishing	2	Shipbuilding	7
Other manufactures	4	Chemicals	2
Gas, electricity, water	1	Textiles	17
Distributive trade	5	Clothing,	2
Banking, insurance, finance	1	Leather, footwear	2

Source: authors' sample.

recruitment to the business family. This is mirrored in the politician and civil service origin of 16 per cent of businessmen, four times the proportion in Britain.[19] The new French industries were most open to upwardly mobile managers[20] whereas traditional sectors were dominated by established business families. Hence we should not be surprised that having a father in business reduced the chances of starting a successful company. A father in business, one way or the other, supplies a less risky means of advancement, inside or outside the business sector, for the average son.

In the Scottish mid-century sample, only one of 92 identifiable cases entered a family firm and did not have a father in business. The comparison with Alsace shows how much more dominated by the family that region was than Scotland. In contrast to the large companies of France as a whole in 1907, only 20 per cent of the Alsatian businessmen lacked a father in business, whereas for the Scots the figure was more than double. More than half of the Scotsmen without a father in business entered an established independent firm, compared with 21 per cent for the few Alsatians in that category (Figures 2.1(a) and (c)). Scottish society was less traditional in this sense, perhaps more impersonal, and presumably more achievement-orientated.

Two-thirds of the Scottish sample were first generation, 21 per cent second generation and 12 per cent, third. By 'first generation' we mean 'in business'. Hence they need not have started their own firm but they might have joined independent firms or married into them; 29 first-generation businessmen did not start their own firms, 38 out of 67 first generation did. The definition of 'family firm' is based on equity ownership, and relationship to the owners by marriage or birth. James Gilchrist (1847–1917) is a Scottish example of the family management of an independent firm. He was second generation, his father (Archibald) was in business (Barclay Curle, shipbuilders), and he worked in an independent firm. All second-generation businessmen must have a father in business but not all those with fathers in business are second (or more) generation. They may have started their own enterprise or joined independent firms.

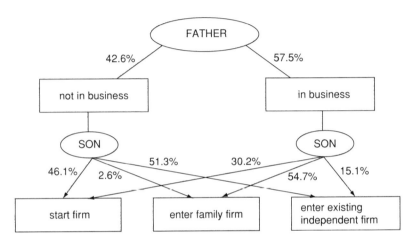

Figure 2.1a   Paternal influences and choice of firm type: Scottish entrepreneurs (active between 1850 and 1870)

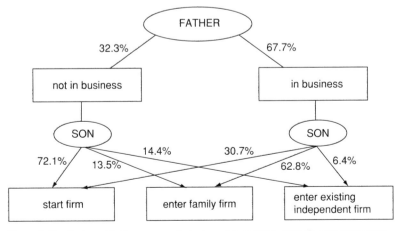

Figure 2.1b   Paternal influences and choice of firm type: French entrepreneurs

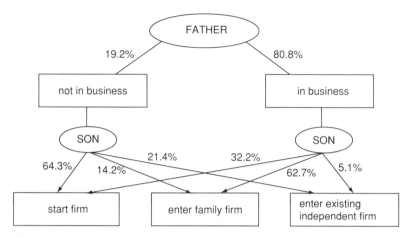

Figure 2.1c   Paternal influences and choice of firm type: Alsatian entrepreneurs

Family and the independent firms

Generalizations about family firm performance have been based upon impression rather than samples. One historian concluded that small British family firms performed well in the nineteenth century whereas large ones were more questionable.[21] Another castigated the amateurism of British personal capitalism.[22] A third asserted that the view that third-generation businessmen failed is not now widely shared.[23]

Family business remained the norm in Britain outside the railways and joint stock banks, for even quotation on the stock exchange did not preclude family control. As late as 1913, 32 of the 51 directors of the three largest British companies (J & P Coats, Imperial Tobacco and Watney Combe Reid) still bore the names of their founding family firms. Survival of family businesses and business families owed something to the loyalty that could be expected from family managers and the commitment that avoided the necessity for monitoring, or for motivating, their performance. But family firms also satisfied the need to provide jobs for the family. Less fertile families might have more room for professional managers in their businesses. Natural selection and the division of labour suggest that professional managers, suitably motivated, will be more competent than those who happen to be born into the business family, since the talent of the founder is unlikely to be transmitted genetically to a wide range of family members. On the other hand, some families may have discovered the secret of socialising their children appropriately. But, by and large, failure to introduce managers selected on merit was likely to be a handicap to business development.

French business was also dominated by family firms. The Compagnie d'Anzin, the largest and oldest coal mining company in northern France, was a family firm and so was the most influential business in the South, the Compagnie des Mines de Carmaux.[24] The De Wendel family created the dominant firm in the Lotharingian iron and steel industry, while Peugeot was a long-established engineering family in Doubs. Another major family firm, Établissement Tiberghien, began as a wool manufacturer at Tourcoing in the mid-nineteenth century and later diversified into cotton. Saint Gobain, founded in 1665 by Louis XIV, maintained a family tradition which could be traced to its rebirth as a private company in 1830. The largest Roubaix woollen firm was François Mesurel Frères, with a capital of 4 million francs and in a sector the businesses of which were closely interlinked by family ties.[25]

The main difference between businesses in Second Empire France was between independent firms and the rest.[26] Independent firms – admittedly a small number – presented an average turnover 13 times that of the average family or start-up firm (Table 2.3). The differences in the size of capital and number of workers employed were less, but nonetheless striking. The capital–labour ratios were higher, and perhaps most surprisingly, the wealth left at death by the businessmen employed in independent firms was, on average, more than double those of family firms. This is consistent with the existence of a managerial elite class in France. It is certainly different from Scotland in the same period. Scottish managers of independent firms left on average little more than one-quarter of a million pounds, whereas family firm businessmen averaged almost half a million. Scottish family firm businessmen were much

Table 2.3   Businesses and businessmen in Second Empire France

	Turnover	*Capital*	*Labour*	*Wealth at death*	*Labour/ capital ratios*
Independent firm	33.00 (9)	7.19 (6)	6094 (18)	5.22m. Fr (17)	0.396
Family firm	2.52 (67)	4.83 (34)	957 (93)	2.43m. Fr (82)	0.624
Start-up	2.47 (52)	4.16 (34)	700 (81)	1.75m. Fr (96)	0.787
Number of observations	128	74	192	195	43

Source: authors' sample.

richer than the French in our sample, but this was much less true of independent firm managers. Their comparatively lower wealth may be a reflection of the liberal Scottish legal environment that offered greater encouragement to the formation of independent enterprises, so that relatively less capital and turnover were needed than in France.

There is only a small difference between French start-up and family firms in the Second Empire – average turnovers are almost identical, capital is a little scarcer in start-ups, and employment somewhat lower – both features suggest that start-ups were more productive than family firms. The overall implication is that family firms did not grow on average very much, since successful start-up firms could almost match their size. Family firms may have been rather more profitable; the average wealth at death of the family firm businessman was almost two-fifths greater than that of a businessman who started a company. On the other hand, this greater wealth may merely reflect larger inheritances from the family business.

Scottish start-up businessmen left more money on average than the French starters or family firms, but also could not match their compatriots in family or independent businesses (Table 2.4). The gap between them and the families was more marked, because the Scottish family firm had a longer and more prosperous tradition. This is certainly reflected in the wealth distribution by generation of businessmen (Table 2.5). Third-generation businessmen in Scotland, but not in France, were on average much richer than first or second generations. Here most probably is the differential impact of the French Revolution and the Industrial Revolution. These have domino effects for private wealth accumulation and strength of family firms. Political instability and the devastation of war at the beginning of the century were more detrimental for France. Earlier business generations were therefore less able to build up their enterprises in France than in Scotland.

Table 2.4   Scots businessmen's wealth at death by firm type, 1850–70

Firm type	Wealth (£)
Independent	279 342
Family	474 000
Start-up	182 850

Table 2.5 Mean wealth left at death by generation of businessmen, 1850–70

	Scots	French
First	£216 590 (63)	2.209m. Fr (122)
Second	£366 800 (21)	2.537m. Fr (61)
Third	£653 020 (12)	2.689m. Fr (12)

Notes: 25 Fr = £1, numbers in parentheses.

Religion

Most managing directors of the largest British companies were Anglicans, the state religion of England. For them the general rule that religion rarely influenced business behaviour was more correct than among the most socially aware Nonconformists, the Quakers.[27] There were marked differences in religous affiliation of British businessmen by region. In Bristol, a late industrializing region, businessmen were predominantly Church of England, whereas in Manchester and Birmingham they were more likely to be Nonconformists.[28] In Scotland, virtually all businessmen were Protestant, though including in that category Episcopalians (corresponding to Anglicans in England). The predominantly Catholic Highlands and Irish immigrants were not notable seedbeds for businessmen. There was only one Catholic out of 61 cases of recorded religion. Compared with the distribution of religious observance in Scotland in 1851 (Table 2.6), the minority Roman Catholics were underrepresented among businessmen.

For the French sample, Catholics (non-Protestants) were significantly more likely than Protestants to start a successful firm (Figure 2.2(b)).

Table 2.6 Percentage distribution of religions in Scotland, 1851

Free Church	34.5
Established Church	30.9
United Presbyterian Church	19.4
Roman Catholics	4.5
Independent or Congregationalist	3.0
Episcopalians	2.9

Total attendants at morning public worship 30 March 740, 794.
25.64 per cent of the population attended places of worship.

Source: UK Census of Population 1851.
Note: Table A also records 28 Jews.

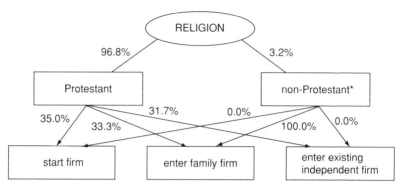

Figure 2.2a   Protestantism and choice of firm type: Scottish entrepreneurs (active between 1850 and 1870)

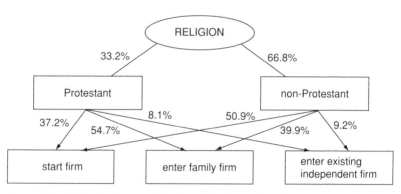

Figure 2.2b   Protestantism and choice of firm type: French entrepreneurs

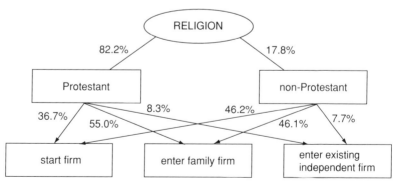

Figure 2.2c   Protestantism and choice of firm type: Alsatian entrepreneurs

However, in the population of France as a whole, rather than in our sample, Protestants were more likely to found successful businesses in this period than Catholics. Statistically, the explanation is simply that in the population there were so few Protestants (about 2 per cent). This created room for politically influential Catholic business dynasties, such as that founded by Henri Bernard (1810–89), sugar refiner, of Lille.

Alsace was different from much of the rest of France and the comparison between the religions of the Alsatian population and that of the entrepreneurs in 1851 is revealing (Table 2.7). Jews are represented proportionately, but the predominance of Protestants is overwhelming: 81 per cent of entrepreneurs, but only 23 per cent of the population. Table 2.7 shows the geographical division by religion in Alsace among entrepreneurs' families; the Lutherans in the north and the Lower Rhine, the Calvinists between Saint-Marie-aux-Mines and Mulhouse, and the Catholics in the Upper Rhine. With the exception of three Huguenot families, the Calvinists were all of Mulhousian or Swiss origin, where land and labour were scarce. Calvinist industrialists did not mind reconstructing factories and moving labour forces, in contrast to their Lutheran colleagues, who deliberately opted for rural settlement. Alsatian non-Protestants, just under 18 per cent of the total, showed a rather higher propensity to form new firms than Protestants, presumably because there were fewer non-Protestant family firms for the prospective businessman to enter (Figure 2.3c).

Religion went hand in hand with philanthropy, carrying possible implications for business performance. William Lever, Lord Leverhulme, was formally a Congregationalist, with a strong taste for ritual that he satisfied by participating in Masonic rites.[29] He created a vast business empire by using vegetable oil for soap instead of tallow (his legacy funded this project), and like many other late Victorian businessmen, devoted a great deal of attention to workers' well-being, building Port

Table 2.7 Religions of sampled Alsatian businessmen and of the regional population(%)

		Catholics	*Lutherans*	*Calvinists*	*Jewish*
Population (1851)	Lower Rhine	64	31	2	3
	Upper Rhine	87	7	3	3
	Total Alsace	74	20	3	3
Entrepreneurs	Lower Rhine	12	76	6	6
	Upper Rhine	17	9	72	2
	Total Alsace	16	27	54	3

Sunlight, a model industrial village in 1888. Quakers, such as the Cadburys and the Rowntrees, were particularly prominent in philanthropy. George Cadbury with his brother Richard, joined the ailing family chocolate business in 1861, founded 30 years earlier. In 1879 he moved the company to Bournville where he established the garden suburb model, being convinced that bad housing lay at the root of many social problems. Another Quaker businessman, Alfred Southall, whose family income and employment were founded on medicines, when out of his office taught in Birmingham schools during the nineteenth century.[30] His teaching experience, as he described it, was time-consuming and diverted him from business. Seebohm Rowntree (1871–1954), from a later generation of Quakers, joined the family firm in 1889, after having (unusually) studied chemistry at Manchester. As well as introducing a corporate pension plan, his wider social concerns prompted his famous 1897–98 survey of poverty in York, and subsequent studies.

This type of social commitment carried a cost for family firms unwilling to delegate authority to salaried managers. As transport costs fell and other economies developed competitive industries, the pressure of business life increased. These trends threatened the businessman who combined running his firm with day-to-day participation in philanthropy.

Education

A fundamental and persistent difference between the two countries of our comparison is that French businessmen were far more likely to have received substantial formal education.[31] Isambard Brunel exploited a French education to innovate in engineering enterprise in Britain.[32] At the age of 14, Isambard was sent back to France, first to the College of Caen in Normandy and then to the Lycée Henri-Quatre in Paris, renowned for its maths teachers. Finally, he was apprenticed to Louis Bréguet (1747–1823), watch and scientific instrument maker. At the age of 16 he returned to England to work with his father. Isambard's building of the Great Western Railway, his bridges and his huge steamship the *Great Eastern*, responsible for his financial ruin and early death, subsequently made him legendary.

Strasburg's commitment to industrial education is demonstrated by the early career of Gottlieb Daimler. As part of a Württemberg government-organized industrial promotion scheme, Daimler received a travel grant in 1853 to work in an engineering firm near Strasburg (F. Rollé and Schwilqué), where regular courses of theoretical instruction were also provided.[33] When the Grafenstaden firm began manufacturing locomotives, Daimler was appointed foreman at the age of 22. After one year he received a scholarship to study engine design and related subjects, including English, between 1857 and 1859 at Stuttgart Polytechnic. Shortly after returning to Strasburg, Daimler's interest in finding a new type of engine encouraged him to resign and travel to Paris, where the Lenoir gas engine had been patented the previous year.

Both Britain and France possessed elite higher education institutions, though they transmitted different traditions. The French *grandes écoles* were technocratic in the service of the state, while Britain's 'Oxbridge' had a reputation for teaching classics and an outdated curriculum. In fact the British story is more complicated, since Oxford's practice differed from that of Cambridge. In 1859, with the establishing of the Natural History Museum, Oxford was in the forefront of European science. But by 1870, the College Fellows were anxious that teaching science would require departments headed by authoritarian professors who would undermine the existing autonomy of College teachers. Oxford science therefore was virtually non-existent by 1914. On the other hand Cambridge, with a strong and active mathematics tradition, was innovative in applied science. Lord Rayleigh, as Professor of Physics, initiated one of the first electricity generating stations in conjunction with the local authority, and the Honourable Charles Parsons studied natural sciences at Cambridge, before inventing the steam turbine and founding a successful company.

French businessmen were much more likely to have been to university, whereas the British more probably served an apprenticeship. Despite significant differences in education patterns, in 1907 big business leaders equally overwhelmingly in both countries entered their firm at the boardroom level. Education does not seem to signify differences in elitism or social mobility. On the other hand, twice the proportion of British 'business leaders' founded their own companies, which is consistent with a more dynamic British industrial sector.

As in their respective nation states, so also formal education was more widespread among Alsatian businessmen than among the Scots, the former being much more likely to have received secondary and university education than the latter (Figures 2.3 (a) and (c)). In both regions, non-university educated businessmen were more liable to have started their own firms. Lower education levels in Scotland again might suggest more business opportunities. The educated, coming from richer families, take the best established positions. But the more options there are, the greater the chances of someone outside the elite getting one. In

Alsace, 70 per cent of university-educated businessmen entered the family firm, and only 3.3 per cent joined an established independent business. For Scotland this position was reversed. Almost half of all

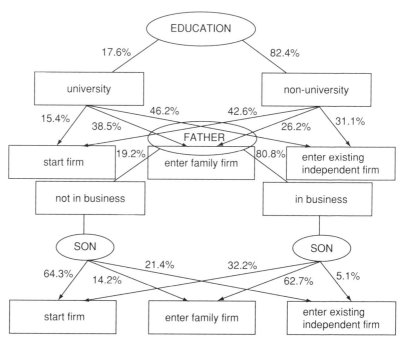

Figure 2.3a Education and choice of firm type: Scottish entrepreneurs (active between 1850 and 1870)

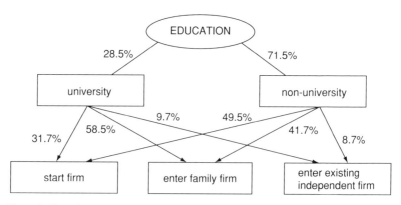

Figure 2.3b Education and choice of firm type: French entrepreneurs

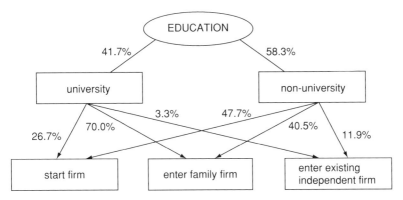

Figure 2.3c Education and choice of firm type: Alsatian entrepreneurs

university-educated businessmen entered independent firms and just under two-fifths joined the family business. It seems as if university education was more of an investment than a consumption good in Scotland and the opposite in Alsace. In Alsace the family business paid for the education whereas in Scotland more often the education paid off with a valuable job.

Alsatian entrepreneurs were distinguished from other French entrepreneurs by their high level of education; 43 per cent had received secondary education as opposed to only 12 per cent in Normandy. Alsatian businessmen with training were more likely to start their own successful firms (Table 2.8). The same cannot be said of Scotland, where it is reasonable to infer training was qualitatively different.

Table 2.8 Training and starting firms in nineteenth-century Alsace and Scotland: a classification of businessmen

	No training	Training	Total
Alsace Existing firm	13	30	43
Starts firm	2	26	28
Total	15	56	71
Chi-squared[1] = 5.42553, Prob value = 0.01984			
Scotland Existing firm	15	43	58
Starts firm	8	27	35
Total	23	70	93
Chi-squared[1] = 0.10588; probability value = 0.74488			

Geographical mobility

If national education or culture was somehow unsympathetic to new technology or innovation, by the later nineteenth century we would expect to find those businessmen educated abroad to flourish. Businessmen founding high-technology firms in later nineteenth-century Britain indeed seem to have disproportionately originated overseas. William Siemens, a younger brother of the founder of the German electrical engineering firm, liked the patent protection for his inventions available in mid-century Britain. Not only did he run the British subsidiary of the German telegraph manufacturing business, eventually to become independent, but he also invented the open hearth furnace and operated a successful steelworks using his process. Reuter's news organization began when Julius Reuter migrated in 1851 from Paris to England, where he found news gathering and transmission far easier. He briefly entered the submarine cable business in the 1860s and was a major user of advanced information technology. One of the founders of Brunner-Mond, the largest constituent company of 1926 ICI, Ludwig Mond (1839–1909), immigrated to England in 1862. Hugo Hirst, who with his partner Byng in 1889 incorporated GEC – which was to be the major electrical engineering, telecoms and defence contractor for much of the twentieth century – was born in Bavaria and emigrated to England. Guglielmo Marconi came from Bologna just before the end of the century to sell his radio technology to the Royal Navy and the Post Office. The pharmaceutical company, Glaxo, originated with a New Zealand business selling dried milk, while its present-day competitor, Wellcome, was founded by two Americans in 1880.

Despite the length of this list of foreign entrepreneurs in the potentially more advanced technology sectors, there were competitive British entrepreneurs and businesses in electrical engineering (Ferranti, Swann), pharmaceuticals (Allen & Hanbury, May & Baker) and chemicals (United Alkali, Brunner). Most likely, liberalism, not the absence of any domestic innovators, encouraged the inflow.

Immigrant entrepreneurs were merely part of the interchange and specialization to be expected in a liberal international economy. There were emigrant entrepreneurs from Britain as well, businessmen who originated in Britain but built their careers overseas in the later nineteenth century. Andrew Carnegie (1835–1919), son of a handloom weaver, left Dunfermline for the United States with his family in 1848 at the age of 15, eventually to become the founder of US Steel. His talents and energies may well have been recognized had he stayed in

Britain, but the opportunity to use them must have been less in a more slowly expanding economy. Alexander Graham Bell (1847–1922) entered the family profession of teaching the deaf to speak, and his failing health prompted the family move to Canada in 1870. Six years later in the United States he invented the telephone and began the Bell organization. The observation that Britain provided a liberal economic and political environment for business is consistent with the United States offering even greater opportunities. Bell's success required him to team up with an assistant with a more practical bent. Supposing he had found one if he had stayed in the United Kingdom, the subsequent history of the telephone in Britain indicates its development would have been much slower until taken up by the United States.

However, new industries in later Victorian Scotland – with one exception, shale oil – were disproportionately founded by foreign entrepreneurs. American capital established the North British Rubber Co. in 1856, the Swede Alfred Nobel started his explosive and chemical works in 1873, and the American Singer Company set up at Clydebank during the next decade. In contrast, the indigenous Scots stuck with ships, locomotives, and traditional textiles.[34]

The smaller economic region of Alsace also drew on a surprisingly large foreign contribution, but at one or more generation removed, suggesting different forces were at work than in Scotland, but more akin to those in Britain as a whole. Only ten entrepreneurs (14 per cent) were born outside Alsace, of whom six outside France. The proportion rises to 30 per cent for the fathers' generation: 15 per cent were born in Switzerland, 9 per cent in Germany and 6 per cent in another French region. Only one entrepreneur's family in three was already settled in the province by 1789. The majority of foreign Alsatian entrepreneurs' families came from Switzerland (admittedly a relatively short distance), among which were the Huguenots. Mulhouse, an independent republic allied with the Swiss cantons until 1798, also supplied many. The Mulhouse bourgeoisie in the nineteenth century continued to send their children to study in Switzerland. Mulhouse owed the starting of printed cotton fabric production, which was then prohibited in France, to its late accession.

Economic liberalism in the first three-quarters of the nineteenth century created better opportunities both for domestic and foreign entrepreneurs in Britain, and in Scotland especially. All types of firms could take advantage of the legal framework and grow larger than otherwise. More businessmen could shake off the shackles of individual or family equity ownership. The downside of such freedom was a good deal of corruption, malpractice and manipulation of government for personal gain – or loss avoidance. Foreign entrepreneurs immigrated to seize the advantages of a liberal environment. That was fortunate, since Scottish businessmen do not seem to have been keen to move into new industries at home by the later nineteenth century.

Informal human capital appears as a contributor to entrepreneurship in both countries, but not always as expected. Fathers in business are often regarded as a major influence on the business acumen of sons. In our samples, a father in business was associated with a lower chance of starting a successful firm, simply because in an economy dominated by family businesses, a common pattern was for sons to follow their fathers. In some cases management could be a family affair even when another family owned most of the equity. Scotland was much less dominated by family businesses than France; because it was more industrial and the scale of economic activity was greater, the demand for management was so much stronger that sons from non-business families were more often drawn in. This finding contrasts with the results obtained considering only the largest companies in Britain and France. There, a father in business was more often associated with (British) business leadership in 1907, most probably reflecting the greater role of higher education in French career mobility.

In Scotland, where Protestants were the majority, Catholics were under-represented in the business class. Possibly this was because many were immigrants, but perhaps minority Catholic under-representation suggests that cultural factors, not merely exclusion from traditional means of personal advancement, accounted for Protestant business precocity. In France as a whole such exclusion before the Revolution conceivably may be an explanation, but not in Alsace, an area of business immigration.

Idealistic impulses, cutting the time businessmen spent in their firms, may have on balance either enhanced or detracted from some wider measure of well-being. A substantial proportion of both entrepreneurs and managers wanted to advance the public interest by good works, such as housing and education schemes. But the majority showed little effective interest and a proportion were interested solely in getting rich quickly.

French businessmen were more likely to have received formal education to a higher level than British entrepreneurs. This seems to mirror national culture rather than indicate more rapid business expansion in the nineteenth century. For in the largest companies of both countries, most top managers entered at the boardroom level, despite very different firms, population dispersion and poor transport. We have less systematic information about Scottish family firms, but unlike the corresponding French businesses, their owners leave more wealth at death than independent firm managers on average, and their wealth increases with the longevity of the business. Both observations are consistent with a better performance of Scottish than French family businesses. Again the explanation is probably based on law and geography; the economic area of Scotland was compact and integrated in the mid-nineteenth century compared with France. Scottish businesses that survived and prospered in this competitive environment needed to be efficient.

Notes

*Research for this essay was supported by a grant from the Leverhulme Trust. We are grateful for comments on an earlier version by conference participants and Peter Solar.

1. C. Fohlen, 'Entrepreneurship and Management in France in the Nineteenth Century' and P. L. Payne, 'Industrial Entrepreneurship and Management in Great Britain', in P. Mathias and M. Postan (eds), *Cambridge Economic History of Europe* (Cambridge: University Press, 1978), vol. 7, part 1, pp. 346–51 and pp. 201–21.
2. E. Jones, *The European Miracle: Environments, Economies, and Geopolitics in the History of Europe and Asia* (Cambridge: University Press, 1987).
3. C. Napier, 'The History of Financial Reporting in the United Kingdom' in P. Walton (ed.), *European Financial Reporting: a History* (Aldershot: Academic Press, 1995).
4. R. H. Campbell, 'The Law and the Joint Stock Company in Scotland' in P. L. Payne (ed.), *Studies in Scottish Business History* (London: Cass, 1967).
5. Only the UK 1856 Act in the nineteenth century applied without qualification in Scotland, two other British Companies Acts did not (those of 1844 and 1855) and the remaining three were inoperative.
6. C. Freedman, *Joint Stock Enterprise in France 1807–1867: From Privileged Company to Modern Corporation* (Chapel Hill, 1979).
7. C. Freedman, *The Triumph of Corporate Capitalism in France 1867–1914* (Rochester, NY, 1993), p. 21.
8. F. Caron, *An Economic History of Modern France* (London: Methuen, 1979), p. 159.
9. Y. Cassis, *Big Business: the European Experience in the Twentieth Century* (Oxford: Oxford University Press, 1997).
10. The French data set is derived primarily from D. Barjot *et al.*, *Les Patrons du Second Empire* (Paris: Picard, 1991–94). With 340 cases, it is larger than that

used in J. Foreman-Peck *et al.*, 'Entrepreneurs and Business Performance in Nineteenth Century France', *European Review of Economic History*, 2 (1998), 235–62.

11. M. Hau, *L'Industrialisation d'Alsace, 1803–1939* (Strasbourg: Presses des Universités de Strasbourg, 1987).

12. The Scottish study is built on the work of S. Checkland and A. Slaven, *Dictionary of Scottish Business Biography 1860–1960* (Aberdeen, 1986). J. Foreman-Peck and J. Smith, 'The Generation and Transmission of Wealth among Victorian Businessmen and Elites' (unpublished, 1998) find statistical evidence of Scottish 'canniness' in their analysis of British elites before 1914. Membership of the Church of Scotland was associated with greater business wealth, other things being equal.

13. Hau, *Industrialisation d'Alsace*, p. 61.

14. Ibid., Table 78.

15. B. Lenman, *An Economic History of Modern Scotland 1660–1976* (London: Batsford, 1977), p. 192.

16. Hau, *Industrialisation d'Alsace*, Table 13.

17. Or perhaps a reflection of the different approaches to sampling the two regions.

18. Lenman, *Economic History of Modern Scotland*, p. 185.

19. There seems to be a significant difference between the two countries, with a chi-square of 9.6(5), but there were some difficulties in reconstructing the underlying numbers in the data taken from Cassis, *Big Business*.

20. M. Lévy-Leboyer, 'Le Patronat Francais 1912–1973', in M. Lévy-Leboyer (ed.), *Le Patronat de la Seconde Industrialisation* (Paris, 1979).

21. P. L. Payne, 'Family Business in Britain: an Historical and Analytical Survey' in A. Okochi and S. Yasuoka (eds), *Family Business in the Era of Industrial Growth* (Tokyo, 1984), pp. 196–7.

22. A. Chandler, *Scale and Scope: the Dynamics of Industrial Capitalism* (Cambridge, 1990) pp. 389–92.

23. R. Church, 'The Family Firm in Industrial Capitalism: International Perspectives on Hypotheses and History', *Business History*, 25(1993).

24. E. Chadeau, 'The Large Family Firm in Twentieth Century France', *Business History*, 37(1995), 184–205.

25. Caron, *Economic History of Modern France*, p. 168.

26. We distinguish 'independence' by the relationship to the businessman. Thus the businessman in an independent firm is not related to the principal equity owners and has not founded the enterprise. The businessman in a family firm may have joined his uncle's or father-in-law's concern, even if his own father was not in business.

27. D. Jeremy, *Capitalists and Christians: Business Leaders and the Churches in Britain, 1900–1960* (Oxford: Clarendon Press, 1990).

28. H. Berghoff, 'Regional Variations in Provincial Business Biography: the Case of Birmingham, Bristol and Manchester 1870–1914', *Business History*, 37(1995), 64–85.

29. Jeremy, *Capitalists and Christians*.

30. J. Foreman-Peck, *Smith & Nephew in the Health Care Industry* (Elgar, 1995).

31. D. Jeremy, *A Business History of Britain* (Oxford: University Press, 1998), pp. 386–408.

32. L. T. C. Rolt, *Isambard Kingdom Brunel: a Biography* (London: Arrow Books, 1961), chapter 1.
33. E. Diesel, G. Goldbeck and F. Schildenberger, *From Engines to Autos: Five Pioneers in Engine Development and Their Contributions to the Automotive Industry* (Chicago: Henry Regnery, 1960).
34. For a conclusion of Scottish entrepreneurial failure from these observations, see, for example, T. Byres, 'Entrepreneurship in the Scottish Heavy Industries 1870–1900' in P. L. Payne (ed.), *Studies in Scottish Business History* (London: Cass, 1967).

3
The End of the Anglo-French Commercial Alliance, 1860–1894[1]

Peter T. Marsh

For most of the 40 years before Fashoda, Anglo-French relations were comparatively cordial. The foundation of that cordiality was commercial. Richard Cobden and Napoleon III laid the cornerstone in 1860 with their agreement on tariff reductions. Like the founders of the European Economic Community a century later, these two mid-nineteenth-century statesmen, in most ways so different from each other, agreed in regarding their economic agreement as a means towards a political end. Both men sought to avert the conflict between their two countries that Napoleon's aggrandizing behaviour around the borders of France seemed otherwise all too likely to precipitate.

The resulting commercial alliance achieved its immediate political objective and also promoted the material well-being of the two countries. Yet neither country was quite convinced of the worth of their commercial agreement; and they abandoned it between 1882 and 1892. No one was more ambivalent about the policy of negotiated tariff reduction than the great British Liberal, Gladstone. As Chancellor of the Exchequer in 1860, he co-operated closely with Cobden in reaching the agreement with the French Emperor, and for the rest of his life Gladstone argued that the commercial treaty of 1860 had saved Britain from the likelihood of war with France.[2] Yet he grew increasingly disenchanted with the bargaining that was indispensable in the making of tariff treaties. In the early 1880s when the treaty of 1860 was about to expire, Gladstone, who was by then Prime Minister, favoured its renewal mainly because of its political implications.

So did Gambetta on the French side. Yet, despite a frantic last-minute effort by Gambetta, in 1882 the two countries failed to renew their treaty. Rather than accept any heightening of the French tariff, which even the most liberal of the French ministers regarded as politically

34

unavoidable, Gladstone's government preferred to let Cobden's treaty lapse. Ten years later the last remnants of the commercial alliance between the two countries disintegrated.

A lot in Europe had hinged on that alliance. It constituted the formative centre of the network of tariff-reducing treaties that the two countries had spread across Europe in the 1860s. Nevertheless, as Britain had done in 1882 in allowing Cobden's treaty to lapse, so France in 1892 with the enactment of the Méline tariff gave up its central position in that network. The two countries thus lost their ability to shape the treaty-based or conventional tariff of Europe in their interests. In a momentous turn of events, Bismarck's successor Caprivi seized the power that France abandoned and reconstructed the European tariff treaty network around the German Empire.

Why did France and Britain allow this to happen? Why did their commercial alliance fall apart? The answer appears to be as follows. While the purposes behind the original treaty were primarily political, the dynamics of disintegration had to do with commercial policy and found their political expression in the legislative concerns of each country with the sore points in its economy rather than in their diplomatic relations.

The British governing elite were never entirely easy about the commercial policy that underlay the treaty of 1860. Its mode of negotiation was irregular both in personnel and in principle. In his discussions with the French Emperor, Cobden operated without any office in, or formal mandate from, the British government. Thereafter he involved British merchants in hammering out the details of the tariff with French officials, setting another precedent from which the Foreign Office soon recoiled. There was more concern in parliamentary circles about the violation of free trade theory implicit in the 1860 treaty. That concern thereafter prevented Britain from participating as effectively as France in securing tariff treaties with other European states as Cobden and Napoleon had envisaged. The form of free trade theory to which the British governing establishment was devoted interpreted agreements to reduce tariffs as a blessing to both contracting parties rather than as an exchange of concessions. But as soon as the British Foreign Secretary, Russell, attempted to reach tariff-reducing agreements with Britain's other trading partners, he discovered that he had to offer compensating equivalents or concessions for the tariff reductions he sought. This need applied even when all that Britain sought was most-favoured-nation access to tariff reductions that France secured by treaty with other European countries in pursuance of the 1860 model with Britain. British merchants also discovered that continental states couched their tariff treaties with each other in terms that benefited only the immediate signatory countries and not those others who were entitled simply to most-favoured-nation treatment. Support in Britain for commercial treaties was nevertheless stronger in mercantile than in governmental circles through most of the 1860s. In fact it was pressure from the chambers of commerce that set the pace of British commercial diplomacy.

In France that situation was reversed. There the pressure for an open European market came from the government, whether imperial or later republican, and it encountered resistance from chambers of commerce especially in the textile-making North. The network of tariff treaties that France, feebly seconded by Britain, spread across western and central Europe between 1860 and 1867 formed part, the main part, of an attempt by Napoleon III to widen his imperium commercially. He supplemented the network of tariff treaties with a monetary union that incorporated the neighbouring economies of Belgium, Switzerland and Italy. This use of commercial approaches towards imperial ends was distinctive of the Second Empire.

Yet it was sustained for 20 years after the fall of the empire by the most effectively liberal ministers in the Third Republic, men such as Léon Say and Pierre-Emmanuel Tirard. Between 1880 and 1882 Say and Tirard took successive charge of the negotiations on the French side for renewal of the treaty that Cobden had reached with Napoleon III. The best efforts of Say, Tirard and also Gambetta were, however, subverted by contrary forces in Britain and France. On one side, the French ministers faced mounting protectionist pressure in the legislature. On the other, the British negotiators refused to accept any increase in the French tariff on textiles, even when the French offered to reduce their tariff on other sectors of British industry, notably on iron and steel.

The chief British trade negotiator in the early 1880s, Sir Charles Dilke, was even more anxious than Tirard to find a mutually acceptable settlement. But the British mercantile community had come to regard the original 1860 treaty as an unequal arrangement. Britain, they now thought, had accepted the treaty in 1860 provisionally on the assumption that it would lead the French on to full free trade. That assumption was discredited by the French demand in the early 1880s for tariff increases. The depression that set in after 1873 had deepened the conflict of interest between merchants on the two sides of the Channel. Falling prices made the burden of those items in the French tariff that carried fixed rather than *ad valorem* rates of duty fall ever more heavily on British exporters. Yet the French negotiators in the early 1880s demanded replacement of their remaining *ad valorem* rates of duty with fixed charges.

British merchants raised a close to universal cry for abandonment of a treaty on those terms. This reaction came as much from firm free traders as from nascent protectionists. The British government felt obliged to comply. Dilke did so with more reluctance than Gladstone. After the failure of the negotiations with France, Gladstone told the House of Commons that he took comfort in 'escaping from the meshes of the Tariff Treaty' because 'those principles of Free Trade on which we stand in our fiscal legislation are no longer disparaged'.[3]

Meanwhile the political elements in the relationship between Britain and France changed in a way that their economic interests could no longer reconcile. In 1859/60 the potential for conflict between them came from European sources, from Britain's fear that Napoleon aimed to extend French power around Europe as his uncle had done. Napoleon III used the economic interest that Britain shared with France in opening up the continental market to allay that political fear. But in the 1880s Britain's political suspicions of France took a different turn, overseas; and there the economic concerns of the two countries only heightened their political antagonism. France, frustrated by its inability to avenge its losses on the continent from the war with Germany, paid increasing attention to its interests further afield, particularly in the northern half of Africa. There they came into conflict with British interests, opening the road to Fashoda. And these conflicting interests were as much economic as political, unlike the conflicts of mid-century. British officialdom was initially reluctant to recognize how the different kinds of conflict combined. Is it true, the Foreign Office asked its commercial attaché in Paris, that France is erecting preferential tariff walls around trade with its overseas possessions even while it continues to promote open trade within the continental European market? What surprises us now is the naivety of that question. Even the liberal members of French ministries after 1882 did not insist on applying their principles to commerce with the French colonies. There was thus little prospect for agreements on colonial commerce to offset the accumulating political confrontations between Britain and France overseas. On the contrary, commercial considerations reinforced the road that led to Fashoda. Those in Britain who were most concerned about cultivating the overseas empire, men such as Lord Salisbury and Joseph Chamberlain, were also inclined to align Britain with the Triple Alliance of Germany, Austria-Hungary and Italy rather than with the emerging Dual Alliance of France and Russia.

These considerations had, however, little to do with the enactment of the Méline tariff and hence with the departure of France from a controlling position in the web of tariff treaties that it had woven around itself. France went its own way in 1892 for its own commercial and domestic political reasons. No attention was paid to the former commercial alliance with Britain. That neglect was understandable since Britain had abandoned the alliance a decade earlier. More surprisingly, the French legislature refused to heed warnings that disregard for former commercial treaty partners would open the way for the advancement of Germany. When Caprivi began to construct a common tariff with Austria-Hungary, Italy and Switzerland, liberal commentators in France raised the alarm. They pointed out that 'a vast Customs League' was in the making, 'created for the sole purpose and with the obvious effect of building up a wall against France and her export trade, of which the French will have furnished the mortar and the stones'.[4] But Méline and his men, though staunchly anti-German, disregarded this objection to their work.

They went on raising the tariff to protect the French domestic market from foreign encroachment and to keep up the prices that French producers could command at home against the threatened flood of cheap produce from abroad. The protectionists who controlled the French legislature raised the minimum tariff in deliberate defiance of the country's current commercial treaty partners. Protectionist legislators denied the executive the right to offer reductions in the French tariff in return for corresponding reductions in foreign rates of duty. Going still further despite pleas from the ministry, the legislature set the duty on wine high enough to make a tariff agreement with Spain, the major French supplier while the ravages of phylloxera had yet to be repaired, absolutely impossible. Méline and his supporters extended their hostility from tariff-setting treaties to most-favoured-nation agreements, arguing that these latter deprived France of steadying control over its own tariff.

On the other side of the Channel the Conservative who had succeeded Gladstone as Prime Minister, Lord Salisbury, paid close attention to the prolonged debate in France. The often daily reports that he received from Sir Joseph Crowe, the commercial attaché in the Paris embassy, made Salisbury perhaps the best-informed statesman outside France on the evolution of the new commercial policy there. He paid similarly close attention to the response to the French tariff in other foreign and commerce ministries across Europe, from the Scandinavian states and the Iberian peninsula to the Balkans. He encouraged Crowe to tour the continent and report on the countries most likely to react to the French venture. From every British embassy and legation on the continent Salisbury demanded detailed assessments of the impact of any tariff treaties or autonomous changes in tariff on British trade and commerce. He attempted, whenever opportunity offered, to orchestrate the European response to protectionist excesses in countries such as Spain that still desired good trading relations with partner economies. Not since the early 1860s, and perhaps not even then, had the chancelleries of Europe been so absorbed with commercial diplomacy as they were in the early 1890s. Never before had a British Foreign Secretary so involved himself with these matters.

It is tempting to interpret the attention Salisbury paid to European tariff making as one more reflection of his keen interest in international diplomacy. He was, by his own choice, Foreign Secretary as well as Prime Minister; and in Britain the responsibility for commercial diplomacy fell to the Foreign Office. His co-operation on tariff matters with the commercial treaty association of central European states coincided nicely with the Mediterranean agreements that he reached with the Triple Alliance. Yet there is no evidence that Salisbury made this connection between high power politics and commercial diplomacy himself. Nor did he expressly interpret the Méline tariff as evidence of, and another reason for, the distance that was developing in the general relationship between Britain and France. It was not the disintegration and loss of the Anglo-French commercial alliance that concerned him. That alliance had been defunct for a decade. Salisbury was interested in the tariff making that was going on in Europe not so much because of its bearing on Britain's diplomatic relationships as for domestic reasons having to do with the kind of Conservative government he wanted to provide in Britain.

What dismayed him in the diplomatic scene so far as commerce was concerned was Britain's ineffectiveness. Amid the flurry of commercial policy-making on the continent, Britain was being simply overlooked. During the 1860s Gladstone had completed the reduction of the British tariff to slim proportions for maximum revenue production. In doing so he had deprived Britain of most of its bargaining chips in commercial diplomacy. Thus disabled, and further prompted by Gladstone's principled distaste for the bargaining that was the lifeblood of tariff treaty making, the British government had largely withdrawn itself from the commercial diplomacy of Europe. Successive governments, mainly but not solely those of Liberal affiliation, took pride in the high-minded morality of the British version of free trade. Reassured by the financial dividends that the City of London reaped from that doctrine, the Treasury enforced it rigidly, undeterred by the refusal of other industrializing countries to follow the British example.

There remained, however, a useful though embarrassing anomaly in the Gladstonian policy. Gladstone retained a high duty on wine and framed it, furthermore, in such a way as to discriminate in favour of the wines of France against the stronger wines of the Iberian peninsula and Italy. This covert bargaining chip could be put to good use. Mediterranean wine producers were eager to overcome their disadvantage in the British market. Though Gladstone refused to acknowledge the discrimination, in 1880 he made a grand offer of reduction all round, to benefit the wines of every producing country. But even-handed treatment of this sort did not satisfy any of the continental contenders. They did not respond to Gladstone's proposal, and he did not repeat it. Opposition from the Treasury was enough to make this a one-time offer only. And free-trade orthodoxy ruled out any threat to heighten the wine duty against countries that discriminated against British exports.

In any case, Salisbury discovered by the early 1890s that the duty on wine was not in itself enough to enable Britain to bargain effectively. He wanted Britain to give itself once again the power to discriminate against the luxury exports of continental countries, particularly the silks and other fine textiles that bulked so large in the calculations of European ministries of commerce. He perceived that, regardless of what the theorists, both free-trading and protectionist, said, the commercial treaty makers of Europe were hammering out a conventional tariff that combined some protection for the vital economic interests of each state with terms that provided access to each other's markets. He also learned in detail how the Germans shaped the tariff of the central European states to discriminate against the goods of countries like Britain and France that were still entitled to most-favoured-nation treatment.

He wanted above all to show the manufacturers and merchants of Britain how the traditional tools of government could advance their economic interests. When it came to the tariff, Salisbury was as much concerned about the economic concerns of British voters as Méline was about the French. Salisbury opened his campaign in the general election of 1892 by appealing for the restoration of a tariff on luxuries, a tariff that could be used to gain greater access to the continental market. He presented the need for this tool of negotiation as a matter of logic and common sense: 'this little island lives as a trading island', he reminded his audience.[5] Britain could not produce enough to feed and employ its population without importing foodstuffs and exporting the products of its main industries. Those exports were under fire.

> We live in an age of a war of tariffs. Every nation is trying how it can, by agreement with its neighbour, get the greatest possible protection for its own industries, and, at the same time, the greatest possible access to the markets of its neighbours. This kind of negotiation... has been going on for the last year and a half with great activity [but] ... what I observe is that while A is very anxious to get a favour of B, and B is anxious to get a favour of C, nobody cares two straws about getting the commercial favour of Great Britain. What is the reason of that? It is that in this great battle Great Britain has deliberately stripped herself of the armour and the weapons by which the battle has to be fought. You cannot do business in this world of evil and suffering on those terms. If you go to market you must bring money with you; if you fight you must fight with the weapons with which those you have to contend against are fighting. ... The weapon with which they all fight is admission to their own markets – that is to say, A says to B, 'if you will make your duties such that I can sell in your market, I will make my duties such that you can sell in my market'. But we begin by saying, 'We will levy no duties on anybody', and we declare that it would be contrary and disloyal to the glorious and sacred doctrine of free trade to levy any duty on anybody for the sake of what we can get by it. It may be noble, but it is not business. On those terms you will get nothing. ... if you intend, in this conflict of commercial treaties, to hold your own, you must be prepared, if need be, to inflict upon the nations which injure you the penalty which is in your hands, that of refusing them access to your markets.

There was one great exception to the commercial policy Salisbury advocated that he fully recognized. If applied to the United States, it would damage vital British interests. The United States was more thoroughly protectionist than any European state save Russia. British commercial policy had focused on Europe for the past 40 years because of impediments to entry into the American market, first the Civil War there, and then the post-war escalations in the tariff.

> The Power we have most reason to complain of is the United States, [yet] what we want the United States to furnish us with mostly are articles of food essential to the feeding of the people, and raw materials necessary to our manufactures, and we cannot exclude one or the

other without serious injury to ourselves.... We must confine ourselves, at least for the present, to those subjects on which we should
not suffer very much whether the importation continued or diminished ... if it is a question of wine, or silk, or spirits, or gloves, or lace,
or anything of that kind ... I should not in the least shrink from
diminishing the consumption ... for the purpose of maintaining
our rights in this commercial war, and of insisting on our rights of
access to the markets of our neighbours.... We must distinguish
between consumer and consumer, and while jealously preserving
the rights of a consumer who is co-extensive with a whole industry,
or with the whole people of the country, we may fairly use our power
over an importation which merely ministers to luxury, in order to
maintain our own in this great commercial battle.

The problem for Britain in common with most other states of Europe
was, as Salisbury said, one of access to each other's markets. Even highly
protectionist countries on the continent made the dual use of tariffs that
he described, to gain access to neighbouring markets as well as to protect
the market at home. France pulled away from this European pattern. But
no other continental state was tempted to follow the French example.
Switzerland, though threatening to retaliate, wished only to demonstrate to the French how much they would hurt themselves by with-
drawing from tariff treaty making. Germany under Caprivi abandoned
Bismarck's unilateralism and returned to commercial treaty making, a
return that was not reversed after Caprivi fell from office. Though all the
continental states except for the Netherlands agreed on the need to
protect their home markets, all except France agreed on the need for
access to each other's markets. Tariffs on the continent were designed to
serve both purposes. The question for the British was whether they
could design a tariff that would open the continental market to them
without damaging the economy at home. European experience convinced Salisbury that Britain could do so if it reimposed tariffs on
luxuries and regained full freedom of manoeuvre over the existing
duty on wine.

But the British electorate rejected Salisbury's plea. Though his speech
heartened his immediate audience of Conservative activists, the electorate as a whole responded with indifference verging on hostility. His
Liberal Unionist ally, Joseph Chamberlain, estimated that Salisbury's
remarks on the tariff at the opening of the campaign cost the Conservative and Unionist forces a dozen seats in the July voting. Whatever the
effect on the Liberal Unionists many of whom were free traders, some of

the losses occurred on the Conservative side and in both rural and urban seats. Though Gladstone's Liberals had to rely on the Irish for the small majority they won in the new House of Commons, the results certainly did not mandate the basic change in British commercial policy that Salisbury advocated. In a message to his prospective successor at the end of the year, Salisbury conceded that henceforth the Conservative Party would have to avoid any taint of protectionism.[6]

Thus in 1892 both Britain and France isolated themselves from the commercial policy-making in which the rest of Europe was engaged. In so doing though without acknowledging the fact, they annulled the commercial alliance that had preserved a basic harmony between them for a generation after 1860. There was nothing now to offset the sharpening imperial disputes that drove them to Fashoda.

Notes

1. This essay draws in large part upon my book, *Bargaining on Europe: Britain and the First Common Market, 1860–1892* (London, 1999).
2. W. E. Gladstone, 'The History of 1852–60, and Greville's Latest Journals', *English Historical Review* (Apr. 1887), 296.
3. Hansard 3rd ser., cclxvii, 1911 (24 Mar. 1882).
4. Reported from the French journal, *Débats*, by the British commercial attaché in Paris, J. A. Crowe, enclosed in Lytton to Salisbury, 13 Apr. 1891, PRO/FO881/6185, p. 185.
5. Speech at Hastings reported in *The Times* of 19 May 1892.
6. R. T. Shannon, *The Age of Salisbury, 1881–1902* (London: Longman, 1996), pp. 350 and 379–80.

4
Théophile Delcassé and the Question of Intervention in the Anglo-Boer War, October 1899–March 1900

Pascal R. Venier

After the humiliation of the Fashoda crisis of 1898, French Foreign Secretary Théophile Delcassé was actively involved in reviewing the priorities of French foreign policy.[1] Working towards strengthening the diplomatic links of France, he initiated a political line which led to the reshaping of the Franco-Russian alliance in 1899, and later to the signature of the Franco-Italian agreements of 1900 and 1901. Delcassé also considered the possibility of a rapprochement with Britain, which eventually led to the colonial settlement of 1904, which would be the starting point for the Franco-British diplomatic collaboration, generally known as the Entente Cordiale.

One of the difficulties in interpreting Delcassé's foreign policy, in the early years of his tenure of office at the Quai d'Orsay, is to establish precisely when he became convinced of the need to radically alter the course of France's policy towards Britain. This question has been the object of many controversies.[2] According to his collaborators, the French Foreign Minister was convinced, as early as February 1899, of the need to pursue a policy of rapprochement with Britain which he consistently took steps to implement.[3] This school of interpretation seems to have been forgotten since the 1960s and the work of Christopher Andrew.

Analysing, in his *Théophile Delcassé and the Making of the Entente Cordiale*, the policy of the French Foreign Minister during the Boer War, Andrew attempted to demonstrate that far from following a policy of rapprochement with Britain, he led a hostile policy against her. Summarizing his conclusions, he did not hesitate to state that 'during the first six months of the Boer War Delcassé made two separate attempts to persuade Germany to join with the Dual Alliance (France and Russia) in demanding that England end her military occupation of Egypt'.[4]

Although Andrew's interpretation has generally been accepted for the last 30 years, it is not irrefutable. Much to the contrary, a careful analysis of available sources suggests a rather different reading of the events. The purpose of this chapter will, therefore, be to re-examine the role played by Théophile Delcassé in the question of the so-called 'intervention in the Boer War'. This episode is so fascinating as much as it remains one of the most obscure of a period of the history of international relations otherwise very well studied, and to a lesser degree because of the controversies it generated in 1908 at the time of the *Daily Telegraph* affair and also during the interwar period and since the Second World War.

Here it is only possible to highlight the main stages of a controversy which arose in the summer of 1908 from the publication of an article in the *National Review*.[5] André Mévil, a journalist close to Delcassé, claimed that 'during the South African War the Germans, profiting from events, projected a Franco-German-Russian *entente* with the object of inducing England to consider the advisability of making peace' but also stressed the contrast in the attitudes of France and Russia, mainly inspired by humanitarian motivations, and that of Germany, whose machiavellian designs were aimed at exploiting France and humiliating Britain.

The debate rebounded in the aftermath of the First World War, when the first relevant diplomatic documents and political memoirs were published. Léon Cahen, for the Ecole Historique Française, argued the intervention initiative was primarily the result of Wilhelm II's intrigues in order to discredit Russia and France in the eyes of Britain.[6] For the German revisionist school, illustrated by Erich Brandenburg, the initiative for intervention came from France and 'the only explanation of this episode seems to be that France and Russia had, all along, aimed at entangling Germany in such a way as to have brought about a permanent estrangement from England'.[7]

In the 1950s and early 1960s, the question remained a subject of deep debate among historians, and the most distinguished specialists, while approaching it in a more serene and detached state of mind, offered deeply conflicting interpretations. Alan Taylor interpreted the proposals for intervention as having been initiated by Germany,[8] while John Hargreaves, in an article published for the centenary of Delcassé's birth, stressed the latter's Anglophobia during the Boer War.[9] For John Grenville, Delcassé had led a hostile policy against Britain during the

conflict, not only playing an essential role in the projects for intervention against her, but also considering at the end of February 1900, no
less than a 'preventive war' against her![10]

Delcassé and the Russian initiative for a continental intervention in the South African War, October–November 1899

Soon after the outbreak of the Anglo-Boer War the possibility of forming
a continental coalition against Britain was considered at the request of
Russia. For some historians, the initiative was actively encouraged by
Delcassé who saw an opportunity to reopen the question of Egypt.[11]
During the visit of the Russian Minister to Paris, in October 1899, it is
said that Delcassé and Count Muraviev would have agreed that the latter
should sound out Germany on the subject of intervention in the South
African War during the forthcoming visit of the Tsar to the Kaiser at
Potsdam.[12] On 8 November, during his conversations with Wilhelm II
and Bülow, Muraviev would have mentioned the possibility of such an
intervention in the conflict and would have attempted to overcome
German fears of British naval superiority, but to no avail, as the Germans
were not then disposed to consider intervention.[13] However, it seems
difficult to accept such a version of events. In the light of available
documents, it is possible to argue that although the Russian Foreign
Minister did discuss with his French counterpart the possibility of a
diplomatic intervention, he, in fact, never actually came to formulate
such a proposal to the Germans, partly due to Delcassé's opposition.

In October 1899, Muraviev undertook a tour of Europe, in order to
secure support for a *combinaison* of European powers against Britain
which he was planning. Visiting Biarritz, he met Spanish Premier Silveva
in San Sebastian and then went on to Paris to discuss the matter with
Delcassé.[14]

From the account that Silveva gave of his conversations with the
Russian Foreign Minister, it is known that although he was confident
of the support of Germany, he expected, by contrast, some difficult
negotiations with his French counterpart.[15]

Delcassé was undoubtedly aware that the position of France was not
favourable to an adventurous policy, as the Fashoda crisis had all too
cruelly revealed that the preparedness of the French Navy was inadequate to risk a possible confrontation with Britain's naval might. The
domestic political climate had further degraded in a rather spectacular
manner, and the priority for the French cabinet, more than an ambi-

tious foreign policy, was fighting for the very survival of the regime. The French government was also preoccupied with ensuring the success of the forthcoming Paris Universal Exhibition of 1900.

After the outbreak of the Anglo-Boer War, Count Bülow made overtures to the Marquis de Noailles, the French ambassador in Berlin, mentioning in particular 'the similitude of interests of France and Germany in extra-European questions'.[16] While welcoming these overtures, Delcassé, who knew that the Alsace-Lorraine question remained an insurmountable obstacle to any understanding with Germany, nevertheless gave to these overtures all the attention they deserved, but remained extremely cautious. He instructed the Marquis de Noailles to find out more and to ask the German authorities to clarify their thoughts.[17] Noailles acted on these instructions, but the State Secretary remained more elusive than ever.[18] While in a conversation with Noailles, the Kaiser expressed his concern at the rise of British power, and did not dissimulate his reluctance towards any further intervention in the South African question: 'When I sent my telegram to Krüger, there was still time. But, in the last 4 years, the English have developed their navy to such an extent that I am paralysed. It is impossible to risk ourselves against them: my trade, my ports, Hamburg, are too exposed.'[19] Germany's support in any diplomatic intervention of such a nature as to allow France to reopen the question of Egypt clearly appeared to be out of the question.

It is very difficult to have a precise idea of the content of the discussions which took place during Muraviev's visit in Paris, but it seems, however, that the French authorities refused to follow the Russian's adventurous proposals.[20] The British ambassador in Paris, Sir Edmund Monson, was himself convinced of that.[21] Delcassé, who remained extremely cautious, seems to have rejected the idea of a hostile intervention against Britain, only accepting the eventuality of a pacific and humanitarian démarche in the traditions of French foreign policy.[22] He himself later wrote that 'During Count Mouravieff's stay in Paris, the Russian Foreign Minister and myself had agreed to try, should the right moment arise, to put an end to the war between England and the Transvaal.' And that 'Count Mouravieff, who was to meet Emperor William and M. de Bülow had undertaken to sound out the imperial Government and to enquire of their dispositions.'[23]

However, no proposals for a common diplomatic intervention were made to the Germans, which plainly spared the Russian minister the humiliation of a refusal.[24] Following a practice common in German diplomacy, 'a semi-official note' had been inserted in the *Kölnische*

Zeitung, and other German newspapers, on the eve of the Tsar's arrival in Potsdam, on 7 November 1899. This note, denying that any intervention scheme had been put to the German government, hinted that such a proposal would not be welcome.[25] Further, on the very morning of Muraviev's arrival in Berlin, the Anglo-German agreement on Samoa, a great success for Bülow's 'Free Hand' policy, was announced, much to Muraviev's annoyance.[26] This announcement, made even before the signature of the document, as it is now known, was clearly 'a slap in the face' for the Russian Foreign Minister.[27] Shortening his visit to Germany, he promptly returned to St Petersburg.[28]

One must stress that the only document which has been used as evidence to support the claim that a proposal was made to the Germans is a letter from Delcassé to Noailles of 4 March 1900.[29] However, intriguingly, although the document does mention that 'Count Mouravieff [...] had undertaken to sound out the imperial Government and to enquire of their dispositions', it also clearly states that they 'seemed to him such that no conversation could be engaged on this matter'.[30]

It is therefore not possible to use this document in support of such a claim. The absence of any reference to a proposal for an intervention in the accounts of the meetings between Nicholas II, Muraviev, Wilhelm II and von Bülow on 8 November 1899, given by the German State Secretary, are also revealing.[31] Much to the contrary he reported that

> about the South African conflict, Muravief remarked that the so-called public opinion in France, in Russia and apparently also in Germany pressed the governments to attempt something against England. But that there was nothing to do. France were not thinking of attempting anything, but would wait to see which course the military events would take. France in any case wanted first [to] consolidate herself internally.[32]

It is also interesting to note that on that occasion Bülow reported that Muraviev was not without expressing some animosity towards the French Foreign Minister: 'Delcassé is a maniac, for whom everything is subordinated to the idea of *Revanche*. He only sees Strasbourg without thinking of the superior interests of Europe.'[33]

March 1900: hostile intervention or offer of *bons offices*

It is a fact that the idea of a diplomatic intervention of the three continental powers was proposed to Germany in March 1900.

However, it seems to have been in a very different spirit than is generally assumed.

It is well established that the Russian ambassador in Berlin approached von Bülow on 2 March 1900 and submitted a note proposing to Germany to join in a tripartite initiative to end the war between Britain and the Boer Republics.[34] The outcome of the initiative was, however, extremely disappointing. Wilhelm II responded on 3 March, that he thought that London should be sounded out beforehand.[35] The Kaiser also asked for a preliminary condition to any negotiation in the form of a guarantee of territorial status quo in Europe, which for France would have meant reiterating her acceptance of the terms of the treaty of Frankfurt and renouncing any claim on Alsace and Lorraine.[36] This immediately brought the Russian initiative to an end.

It has been argued that Delcassé's desire to profit from Britain's difficulties remained very strong and that he hoped to broaden the scope of a possible intervention to include the question of Egypt and force the British to evacuate the Khedivate.[37] This initiative would have been conceived by its protagonists as hostile intervention and probably as a stage towards the formation of a continental coalition against Britain.[38] There are difficulties with following this interpretation and its seems essential to analyse both the context and nature of the initiative to understand its significance.

It seems extremely revealing that, in mid-January 1900, when, in the context of the *Bundesrath* affair which had created a climate of acute tension between Britain and Germany, von Bülow and Wilhelm II made overtures which Russian ambassador, Count Osten-Sacken, interpreted as indicating that Germany would be prepared to consider the eventuality of a continental coalition against Britain, Delcassé unambiguously refused to envisage the possibility of an entente with Germany.[39] As Prince Urusov, the Russian ambassador in Paris reported, Delcassé 'saw in the German's apparent fluctuations, the intent to push France to compromise herself in the eyes of England and the French minister was not far to consider the vague overtures made by emperor Wilhelm to Count Osten-Sacken as a similar attempt directed towards Russia this time'.[40] Approached by Muraviev about the opportunity of reopening the question of Egypt, Delcassé was extremely reserved, stressing, on 25 January, how damaging such a move could potentially be for the 'prestige and the dignity of the Powers who would have attempted it'.[41]

It is nevertheless clear that, as Christopher Andrew has shown, Delcassé did seriously envisage in early February 1900, the possibility of reopening the question of Egypt.[42] He did so, after Cogordan, the

French consul-general in Cairo, suggested pressing London not to evacuate Egypt, but, more modestly, to enforce the dispositions of the International Convention on the Suez Canal of 1888, which provided for its 'neutralisation', but which the British had refused to implement since 1889.[43] Paris daily *Le Matin*, Delcassé's mouthpiece, was employed, as was often the case, to float a trial balloon.[44] It was in the form of a leader entitled 'L'Égypte' published in its issue of 6 February, which 'encouraged Germany to take part with the support of France and Russia in an initiative to secure the neutralisation of the Suez canal'.[45]

The French Foreign Secretary does not however seem to have stuck with such intentions for very long. The Germans were not very receptive to these overtures; much to the contrary, it was reported from Berlin that a violent anti-French campaign, which was believed to be orchestrated by the Wilhelmstrasse, was developing in the German semi-official press.[46] At the same time the enthusiasm of the Russians for intervention was cooling down, as they had been able to exploit British weakness to their advantage, notably with two diplomatic successes in Afghanistan and Persia.[47] Revealingly, Montebello, the French ambassador in St Petersburg, reported on 15 February that both General Kuropatkin and Muraviev 'believe that we cannot count on any real and efficient support from Germany, in any circumstance, at least in the current state of affairs, and they both seem [. . .] to be in perfect agreement on this matter'.[48] Count Muraviev concluded in an important memorandum of 7 February 1900, that a continental league against Britain was impossible and that diplomatic action against her was far too risky.[49]

If both French and Russians were, by mid-February, ruling out the possibility of a hostile intervention, how can the initiative of March 1900 be accounted for? Could this proposition be of a totally different nature from the one it is generally believed to be?

The most likely explanation for the approach made to the Germans in March 1900 is that it was the result of a personal intervention by Nicholas II, who, after a series of British victories, saw a momentum for a peaceful resolution of the conflict.[50] Such an initiative was pretty much in the logic of the behaviour of the monarch who saw himself as the champion of the cause of peace and had already been instrumental in bringing about The Hague peace conference of 1899.[51] It is well established that the Tsar, who had been deeply shocked by the South African bloodshed, had also been particularly sympathetic with the Boer cause and was perhaps also influenced, to a point, by the violently pro-Boer feelings of Russian public opinion.[52] It is quite clear that Delcassé, far from being instrumental in bringing about this diplomatic initiative, only followed the movement with strong reservations. He notably insisted that the United States be associated with the démarche in order to avoid any ambiguity as to its nature.

A careful reading of the nature of the proposal of March 1900 completely dissipates the idea that the proposal was intended as a hostile intervention, or as a step towards the formation of a continental coalition against Britain. The documents of the French diplomatic archives are, in this respect, very revealing. For the Marquis de Montebello, it was nothing but a 'friendly intervention',[53] while Delcassé stressed in his correspondence that it was primarily intended as a 'friendly *démarche*' inspired by humanitarian motives, undertaken in the spirit of Article 3 of The Hague Convention, which provided for third parties to engage in *bons offices*, mediation and arbitration.[54] Interestingly, the French Foreign Secretary drew a parallel between this initiative and that of France in the conflict between Spain and the United States in 1898.[55] The French ambassador in St Petersburg, the Marquis de Montebello, showed, for his part, that it was neither an offer of 'intervention' nor even of 'mediation', but was strictly and solely 'an offer of *bons offices*', meant as 'a peaceful and friendly *démarche*'.[56]

It is also revealing that the very disappointing German response did not immediately bring the Russian initiative to a halt. Much to the contrary, Muraviev persevered and on 14 March nourished the design to send the powers a circular on the possibility of an intervention in favour of the Boer Republics.[57] The Russian Foreign Minister only withdrew his offer of mediation after the request formulated by the South African Republics to eight European powers and the United States to seek their friendly intervention.[58] The initiative of March 1900 does not seem dissimilar in nature to other Russian initiatives such as the plea for the cessation of the war sent by the Tsar to King Edward VII in 1901.[59]

Conclusion

This re-examination of the question of intervention in the Anglo-Boer War led to the rejection of the interpretation, according to which Delcassé was instrumental in orchestrating the formation of a continental coalition against Britain in order to force her to evacuate Egypt. Far from having led a hostile policy against Britain during the six first months of the Anglo-Boer War, it seems entirely feasible to claim rather that he had a moderating influence on the Russian ally.

Following a policy which can be qualified as détente towards Britain, he may even have sought a rapprochement with her. During his conversations with the British ambassador, Delcassé confided that he felt that

> the policy of France should be that of friendship with England.... There are undoubtedly outstanding questions to be settled between the two countries; but looking all round the world, he could not see one which could not be arranged amicably; if both parties are actuated by an honest wish for peace.[60]

While French public opinion enthused over the Boer cause, the official attitude of the French cabinet remained extremely cautious and Sir Edmund Monson recognized, in November 1899, that 'the attitude of the French Government had been quite correct'.[61] Delcassé resisted the pressure of public opinion and took great care to clearly dissociate himself from the attacks of the press against England.[62]

Should we, for so much, conclude as Delcassé's collaborators did, that as early as February 1899, he had undertaken to follow one of the main axes of his *grande politique* which led to the 1904 Entente Cordiale? At this stage of our research project it would perhaps be premature to reach firm conclusions and we would limit ourselves to asking the question.

Two main arguments remain which make it difficult to accept such a claim. A first discordant note to such a line of argumentation is that the revisions introduced in the Franco-Russian alliance in 1900–1, gave – as French historian Pierre Renouvin put it – 'an anti-English twist' to it.[63] For the first time, in the General Staff protocols of 2 July 1900 confirmed by the exchange of letters of 16 and 30 May 1901, Britain was treated as a potential enemy and the two allies considered measures to be taken to give each other mutual support in case of a war with her. Furthermore, Christopher Andrew has shown that despite understanding the impossibility of a new initiative on Egypt to end British occupation, Delcassé nevertheless remained opposed to seeking an arrangement with Britain based on an exchange of interests in Egypt and Morocco and continued to regard England as 'the implacable opponent of French policy in Morocco', until 1903 when he took the first steps towards the Entente Cordiale. This, at the very least, suggests the interest of conducting a systematic study of the policy of Delcassé during his early years at the Quai d'Orsay.

Notes

1. On the *grande politique* of Théophile Delcassé, see Pierre Renouvin, *La Politique Extérieure de Th. Delcassé 1898–1905* (Paris: CDU/SEDES, 1953); Christopher M. Andrew, *Théophile Delcassé and the Making of the Entente Cordiale, a Reappraisal of French Foreign Policy 1898–1905* (London: Macmillan – now Palgrave, 1968) and Jean-Baptiste Duroselle, *La France de la 'Belle Epoque'* (Paris: Presses de la FNSP, 1992), pp. 239–80.
2. Pierre Renouvin, *Histoire des Relations Internationales* (Paris: Hachette, 1955), vol. 6, p. 171 and Bertha R. Leaman, 'The Influence of Domestic Politics on Foreign Affairs in France, 1898–1905', *Journal of Modern History* (hereafter *JMH*), XIV (1942), 449–79.
3. Cf. Albéric Néton, *Delcassé (1852–1923)* (Paris: Académie Diplomatique Internationale, 1952), pp. 204–6.
4. Christopher M. Andrew, 'The Entente Cordiale from Its Origins to 1914', in Neville H. Waites (ed.), *Troubled Neighbours, Franco-British Relations in the Twentieth Century* (London: Weidenfeld and Nicolson, 1971), p. 15.
5. André Mévil, 'Delcassé and the Entente Cordiale', *National Review*, July 1908, 714–15.
6. Léon Cahen, 'Les embarras de l'Angleterre en Afrique et en Orient', in Henri Hauser (ed.), *Manuel de politique européenne, Histoire diplomatique de l'Europe (1871–1914)* (Paris: PUF, 1929), vol. 1, pp. 375 and 388–90.
7. Erich Brandenburg, *From Bismarck to the World War* (London: OUP, 1934, German original published in 1924), pp. 136 and 143.
8. A. J. P. Taylor, *The Struggle for Mastery in Europe, 1848–1918* (Oxford: OUP, 1954), pp. 401–2.
9. John D. Hargreaves, 'Delcassé and the Entente, a Revolution in French Foreign Policy', *The Guardian*, 18 March 1952.
10. John A.S. Grenville, *Lord Salisbury and Foreign Policy: the Close of the Nineteenth Century* (London: The Athlone Press, 1964), pp. 269–90.
11. Ibid., p. 270 and Andrew, *Théophile Delcassé*, p. 164.
12. Andrew, *Théophile Delcassé*, p. 164.
13. Cf. Grenville, *Lord Salisbury*, pp. 270–4 and Andrew, *Théophile Delcassé*, pp. 163–5.
14. Sir E. Monson to Salisbury, 27 October 1899. George P. Gooch and Harold Temperley (eds), *British Documents on the Origins of the War, 1898–1914* (hereafter BD) (London: HMSO, 1926), vol. I, pp. 234–5.
15. Sir E. Monson to Salisbury, 27 October 1899. BD, I, pp. 234–5.
16. MAE, Allemagne NS 26, telegram from Noailles to Delcassé, 18 October 1899.
17. Letter from Delcassé to Noailles, Paris, 30 October 1899, DDF, 1, XV, no. 288, pp. 503–4.
18. Letter from Noailles to Delcassé, Berlin, 6 November 1899, DDF, 1, XV, no. 291, p. 508.
19. Letter from Noailles to Delcassé, Berlin, 29 October 1899, DDF, i, XV, no. 287, pp. 502–3.
20. This was revealed a few weeks later by an article written by Delcassé's confidant, Louis Jesierski, under his usual pseudonym: Jean Fontaine, 'L'accord anglo-allemand', 14 November 1899. See also Mévil, 'Delcassé', pp. 55–6.

21. Monson to Salisbury, 9 November 1899, in John F. V. Keiger (ed.), *France 1891–1904, British Documents on Foreign Affairs* (hereafter BDFA), Part I, Serie F, vol. 11 (Frederick: University Press of America, 1989), p. 237.
22. Mévil, 'Delcassé', p. 55.
23. Letter from Delcassé to Noailles, 4 March 1900, DDF I, XVI, no. 90, p. 140.
24. The idea that such a proposal never actually took place was put forward by William L. Langer, *The Diplomacy of Imperialism* (New York, Knopf, 2nd edn, 1951), p. 652 and Taylor, *The Struggle for Mastery in Europe*, p. 401.
25. See Diplomaticus [Lucien Wolf], 'Count Muraviev's Indiscretion', *Fortnightly Review*, December 1899, 1036–45.
26. On the Samoa agreement see Paul M. Kennedy, *The Samoan Tangle, a Study in Anglo-German–American Relations, 1878–1900* (Dublin: Irish University Press, 1974), pp. 225–39.
27. Hermann von Eckardstein, *Ten Years at the Court of St. James, 1895–1905* (London: Thornton Butterworth, 1921), p. 127.
28. Ibid.
29. Cf. Grenville, *Lord Salisbury*, p. 271 and Andrew, *Théophile Delcassé*, p. 164.
30. DDF i, XVI, no. 90. Letter from Delcassé to Noailles, 4 March 1900, p. 140. 'Pendant le séjour du comte Mouravieff à Paris nous nous étions mis d'accord, le Ministre des Affaires étrangères de Russie et moi, pour tenter de mettre fin au moment opportun à la guerre anglo-transvaalienne. Le comte Mouravieff, qui devait voir à Potsdam l'Empereur Guillaume et M. de Bülow s'était chargé de sonder le Gouvernement impérial et de s'assurer de ses dispositions. Elles lui parurent telles qu'aucune conversation ne pût s'engager à ce sujet.'
31. Bülow's notes, Berlin, 8 November 1899, in *La Politique extérieure de l'Allemagne, 1870–1914, Documents officiels publiés par le ministère allemand des Affaires étrangères* (hereafter PEA) (Paris: Alfred Costes, 1932), vol. XVII, no. 4309, pp. 133–4, and Prince von Bülow, *Memoirs 1897–1903* (London: Putman, 1931), p. 300.
32. Bülow's notes, Berlin, 8 November 1899, PEA, vol. XVII, no. 4310 [GP 3338 and 3990], p. 135.
33. Prince von Bülow, *Memoirs 1897–1903*, p. 300.
34. Noailles to Delcassé, Berlin 5 March 1900, DDF, 1, XVI, no. 91, p. 142, Abel Combarieu, *Sept ans à l'Elysée avec le Président Emile Loubet* (Paris: Hachette, 1932) p. 52 and telegram from Bülow to Prince Radolin, Berlin, 3 March 1900, in *Die Grosse Politik der Europäischen Kabinette, 1871–1914* (Berlin: Deutsche Verlagsgesellschaft für Politik und Geschichte, 1922–27), vol. 15, no. 4472, p. 516.
35. Note of the Russian embassy in Paris, 6 March 1900. DDF 1, XVI, no. 93, pp. 143–4 and letter from Wilhelm II to Sir Frank Lascelles, 3 March 1900, *German Diplomatic Documents 1871–1914* (London: Methuen, 1930), vol. III, p. 124.
36. Delcassé to Paul Cambon, 14 March 1900, DDF 1, XVI, no. 102, pp. 161–2; and Delcassé to Noailles, Paris 26 March 1900, DDF 1, XVI, no. 107, pp. 172–3.
37. Andrew, *Théophile Delcassé*, p. 172.
38. Ibid.
39. Combarieu, *Sept ans*, pp. 50–2.
40. Very confidential letter from Prince Urusov, 19/31 January 1900. Baron A.-F. de Meyendorff, *Correspondance diplomatique de M. de Staal 1884–1900* (Paris: Marcel Rivière, 1929), vol. 2, p. 453.

41. Delcassé to Montebello, Paris, 25 January 1900, DDF, 1, XVI, no. 59, p. 86.
42. Andrew, *Théophile Delcassé*, pp. 166–9.
43. Dispatch from Cogordan to Delcassé, Cairo 29 January 1900. DDF i, XVI, pp. 89–91.
44. Andrew, *Théophile Delcassé*, p. 168 and C. Andrew, 'France and the Making of the Entente Cordiale', *Historical Journal*, X (1967), 97.
45. 'L'Egypte', *Le Matin*, 6 February 1900.
46. A. D. Paris, NS Allemagne 15, Noailles to Delcassé, 6 February 1900.
47. Taylor, *The Struggle for Mastery in Europe*, p. 388; Langer, *The Diplomacy of Imperialism*, pp. 665–6 and A. V. Ignat'ev, 'The Foreign Policy of Russia in the Far East at the Turn of the Nineteenth and Twentieth Centuries', in Hugh Ragsdale (ed.), *Imperial Russia and Foreign Policy* (Cambridge: Cambridge University Press, 1993), p. 254.
48. Montebello to Delcassé, St Petersburg, 15 February 1900. DDF, 1, XVI, no 78, pp. 122–3.
49. M. Pokrovski (ed.), 'Die Saristische Diplomatie über Russlands Aufgaben im Orient im Jahre 1900', *Berliner Monatshefte*, July 1928, 638–69.
50. Sir Sydney Lee, *King Edward VII*, 2 vols (London, 1925), vol. 2, pp. 765–6; Meyendorff, *Correspondance diplomatique*, p. 446; Bülow to Radolin, Berlin, 3 March 1900, PEA, vol. XVIII, no. 4423, p. 35, et MAE, Delcassé papers, 10, Montebello to Delcassé, St Petersburg, 15 March 1900. In a conversation with Prince Radolin, the German ambassador in St Petersburg, Muraviev later stressed the fact that the initiative came from the Tsar himself. Radolin to Hohenlohe, 11 March 1900, PEA, XVIII, no. 4440, pp. 48–9.
51. On Nicholas II's pacifist ideals, see Dan L. Morrill, 'Nicholas II and the Call for the First Hague Conference', *JMH*, 46 (1974), 299–300.
52. Lee, *King Edward VII*, pp. 765–6; Meyendorff, *Correspondance diplomatique*, p. 446.
53. MAE, Papiers Delcassé, vol. 10, Montebello to Delcassé, St Petersburg, 3 March 1900.
54. Telegram from Delcassé to Paul Cambon, Paris, 14 March 1900. DDF, 1, XVI, no. 102, p.161.
55. Telegram from Delcassé to Noailles, Paris, 4 March 1900, DDF i, XVI, no. 90, pp. 140–1.
56. MAE, Delcassé papers, vol. 10, letter from Montebello to Delcassé, St Petersburg, 15 March 1900.
57. Radolin to Auswärtiges Amt, 14 March 1900, PEA, vol. XVIII, no. 4445, p. 53.
58. Note from Bülow, 20 March 1900, PEA, vol. XVIII, no. 4448, p. 60 and Delcassé to Noailles, Paris, 26 March 1900, DDF, 1, XVI, no. 107, pp. 172–3.
59. Lee, *King Edward VII*, pp. 765–6.
60. Sir Edmund Monson to Salisbury, 8 December 1899. BDFA, *France 1891–1904*, p. 242.
61. Sir Edmund Monson to Salisbury, 20 November 1899. BDFA, *France 1891–1904*, p. 238.
62. Sir Edmund Monson to Salisbury, 1 December 1899. BDFA, *France 1891–1904*, p. 239.
63. Pierre Renouvin, 'L'orientation de l'Alliance Franco-Russe en 1900–1901', *Revue d'Histoire Diplomatique*, LXXX (1966), 193–204.

5
Anglo-French Rivalry over Siam and the Treaties of April 1904

Nigel J. Brailey

The nature and importance of the 1893 Siam crisis

In 1909, Sir Edward Grey remarked that, 'before 1904 we had constantly been on the brink of war with either France or Russia; for instance, when I was at the Foreign Office in 1893, we had been thought to be on the brink of war with France about Siam...'.[1] And after the 1914–18 war, in his autobiography, he concluded that 'The controversy that arose about Siam in 1893 is an instance of how quickly and suddenly a catastrophe might have been caused by something that had little real importance.'[2] A more helpful comment appeared in a *Times* editorial in 1907, on the occasion of the second visit to England of King Chulalongkorn of Siam:

> HIS MAJESTY's present visit is not political, but the fact that he comes to us directly from Paris serves to recall the serious international questions with which Siam has been connected in the past, and to emphasize the great progress towards the final solution of those questions which has been made within the last fifteen years. The first and most important step in this direction was taken by the Anglo-French Siamese Agreement of January, 1896, and it is only a few days since the ratifications of the latest Franco-Siamese treaty were exchanged in Paris.[3]

This editorial made no reference to the treaties of April 1904, one of which was specifically concerned with Siam, but stresses the importance of the so-called 'Siam Question'.[4] By contrast, Grey, who had been Under-Secretary at the Foreign Office in 1893, later, as a champion of Anglo-French collaboration, clearly became concerned to minimize its significance, while the success of the Siamese in themselves 'reforming'

56

their country, and thereby improving its stability, was also recognized in *The Times*. But Grey's chief in 1892–94, Lord Rosebery, no Francophile and distinctly more sympathetic to Germany, seems to have agreed that he had confronted war across the Channel at the height of the Siam crisis, known as the Paknam Incident, in July 1893.[5] Rightly or wrongly, 'catastrophe' is not a word he would have used for it.

There had of course been fears at that time of intervention on the side of France by its ally Russia, closely coincident with the morale-boosting visit of the Russian Black Sea fleet to Toulon. And if there is little indication that Gladstone's last Cabinet would have been prepared to back Rosebery to the point of war over Siam, following the crisis, Lord Spencer, his colleague at the Admiralty, was to bring on Gladstone's retirement by insisting on reinforcing the Royal Navy to maintain the two-power standard.[6] *Le Temps* of Paris derided Britain as a 'Great Power with nerves',[7] and all in all, the crisis might be viewed as the twin of Fashoda, which came five years later. Despite the presence of British gunboats, for nine days a French squadron blockaded the mouth of the Bangkok river. Then, on Rosebery's imperfectly conveyed advice, the Siamese came to terms, agreeing ultimately by a treaty of 3 October 1893 to the cession of all their territories east of the Mekong river (the modern 'Laos'), a 25-kilometre demilitarized zone on the west bank, which seemed to expose it to creeping French control, and a substantial indemnity.

In 1893, as Siam's effective patron over the previous four decades, Britain suffered a humiliation, even if it did not spell the complete disintegration and colonial takeover of a country of some significance, then and now. Some saw the Siam of the time as the last remaining really attractive piece of potential colonial real estate in the world, on a par with already colonized Burma and Indochina.[8] But the humiliation involved, with the consequent transfer to Peru of Captain H.M. Jones VC, Britain's minister in Bangkok, has doubtless been one cause of its historiographical neglect in Britain. This contrasts with Fashoda, a classic dispute over, in Lord Salisbury's favourite words, 'a little bit of desert' (or perhaps not *so* little), and so satisfying to Britain in its outcome. At the same time, it may have required Britain's assertion of its overwhelming physical superiority at Fashoda to render practicable the growing Anglo-French understanding between 1903 and 1914.

However, the traditional British view is that Siam was ultimately saved from French takeover largely by British action, commencing with interest shown during the Paknam crisis in 1893, but principally through the Anglo-French agreement announced on 16 January 1896, negotiated by

Lord Salisbury with the French ambassador to London, the Baron de Courcel. The latest and most comprehensive expression of this is Patrick Tuck's *The French Wolf and the Siamese Lamb: the French Threat to Siamese Independence 1858–1907* (Bangkok: White Lotus, 1995). The book was reviewed with some hostility by Professor Denys Lombard, late Director of the Ecole Française d'Extrême Orient, and apparently displeasure was also displayed at the French embassy in Bangkok.

Yet there is some reason to argue that, in the aftermath of the extinction of the neighbouring kingdoms of Burma and Annam in 1885, respectively by Britain and France, Britain was the greater threat to Siam's survival.[9] At all events, it was the British authorities in Singapore, currently extending their control up the Malay peninsula, who most favoured a partition of the country with France, and continued to do so at least through to 1901. The staff at the Colonial Office in London clearly sympathized with Singapore while, during the phase of revolving-door British governments in 1885–86, the Foreign Office staff nearly reached the point of supporting them, and agreeing to a proposal for a 'division' (of spheres of influence) emanating from the French consul in Calcutta, Jules Harmand. This was also an era of considerable commercial and economic activity in the country on the part of nationals of both Britain and France, including schemes with which de Lesseps was connected, for a maritime canal across the Kra Isthmus, a Burma–China railway through northern Siam, and the general development of the Siamese northern section of the Malay peninsula, all quite oblivious to the interests of Siam itself. Particularly intriguing are the indications of Anglo-French collaboration in such schemes.[10]

British support for Siam's territorial integrity in these years seems to have been restricted to the then minister in Bangkok, Ernest Satow alone, who was able in this respect to act as a bridge to the point at which Lord Salisbury properly resumed the reins of British foreign policy in 1887. 'Division' or 'partition' was then rejected, and London reverted to hoping that Siam could maintain her independence unaided. In 1893, Salisbury was out of power, only to return in July 1895, amid complaints of Rosebery's misguided obsession with creating a mini 'buffer-state' between British and French colonial territories astride the upper Mekong.[11] Then seeing the Siam question as the 'crux' of Anglo-French difficulties, Salisbury seems to have taken the lead in arranging a strange kind of hybrid settlement. This combined a guarantee of the independence of central Siam with a division of the rest of the country into respective British and French spheres of influence, albeit protected from immediate annexation by declarations of intent on the part of

Salisbury in published letters of his to his ambassador in Paris, Lord Dufferin.[12] However, the settlement made no reference to Siamese sensibilities, and Bangkok was not in the least consulted over it. At best it could be said to have offered Siam a breathing-space in which to diminish, by its own actions, the case for its partition favoured by British and French imperialists, including a number of Salisbury's Cabinet colleagues. But thereby, providing there was effective domestic reorganization in Siam, which should not necessarily be termed 'reform', the basis for longer-term Anglo-French agreement on its survival was laid.

Indeed, it has been argued that the Joint Declaration of January 1896 presaged a new 'entente' between Britain and France, disappointed by subsequent events.[13] In fact, the best explanation for the acquiescence to it of the French government seems to be the temporary absence from the French Foreign Ministry at the Quai d'Orsay of Gabriel Hanotaux in favour of Marcellin Berthelot, more famous as a chemist. De Courcel was thereby enabled to pursue his enthusiasm for an Anglo-French rapprochement, a policy supported by other French diplomats such as the Cambon brothers. But given the expected hostility to the arrangement of the Groupe Colonial, as active as ever in the Chamber of Deputies, the relevant papers were merely laid before the Chamber, thereby avoiding the full-scale debate required in the case of a treaty which might well have blocked it. There was no confirmation of French acceptance of Salisbury's interpretation of the declaration with respect to Siam's outlying territories. And when Hanotaux returned to the Quai as a member of the government in March 1896, French colonial policy resumed its unfriendly slant towards Britain.

Another connection between the Siam and Fashoda crises is represented by the originally somewhat Anglophobe Théophile Delcassé. As Under-Secretary for Marine in the then French Ministry of Marine and Colonies, Delcassé had secured the right to attend, though not vote, at Cabinet meetings of the Ribot government, with a view to pressing French territorial demands in Bangkok during the 1893 crisis.[14] Thereafter, responsibility for France's colonies was separated from the Navy, and Delcassé became a fully fledged minister. Before he left office in 1895 for an interval of three years, he was responsible for planning the Marchand expedition, that from its base in the French Congo, finally turned up on the banks of the Nile in August 1898, to dispute with Herbert Kitchener and his army recently victorious over the Dervishes at Khartoum control of the Sudan. By that time, Delcassé had returned to government as Hanotaux's successor as French Foreign Minister, to serve through continuously to 1905. But it was the previous interval, along with Delcassé's acceptance by October of unavoidable retreat at Fashoda, that is reckoned to have marked the beginning of his conversion from an uncompromising colonial expansionist to a calculating accommodationist, pursuing French interests around the world without risking outright conflict with Britain.[15] However, his tenure of the Foreign Ministry also had to begin with the frustration not to say agony of withdrawal from Fashoda, and acceptance that even East Africa, with its access to the sea lanes from Europe to the East, was to be considered a British preserve.

Siam in the Entente deal

That the 'Entente' treaties of 8 April 1904 were, as they stood, essentially just a 'colonial deal' has surely become widely accepted, albeit with principal respect to Morocco and Egypt.[16] The first and longest of the three treaties resolved Anglo-French differences regarding Newfoundland and West and Central Africa, the second, the one traditionally commanding most interest, represented the Egypt and Morocco deal, and the third and shortest dealt with Siam, Madagascar and the New Hebrides, a truly globe-spanning arrangement *in toto*.

Who on the French side was chiefly responsible for the treaties and the rapprochement they expressed has provoked some disagreement. Among British historians, Christopher Andrew predictably points to Delcassé, but P.J.V. Rolo seems to favour his ambassador in London in succession to de Courcel, Paul Cambon.[17] After all, as late as 1900 in the context of the Boer War, Delcassé himself had been discussing proposals for a European Grand Alliance against Britain, and prospectively also Japan,[18] which Paul Cambon and his brother Jules would not in the least have supported. But with regard to the basis of the agreement, as early as 1893, Lord Salisbury had apparently favoured a Morocco–Siam deal,[19] at a time when any compromise over British domination of Egypt was still out of the question. And in the context of the negotiations that began properly in 1902, when previous approaches to Germany and Japan had ended merely in the alliance with Japan alone, and well before the visit to Paris in April 1903 of King Edward VII, Rolo argues that 'The situation in Siam provided an opening', i.e. the acceptable common ground. Admittedly it was Morocco with regard to which Delcassé had already been negotiating for several years with the Italians and Spanish, which 'by postulating a major issue between the two countries, eventually prepared the way for serious bargaining'.[20] But not until October 1903 was Egypt seriously discussed as the counterweight, and Delcassé persuaded to recognize France's bargaining position there as 'a dwindling asset', two decades on from the Wolseley expedition which the French had refused to join.[21]

The real importance of such an 'opening' as that provided by Siam, as might earlier have been the case in 1896, should not be dismissed. B.C. Busch, American biographer of Sir Charles Hardinge, Under-Secretary at the Foreign Office 1906–10 and 1916–20, comments regarding the sad sequel to the Entente, 'The difficulty of Anglo-German relations was that there were few precise issues which could be discussed like Newfoundland fisheries or Persian concessions.'[22] Egypt and Morocco clearly did represent the real substance of the Anglo-French 'deal' as it finally emerged in 1904. But the question of Siam, as something that by 1903 could easily be accommodated, was an essential starting-point. The most picturesque expression of Siam's importance in this respect is probably that of Julian Amery in his completion of the J.L. Garvin multi-volume biography of Joseph Chamberlain, where he observes that 'it was in the swamps of the Mekong and the jungles of Kelantan and Trengganu that the Entente first began to take shape'.[23]

For that matter, there was clearly a parallel between Egypt and Siam as dwindling French assets, countries where France had certain legitimate but no longer realizable claims. At the time, the Groupe Colonial in particular, in its late 1890s heyday,[24] had never accepted the implications of the 1896 Joint Declaration on Siam, let alone Lord Salisbury's accompanying letters qualifying any consequent French (or English) claims to Siam's outlying regions. But not even Britain's isolation at the time of the Boer War had enabled France to annex further territory at Siam's expense. By 1901, Bangkok's repeated efforts at internationalizing the Siam question by involving Germany, inspired by its General Adviser, Gustave Rolin-Jaequemyns, had aroused apprehension in both London and Paris.[25] And in 1902, Delcassé had been seeking to negotiate a treaty with Bangkok which regularized its frontier with French Indochina in line with his new espousal of the slogan 'lâchons l'Asie, prenons l'Afrique'. The demilitarized zone was to be dispensed with, and even the eastern Siamese port of Chantabun, occupied by French troops to guarantee Bangkok's observance of the terms of the treaty of 3 October 1893, was at last to be handed back. But this the Groupe Colonial still rejected, opposing the very idea of restoring territory to a supposedly 'uncivilized' oriental monarchy, and claiming in Chailley-Bert's words that 'l'Indochine a besoin de Siam'.

Eugène Etienne, Delcassé's erstwhile ally from Oran in Algeria, several times Minister for the Colonies and future Minister for War, took the lead in the Chamber in rejecting Delcassé's Siam convention. And this was for Delcassé such a blow that already, three years prior to his eventual notorious resignation at the instance of Berlin, he seems to have been considering terminating his stint at the Quai d'Orsay. But in the spring of 1903, reassured by British indications the year before that he would not be forced to entirely reconsider his policy, he settled on renegotiation. It was bound to be a limited renegotiation at best, as British Foreign Secretary Lansdowne at least, was clearly determined that any decisions on Siam would have the effect essentially of merely confirming the Joint Declaration of 1896. However, in July 1903, in his current role as Vice-President of the National Assembly, Etienne paid a goodwill visit to London, parallel but separate from that of Delcassé and President Loubet. The latter were of course returning the April visit to Paris of King Edward VII which made such a contribution to the mood of entente. Finally in a treaty of 13 February 1904, arranged between Delcassé and the Siamese minister in Paris less than two months prior to the Entente treaties, with the acceptance of Étienne, and in return for the cession of the Gulf of Siam port of Trat, Chantabun was returned to Siam while two small Lao enclaves on the west bank of the Mekong also became French.

Britain, France and 'Thailand the new Siam', 1904–54

That by early 1904, on the eve of the Entente treaties, the Far East was beginning to count in world affairs was pointed out long ago even by as Eurocentric a historian as A.J.P. Taylor.[26] The era of imperial 'questions' was largely over, and eastern Asia at least, could no longer be taken for granted as just a playground for Western imperial rivalry. But with regard to South-east Asia and even other parts of the continent, whatever the vicissitudes of relations between Britain and France in Europe, the sequel was a 'colonial' united front aimed at maintaining Western imperial hegemony. Their relations with 'Siam' as it turned gradually into the modern 'Thailand' serve to point up this change quite effectively.

The most important context to this transformation is how 'Little Japan', still viewed as a lightweight up to 1904, had the temerity to go to war, voluntarily, with Russia. What is more, far from suffering defeat as was widely expected, she humbled the 'Great Bear', seen by many over at least the previous decade as the world's leading power, and in an era of Western imperial hegemony, upset the global balance by destroying most of her navy.[27] Even many Anglo-Saxons who had urged her on, then reversed their position. Others, even in the decade since Japan's signal victory over China in the war of 1894–95, had already begun to see her as an obstacle to their own expansion and been talking intermittently of a Japan-led or sponsored 'Yellow Peril'. By 1907, contemporary with the Second Hague Peace Conference which the United States had most actively promoted, Washington was planning the despatch across the Pacific of the 'Great White Fleet' to intimidate Tokyo over the issue of Japanese immigration which threatened to destabilize California.[28] But at the very least, fear of being dragged into the war of 1904–5 on opposing sides by their respective allies added impetus to Britain and France to reconcile their own differences. Paris seems to have been specially upset by the way Britain had broken ranks with the 'Triple Intervention' powers of April 1895, Russia, Germany and France, in aligning herself with an Asian state. The French also increasingly suspected Japan of having an acquisitive interest in their Indochinese empire, and were probably inclined to do anything they could to detach Britain from her ally. However, the end of the war was quickly followed by an extension of the Anglo-Japanese alliance at the particular instance of Premier Arthur Balfour.

As for the years after the Russo-Japanese War, as Europe marched forward to 'the war to end all wars' in 1914, their main feature was the retreat of the European powers back into their own continent. And while most familiar is the growing neurosis among her rivals regarding the rise of Europe's newest power, Germany, most peculiar was the continuing apparent respect for Russia, so demonstrably revealed by Japan as a paper tiger.[29] At least prior to around 1912–13 when she [*Russia*] began to show some signs of recovery, the real policy-makers in Britain and France appear to have been more concerned to bolster her for fear of what might eventuate if she gravitated towards Germany or completely collapsed, even to the extent in Britain's case for instance, of nearly sacrificing Persia/Iran to St Petersburg in the process of arranging the 1907 Anglo-Russian entente. But this too dovetailed with Britain's new fear of imperial overreach which limited her interest in India's periphery, while the Anglo-Japanese alliance quickly began to seem redundant if not a downright embarrassment given its anti-Russian character.[30] For that matter, with those in Britain who had believed in 'splendid isolation', or at least the 'free hand', at last overruled after 1900, their successors were thereafter the more apprehensive of being forced back to it, and clearly came to regard the maintenance of the entente as it developed after 1905 as the yardstick of their success.

So having been employed as a useful starting-point during 1902–3, for the arrangement of the Entente, what was it to signify for Siam? On the one hand, the general Western decline of interest in empire-building suited her admirably. Outside Europe, Germany's never truly imperial focus was on the Middle East and Persian Gulf, while the inability of France, like Russia, to expand anywhere except by negotiation with Britain, meant that Siam was now properly out of the firing line. The years 1894–1905 anyhow see her making the most of her breathing-space, in the form of the so-called 'Chakri Reformation', during which central government authority was developed and extended right up to the frontiers created by the colonial powers, and a set of functional ministries, set up in Bangkok even before 1893, including Justice, Finance, Education and Public Works, gradually enlarged their influence throughout the kingdom. And if 'reform' then largely ceased for a time, the basis had thereby been laid for the 'modern' Thai nation-state which more properly emerged after the Revolution of 1932–33.

However, 'truth' like much else is ultimately in the eye of the be-holder, and it should be noted that despite the above, and after further final adjustments had been made to their borders with French Indo-china and British Malaya, it still appeared to the 'Thai' that they con-tinued to face a Western imperial threat until at least the late 1940s if not the early 1950s. In other words, they never felt genuinely safe until the Western empires were in active process of dissolution.

Why was this? In 1907, the irredentum province of Battambang, under Bangkok's control since the end of the eighteenth century, was returned to the French protectorate of Cambodia in return for the briefly held Trat and French alignment with Britain in abandoning its extrater-ritorial rights over its Asian subjects in Siam. And in 1909, Bangkok ceded its claims to four northern Malay sultanates to Britain in return for a hefty sterling loan to finance the building of a railway down to the new frontier and the consolidation thereby of its authority in the pen-insular provinces that remained to her, both Malay and Thai. In 1917, under the English-educated King Wachirawut, Siam followed the United States into the European war, ironically at the urging of France and to the displeasure of Britain. And perhaps to an extent in return, though quite unwillingly, with Wachirawut on his deathbed in 1925, Britain followed the lead of others and conceded the almost final elimination of its unequal treaty rights dating back to the visit of the then Governor of Hongkong, Sir John Bowring, in 1855.

But the basic nature of her relations with the two imperial powers still left Siam with something a little short of true sovereignty as it is gener-ally understood in the West. In particular, she felt bound to continue to employ Bank of England-appointed British financial advisers right through to 1950, bar only the years of the alliance with Japan, 1941–45, despite their close involvement in the financial crisis of 1931 which led to a political revolution and the overthrow of the absolute monarchy regime in 1933. Many of the younger generation of revolutionaries, led by Dr Pridi Phanomyong, were French (and not British)-educated. But in this period, Siam, rather like Japan earlier on, often played host to a variety of colonial subversives, for instance Tan Melaka and Ho Chi Minh, and whatever the strains in interwar Anglo-French relations going right back to the Paris Peace Conference, and often relating in particular to imperial issues, by the 1930s Britain and France tended to stand shoulder to shoulder in defence of their colonies. In 1934, there were fears of Anglo-French intervention against the new revolutionary government in Siam, and the country attracted much criticism in the British and French press for its willingness to afford access to Japanese business excluded from the colonies by imperial preference schemes. After September 1939, tension naturally increased, and in June, 1940, shortly following the fall of France, a joint colonial conference was held in Singapore involving representatives of Admiral Decoux's Vichy administration in Hanoi, to decide how they might co-operate in defence of their empires. Bangkok representatives were permitted to attend, though as extremely suspect observers. In December 1940–January 1941, Thailand and French Indochina fought a brief border war, terminated by Japanese intervention largely to French colonial benefit. And when Thailand under Marshal Phibun did ally itself with Japan and went to war with 'the Allies' in December 1941–January 1942 (though not with France), allowing Japan to use it as the launch pad for the capture of Singapore and the invasion of Burma, Anthony Eden proclaimed Britain's refusal to employ any longer the 'new' name of 'Thailand' announced 18 months earlier, and its determination to revert to the old 'client-state' name of 'Siam'.

Understandably, therefore, throughout all these years, the main aim of most of Bangkok's governments of whatever political hue seems to have been to maintain a low profile.[31] In the eyes of its elite diplomatic service, until very recently the envy of the rest of South-east Asia, the best means of evading the Western threat seemed to be to assume the posture of a 'never-never land', a place which did not really exist at all. Even after the war, despite the patronage of the United States, there were fears for a time of Britain realizing Churchill's wartime threat of seizing her southernmost provinces to render British Malaya properly secure, the more so as the frontier was affected by the growing Communist insurgency in Malaya.[32] And French demands for the return of border territories annexed by Thailand in 1940, in effect part of the irredenta claimed by her going back to 1893, were accepted by Washington. Thanks to Dr Pridi in particular, and in the context of British plans to evacuate India and Burma, Bangkok for a time gave support to the movements for self-determination in Indochina, but the first really firm sign of Thailand's security in face of the old Entente powers was the signing in Manila, under American auspices in September 1954, of the SEATO treaty. Not only were Britain and France co-signatories with Thailand, but the treaty came three months after the Geneva conference at which France had signified its agreement to withdraw permanently from Indochina. A mere three years later, Britain had also withdrawn from Malaya.

Increasingly during the nineteenth century up until the 1890s, the smaller Asian countries operated as little better than pawns in the international relations of the major Western powers. 'Survival diplomacy' is the best that Western historians have been willing to attribute to them in the way of foreign policy of their own.

However, this may be unfair, if only because standard Western diplomacy simply did not mesh with traditional Asian ideas of international relations. For that matter, as supposedly 'uncivilized' polities, they were threatened with genuine elimination by Western states disposing of technological and military power hitherto unheard of in their continent.

Yet the old 'Siam' surely did function significantly in the course of Anglo-French relations leading up to and culminating in the Entente. Having apparently adjusted to the Western international system, it thereby secured respect, and even its very survival, though domestic reorganization did also help to deprive the Western powers of the sort of excuses they were accustomed to employ to justify their imperial expansion. And it was all at the cost of substantially betraying many of its own traditions, political and social, in the cause of so-called 'reform'.

The early twentieth-century game of musical chairs among the Western powers having been largely concluded by 1904–5, the various players then adjusted to the new version of the 'armed camp' which had already emerged in Europe by the 1890s, with little apparent confidence that they could for too long avoid the trial of strength which ultimately eventuated in 1914. But this was not a game that only affected Europe. Not only the United States but many other countries around the world were drawn into it as European colonies, including most of the emerging Thailand's neighbours. Thailand itself never actually *fought* in the war, but even it, like Japan, did not by any means

escape a decade later the effects of *the West's* Great Depression in the
'new world' created by Western imperialism. In the end, it doubtless
made the right choice in aligning itself with Japan, the principal anti-
Western colonial force, and thereby helped to create the much more
equal world that we have today, even if the heyday of Britain and France
seems gone for ever.

Notes

1. Quoted by Wilson in K. W. Wilson (ed.), *British Foreign Secretaries and Foreign Policy* (London: Croom Helm, 1987), p. 176.
2. Viscount Grey of Fallodon, *Twenty-Five Years, 1892–1916* (London: Hodder, 1925), p. 12.
3. Leader of 24 June, presumably written by the foreign editor, Valentine Chirol, who had visited Siam in 1897.
4. So-called 'questions', like those of 'Persia', 'China', 'Morocco', the Ottoman Empire, etc., invariably signified in this era of non-Western so-called 'dying nations', a debate over what Western Powers should do with them.
5. See his Liberal leadership retirement speech of October 1896, in Anon., *The Foreign Policy of Lord Rosebery: Two Chapters in Recent Politics, 1886, and 1892– 95* (London: A. L. Humphreys, 1901), p. 82.
6. M. Bentley, *Politics without Democracy, 1815–1914* (London: Fontana, 1984), p. 288.
7. Translated in *The Times*, 4 August 1893.
8. H. Norman, 'The Future of Siam', *Contemporary Review* LXIV (July 1893), 1–13.
9. See my 'Protection or Partition: Ernest Satow and the 1880s Crisis in Britain's Siam Policy', in *The Journal of Southeast Asian Studies*, 29, 1 (March 1998), 63–85.
10. See my 'The Scramble for Concessions in 1880s Siam', *Modern Asian Studies*, 33, 3 (1999), 513–49.
11. The so-called 'Buffer-state Bubble', see the *Pall Mall Gazette*, 9 August 1895.
12. For Salisbury's Siam policy in 1895, see J. D. Hargreaves, 'Entente Manquée: Anglo-French Relations 1895–1896', *Historical Journal*, 9 (1953), 65–92, Chandran Jeshurun, *The Contest for Siam, 1889–1902* (Kuala Lumpur: University of Malaya, 1977), and the particularly Sinocentric L. K. Young, *British Policy in China, 1895–1902* (Oxford: Clarendon Press, 1970), pp. 31–3. Also especially, Salisbury to J. Chamberlain, 4 September 1895 in Chamberlain Papers, Univ. of Birmingham.
13. Hargreaves, 'Entente Manquée'.
14. Chandran, *The Contest for Siam*, pp. 39, 67.
15. C. Andrew, *Theophile Delcassé and the Entente Cordiale* (London: Macmillan – now Palgrave, 1968), p. 87.
16. See I. H. Nish, *The Anglo-Japanese Alliance* (London: Athlone, 1966), p. 286, and Z. Steiner, *Britain and the Origins of the First World War* (London: Macmillan – now Palgrave, 1977), p. 29. Also M. Hurst (ed.), *Key Treaties for the Great Powers 1814–1914* (Newton Abbot: David & Charles, 1972), pp. 756–65.

17. Andrew, *Théophile Delcassé*, P. J. V. Rolo, *Entente Cordiale: the Origins and Negotiation of the Anglo-French Agreements of 8 April 1904* (London: Macmillan – now Palgrave, 1969), esp. pp. 130–55.
18. J. A. S. Grenville, *Lord Salisbury and Foreign Policy: the Close of the Nineteenth Century* (London: Athlone, 1964), p. 289 and Andrew, *Théophile Delcassé*, ch. VIII.
19. Frederick Verney, secretary to the Siamese London Legation, to Florence Nightingale, 3 June 1893, cited in my *Two Views of Siam on the Eve of the Chakri Reformation* (Arran: Kiscadale, 1989), 7n.
20. Rolo, *Entente Cordiale*, p. 123.
21. Ibid., p. 211.
22. B. C. Busch, *Hardinge of Penshurst: a Study in the Old Diplomacy* (Hamden, Conn.: Archon, 1980), p. 106. Hardinge was of course ennobled as Viceroy of India, 1910–16.
23. Vol. IV (London: Macmillan – now Palgrave, 1951), p. 186.
24. See C. Andrew and A. S. Kanya-Forstner, 'The French "Colonial Party": its Composition, Aims and Influence, 1885–1914', in J. C. Cairns (ed.), *Contemporary France* (New York: New Viewpoints, 1978), pp. 26–64.
25. G. Monger, *The End of Isolation: British Foreign Policy 1900–1907* (London: Nelson, 1963), pp. 44–5. 'Rolin' had been Belgian Interior Minister in the famous Frère-Orban Cabinet in the 1880s, and even earlier, founder of the Ghent-based Institut du Droit International.
26. In his *The Struggle for Mastery in Europe, 1848–1918* (Oxford: Oxford UP, 1954), p. 417. Cf. J. Lowe, *The Great Powers, Imperialism and the German Problem, 1865–1925* (London: Routledge, 1994), p. 123.
27. See G. R. Storry, *Japan and the Decline of the West in Asia, 1894–1943* (London: Macmillan – now Palgrave, 1977), ch. IV, and for Russia's place in the world, Young, *British Policy in China*, p. 39, or J. A. Hobson, *Imperialism: a Critical Study* (London: Nisbet, 1902), p. 139.
28. R. A. Esthus, *Theodore Roosevelt and Japan* (Seattle: Univ. of Washington, 1966), ch. XI.
29. James Joll, *The Origins of the First World War* (Longman: London, 1992 edn), pp. 82, 121, 124.
30. I. H. Nish, *The Anglo-Japanese Alliance* and *Alliance in Decline* (London: Athlone, 1972).
31. Cf. introduction to V. Thompson, *Thailand: the New Siam* (New York: Institute of Pacific Relations, 1941).
32. Even in 1953, Churchill is reported to have complained that he had lived more than four score years without ever having to acknowledge the existence of Cambodia, and objected to starting then!

6
Elie Halévy and Anglo-French Relations, 1898–1905

François Crouzet

The *Correspondance* of Elie Halévy, which was published in 1996, is a fascinating book which can be read at a stretch.[1] One reason is that it contains a large number of remarks and comments about Britain, written during the many stays in the latter country by the historian of the English people in the nineteenth century.

The first of those stays took place in late 1892 and early 1893. Halévy, then only 22, had just completed his studies at the Ecole Normale Supérieure and had succeeded in the *agrégation* of philosophy. He made a kind of 'philosophical journey', with the object of examining the state of philosophy in Britain and recruiting British contributors to the *Revue de métaphysique et de morale*, which several of his friends had just founded. His letters, during this period, do not display much interest in British institutions and politics. On the other hand, they contain many peremptory, nay arrogant judgements, not only about English philosophers (like this 'professor of Greek and commentator of Aristotle', who is 'an intelligent and interesting man, but loses both qualities as soon as he comments on Aristotle'), but also about the British. Two, rather contradictory, quotations will be enough. On the one hand, 'the English are a people of calves'; General de Gaulle was to use the same comparison with young cattle, who are supposed to be timorous, but about the French people! On the other hand,

> the English people are brute beasts; I say brute in the noblest sense of the word. They are brute because they are unable to think, because they despise theories, because of their frankness, of their courage, of their love for the open air, of their pride. . . .They are not merchants. . . .They are pirates, adventurers, soldiers; they are, above all, in need of daring, of being in danger, of doing things.

This view is not unrelated to some remarks, which will be mentioned later, about the bellicose trend of British foreign policy, but one must take into account, about such blunt statements, the *normalien's* taste for paradox and *canular* (rough humour). Still, it is obvious at this stage that Halévy, even though he appreciated the *douceur de vivre* (in his own words) in England, was not an Anglophile. Indeed, one has to wait for some years before discerning on his part attitudes which are more friendly to the British.

This change was obvious neither in 1898, during the second long stay in England by Halévy, nor during the two years which followed. During this period – on which this short study will concentrate – Halévy's letters have many references to the international situation and to British foreign policy, but their major theme is the fear of an English aggression against France.[2] They are thus directly relevant to the theme of this volume, but they cannot be considered as representative of French public opinion, or of one of its factions. As François Furet rightly remarked, Halévy escapes every classification: a man of the Left, a republican, a free-thinker, a passionate *Dreyfusard*, but also a staunch patriot, who much despised the politicians of the Third Republic and their behaviour. He was one of his kind . . . ; but, for this very reason, the views of a very clever man, who was to become a great historian, are worth recalling.

Halévy resided in England from January to May 1898, doing research on the Utilitarians in order to prepare his book on the formation of philosophical radicalism. He was thus in England when the Hispano-American War broke out on 25 April. He was greatly worried by this conflict, though he had a 'reasoned aversion' for the Spaniards, 'a people of stupid brigands'. On 25 April, he had dinner with Basil Williams, then a young historian (he later wrote *The Whig Supremacy*), and he was alarmed

> at the bellicose tone of the latter's talking. He would be glad if the Cuban War was extended to the whole world, and if Europe was ablaze. When one observes that, presently, all newspapers in England (and also in France) are chauvinistic, colonialist, conquering, and when one realises that, for England, any war is only a colonial war, an expedition to remote places, one cannot but be disturbed by such a state of mind.

On 4 May, he was more explicit:

> The Cuban War worries me unceasingly. I am afraid that Europe will, sooner or later, get involved, and only God knows in which chaos we

shall then fall. In short, the English are excited and a general war would be more profitable to them than to anybody else, despite the danger for their trade, and the universal reluctance among civilized people to declare war.

Halévy feared that the 'Radicals' would put on again Palmerston's belli-cose cloak, in order to recover 'from the discredit in which their policy of little-Englanders [in English in the text] . . . had thrown them', inas-much as their supporters, among the 'Methodist lower middle class' and among working men, were in sympathy with the United States.[3] On the Conservative side, there was Joseph Chamberlain, 'the man upon whom England relies for the day on which some major piece of international blackguardism would be necessary'; as early as 1893, Halévy had called him a 'viper'.

Shortly afterwards, on 13 May, Chamberlain happened to make a speech that aroused universal interest; he condemned 'splendid isol-ation', expressed his wishes for an alliance with the United States and – cryptically – with Germany (to which he had proposed an alliance but two months before); he sharply attacked Russia (and France, by implica-tion).[4] On 17 May, Elie Halévy wrote to his father: 'Chamberlain is a charlatan, but do not trust the English'. Two days later, he related a conversation he had overheard at Simpson's in the Strand, between four 'quiet quadragenarians'; one of them stated 'as phlegmatically as it is possible – This means a war in Europe before long . . . . We must have it, sooner or later. We must, if we want to retain our rank'. 'This is the first time', Halévy commented, 'that I see a nation in such a state of mind . . . . We must stand on our guard and be extremely prudent; let us settle quickly the Nigerian question and, above all, we must wish for a quick liquidation of the Cuban War'.

Actually, the latter did not spread and the problem of the borders between English and French colonies in West Africa was settled by a compromise – in the convention of 14 June 1898.[5] But the question of the Upper Nile remained unsolved and led, in the autumn of 1898, to the Fashoda crisis. Unfortunately, Halévy was by then in France and his few letters of late 1898 only deal with the Dreyfus affair and French internal politics. Nonetheless, one can assume that he was very worried and feared the worst.

His letters from England only start again in October 1899, just after the Boer War had broken out. Up to 1902, it was to take up a lot of space in Halévy's correspondence.[6] On 4 November, he wrote: 'I express ardent wishes for the Boers'; on the other hand, a few days earlier, he had considered 'absurd' the idea that they could 'as an organized army hold out for a month' against an English force of 70 000 men; he was rather surprised by the victories which the Boers won at the beginning of the war, and by their protracted resistance up to 1902. On the other hand, he made various unflattering comments about the attitudes of the British people. Admittedly, he was impressed by the complete calm which prevailed: 'No assemblies in the streets, no demonstrations in music-halls; popular turmoil does not occur any more in the public places, but in the newspapers'; this was his remark on 19 October.[7] Then, after the first British setbacks:

Anglo-Saxon phlegm is, for all that, really baffling for us; I imagine how the news of a disaster would be received on the *boulevards*, how the press would comment it, how the Opposition would trade upon it in Parliament. Here I see unruffled bourgeois, who carefully fold their newspaper in order to read it at home in an armchair. Two days later, however, he was wondering 'how can be made the brains of men who are content to read in their newspapers' information which is ambiguous. 'If you did see', he wrote to his brother, 'the placidity of public opinion, the facility with which official explanations are accepted, the imperturbable confidence in final success, and the indifference to accidents on the way'.

Halévy returned to England one year later, in November 1900, when the war had at last turned in favour of British arms, though the latter had not managed to break down Boer resistance. He then wrote:

Every Englishman, if taken separately, will repudiate any solidarity with Chamberlain. As a body, however, they will be, at bottom, very grateful to Chamberlain to know how to initiate pieces of black-guardism, to which they unconsciously aspire, as a great nation, but which they do not dare to own. I have hitherto met only one genuine pro-Boer: Fisher Unwin... who, with his wife and his sister-in-law, had left his card before the bust of Kruger, at the Trocadero.[8]

Actually, Halévy was unable to hide his admiration for the self-control of the British ('uncommunicative and difficult to understand people'), who looked without anger and only with irony at the 'triumphal progress' of President Kruger across Europe. They knew 'that the war would last long and be expensive (but they will go on and pay)'; as 'sensible people . . . [they] know how to attend to one thing only at one and the same time. If fifty *cives anglicos* were burnt alive on the *place de la Concorde*, they would not stir – for the time being.'[9] He was wondering whether the English would make 'South Africa another Ireland or another Canada. Another Ireland, unfortunately, I am afraid', but he added: 'The Anglo-Saxons certainly have a genius for pacification. They are not really vindictive.'

Admittedly, in 1901, Halévy was impressed by the growing campaign of protest 'against concentration camps, against Chamberlain's policy and *almost* against the war itself'. Still he did not think that a compromise between the Boers and England was possible. And when the Peace of Vereeniging had been signed he wrote, in May 1902: 'Do not believe that peace had been expected here with nervosity and welcomed with enthusiasm. . . . People are satisfied that it is all over, that's all; but they would have waited one more year for the end without growing weary.' And he concluded:

> This is the perpetual mystery, which always surrounds the doings of this silent, fatalistic, optimistic nation, which dispenses with overexcitement both at work and in leisure. Something is now sure: the English people can bear, without any scandal, any upheaval in their tax system, and without any discomfort, some extraordinary increase in taxation. Chamberlain will therefore be more light-hearted than ever, when he resumes towards us his brutal manners, as soon as necessary, i.e. to-morrow or the day after to-morrow.

As the Boer War was coming to its end, Halévy was thus feeling the same anxiety as when it had started (just like in 1898, during the Cuban War): the fear that it would result in a general war, or at least in an attack by England against France. After lunching with Basil Williams (who, definitely, was an anxiety-maker), he wrote on 21 October 1899:

> Where will they [the English] look for a stimulus to their national pride, after they will have swallowed Transvaal? The attitude of the German Emperor worries me:[10] which compensation can the English offer him in Africa, which is occupied from top to bottom? What about England and Germany coming some day to an agreement to partition French colonies? This would be stupid on the part of England, but who knows? And what would we able to do? To resist would be madness and to surrender would be demoralizing.

Halévy was also wondering what use England would make of her power-ful army, once the war in South Africa had come to an end, and 'where she will divert the militarist excitement which now has fallen into a trance'. On 23 October, he advised his father to ponder a newspaper article which attacked the French press for its pro-Boer attitude and suggested that the Admiralty was ready for all contingencies.

> You must consider that it brutally expresses the opinion of the gen-eral public. The English alone in Europe want a war; they alone can want it, while being sure it will be profitable; and they alone do not have to fear to see their houses on fire. I am returning to the absolute pessimism, in which I fell on everyone of my visits to London, during the last two years. You must foresee anything, and trust England as little as you can. I have come to the point of relying upon the Emperor of Germany to try to settle things.[11]

On 25 October 1899, Halévy wrote to his father a long and interesting letter. He expressed his wish that the Boers would continue their resist-ance because, after its end, 'I shall begin to worry seriously'. He repeated that

> the English, or, if you prefer, the ruling classes, with no resistance from public opinion, want a war. They do not want it in order to reach such or such concrete result; we could then manage, through some concessions. But each concession will result into a new demand, until the day they will have the war they want...not as a last resort, in order to reach an objective, but as an energetic way to assert to others, and to themselves, that they do exist.

Halévy was explaining this attitude by two factors. The first was eco-nomic: 'England...is worried by Germany's progress in industry and trade; though there is no sign of decay at home..., she feels that neither her industry nor her trade progress any more at the same pace as formerly.'[12] The second factor was geopolitical: England

> is conscious that in all parts of the world new Englands have de-veloped, an Anglo-Saxon world which might some day...include, through a federation or an alliance, the United States themselves. Now she feels it is presently necessary to assert through a war the existence of this new and immense England, a world which is self-sufficient.[13]

'For the time being, Chamberlain, whom everybody loathes and everybody accepts, expresses more clearly than anybody the desire, which is more or less conscious with all Englishmen, for a war and, if necessary, for a universal massacre.'

On 25 October, Halévy returned to the same theme:

> I do not think I exaggerate, and I believe that it is not properly realized in France, i.e. in the country that will suffer, with the least delay and the most certainty, from the events which are preparing.... I am writing all this so that you will spread the news around you. God knows how it disturbs many of my ideas, and whether I rejoice to see France pushed by fatality into a system of European coalition,[14] which will inevitably be military and religious and all the rest of it.

And on 4 November, he wrote to his brother:

> I am willing to be optimistic and to believe that the 'liberal' ideal of the 19th century retains some meaning for the people of Europe; but I doubt it. I see here *one* civilization, which is increasingly convinced that it makes up the whole of civilization, and increasingly anxious to have this view accepted by the whole of Europe through violent challenges and insults. No serious protest from public opinion.... No agitation, neither in politics, nor in literature, nor in the arts, nor in religion: a great nation which follows its instinct and wants to get greater. Thence, in my view, war is certain, with in all likelihood profits for Russia ... and losses for us (ruin of our trade with England, which is the largest share of our foreign trade; definitive ruin for our merchant fleet; disappearance of our Navy; and loss of our colonies, which have cost us such a lot of money).

Admittedly, on 30 November 1899, Chamberlain made a speech which sharply attacked France and suggested 'a triple alliance of the teutonic race'.[15] Nonetheless, we can be surprised that Halévy did believe in *la guerre fatale*, the inevitable war between England and France, to use the title of the war-fiction book by Captain Danrit, one of those 'mountebanks in red breeches' whom he detested, and that he had apocalyptic visions (which were also prophetic of the 'era of tyrannies').[16] On the other hand, he had observed on 4 November that 'the Boers are likely to absorb the military activity of Anglo-Saxons for a longer period than they had believed'.

Actually, the long and expensive Boer War was the paroxysm of imperialist passions in Britain, but also the beginning of their decline. Halévy became conscious of this change in the year which followed. On 26 November 1900, he wrote from London: 'The unfortunate Boers are doing me, anyway, a good turn: my stay here is infinitely more pleasant than last year. Not a word against France; everybody seems to accept my vision on the Transvaal war as a point of view which is at least allowable'. And a few days later: 'Presently, the English are charming, and they will stay so as long as the war in South Africa will last, i.e. a very long time.' Nonetheless, Halévy wrote: 'I remain ... pessimistic for the future. Chamberlain remains indestructible.'[17]

Indeed, the distrust of British foreign policy, which Halévy felt, persisted, though it had been reduced.[18] He expressed it again at the very time when the Entente Cordiale was being achieved. He was in London during the state visit by the President of the French Republic in July 1903 and he wrote: 'I have seen the King; I have seen Loubet. It was sunny; one can not imagine something more splendid than the escort of Horse Guards. But the King, in his red uniform, looked like the porter of a big hotel; Loubet looked like his friend, the French chef of the same hotel, who had put on an evening dress .... Oxford Street is everywhere crossed by huge banderoles 'Vive la France – Dieu vous garde – Soyez le bienvenu' .... The English press is enthusiastic, without any exception.' Halévy added that he had overheard two Frenchwomen; one of them said: 'Who would have believed this five years ago?' ... 'I was also here five years ago. How will things be five years ahead?' Three weeks later, he wrote that 'Chamberlain pulls behind him, willy-nilly, his fellow countrymen, in a way which is both absurd and very logical.' The kind of obsession which Halévy felt about Chamberlain still persisted in 1906, despite the Conservatives' recent electoral rout; on 23 May, he wrote from Birmingham: 'The shadow of this terrible individual hovers over this blackish and ill-built town. Anyway it hovers over all England; and Chamberlain looks – am I wrong? – to prepare, even to start his return to the stage, in Parliament. Yesterday, he posed as the leader of the Opposition.' Actually, on 10 July, Chamberlain, who had just reached the age of 70, suffered a stroke which left him a cripple until his death in 1914. There is no allusion to this fatal accident in Halévy's letters and we shall not know whether he rejoiced at the punishment which struck his archenemy.

Anyway, in the letters which Halévy wrote during the early years of the twentieth century, the danger of English aggression against France is no longer mentioned. During the first Moroccan crisis, in 1905, he only deplored that France had 'become a buffer-state between Germany and England', a situation which he inclined 'to find dangerous' because of the 'wicked schemes' of the 'English nation' and of the German government. 'Between England and Germany, France's true interest would be to remain neutral.' Besides, the letters which were then written from England or about England have a new tone and contain judgements which were more pertinent than formerly. 'The English', Halévy wrote in July 1903 after an evening at the Webbs,

> have transformed England in a large *debating society* [in English in the text] where, by dint of discussing all questions, none of them is worth dying for. They have domesticated rioting, domesticated civil war; and they have come to a result which is quite amazing for a Continental, and above all for a Frenchman: an absolute government with the semblance of absolute freedom, or the sovereignty of public opinion, with abdication by the opinion into the hands of a demagogue, like Chamberlain, – of an aristocracy of financiers and merchants. Indeed, extremes do meet.

And a few months later:

> In England, many organized interests are at work. The aristocratic interest, enormously strong, as, presently, the leaders of the Liberal party are Peers, and as, after so many supposedly democratic reforms, Parliament remains a syndicate of patricians, more or less businessmen. Religious interests – the Church and the Dissenters. Interests of the trade unions which are a kind of proletarian aristocracy.

Actually, Halévy was no longer a philosopher, and for some years he had been working on English history for his *Formation du radicalisme philosophique* (the third and last volume was published in 1904), for his lectures at the School of Political Sciences in Paris, for two small books[19] and for a study on Methodism, which he had to give up when he discovered that two French scholars had 'confiscated' the subject. This rather depressed him and to recover his equilibrium, he resolved to undertake what was to be his *magnum opus*: 'the history of the English people in the 19th century'. He had thought about it as early as 1896, but his philosopher friends had dissuaded him from starting such a book; but, on 14 September 1905, he announced to Célestin Bouglé (later a distinguished sociologist), his definitive decision to write this history, 'the design of which takes shape from year to year'. Then comes this remarkable passage:

> The genuine danger, which one runs when studying England too exclusively, is to become an anglophile. But what can I do? It is inevitable for intelligence to be influenced by the objects to which it applies itself and, on the other hand, it is sure that, during the last two centuries, England has given Europe some lessons in politics. Therefore, by studying the history of England, I am losing the feeling that revolutions are beautiful.[20]

This was the confession that the arrogant *normalien* of 1892 and the worried patriot of 1898 and 1899 had become a staunch Anglophile.

Notes

1. Elie Halévy, *Correspondance (1891–1937)*, Henriette Guy-Loë *et al.* (eds), Preface by François Furet (Paris: de Fallois, 1996), 803 pp. A more elaborate version of this study has been published in *The Tocqueville Review*, XVIII, no. 2 (1997), 129–56.
2. Halévy returned at length to these episodes in the *Epilogue (1895–1914)* of his *Histoire du peuple anglais au XIXe siècle*, vol. I, *Les Impérialistes au pouvoir (1895–1905)* (Paris, 1926).
3. See *Epilogue*, I, pp. 41–2, on the pro-American attitude of the Radical press and of the Nonconformists, who called for an 'Anglo-Saxon alliance'.
4. *Epilogue*, I, pp. 44–8, 53.
5. On 17 May, Chamberlain was said to have asked the Cabinet to send France an ultimatum; *Epilogue*, I, pp. 53–4.
6. Who, actually, in *Epilogue*, I, pp. 74–5, evokes his own recollections of the war's beginning: 'I was in London. I remember I did see regiments marching through the town . . . '.
7. Halévy did not forecast the orgiastic explosion which was caused, in May 1900, by the news that the Boers had been forced to raise the siege of Mafeking.
8. This letter was written after a weekend spent with Bertrand Russell and his wife: 'I would not have dared to speak in front of them about Rhodes and Chamberlain, in words as blasphemous as the ones they used in front of me. If, nonetheless, they are "patriots", this is because of the unfortunate period in which we are.' See *Epilogue*, I, p. 100, about the rapprochement between the Webbs and the liberal imperialists. However, the pro-Boer prevailed within the Liberal Party (ibid., pp. 101–3).
9. This refers to a famous statement by Lord Palmerston during the Don Pacifico incident.
10. Kaiser Wilhelm was to come to England, on a state visit, the following month.

11. In the spring of 1899, 'there was undoubtedly in London a party in favour of war against France'; and on 30 August 1898, an agreement had been signed between England and Germany about a possible partition of Portuguese colonies; *Epilogue*, I, pp. 52–3, 59, 108.
12. This is a brilliant intuition about the 'slowing down' of the British economy in the late nineteenth century.
13. Halévy added: 'Europe is increasingly unimportant for men who are not any more Europeans, but citizens of the Anglo-Saxon world'. Already, in May 1898, he had been impressed by the unity of the Anglo-Saxon world, by its indifference to Europe, and he had written this rather prophetic passage: 'When an Anglo-Saxon Federation would have been established, England would become a kind of historical museum, where young Americans, Australians, Rhodesians would come to study...the origins of Americanism.'
14. Or, more exactly, continental, directed against England. On 4 November, Elie wrote to his brother: 'How to avoid...within a system of continental alliances, the triumph of religious brutality, the destruction of all ideas we love?'
15. *Epilogue*, I, p. 109.
16. On 29 August 1899, he ironically asked Célestin Bouglé what would be the attitude of the French Left when, in a not distant future, would begin 'a universal turmoil, unprecedented in world history. There will be slaughter in Africa, in Oceania, in China, in America, in Europe....'
17. Indeed, early in 1901, Chamberlain was to try again to negotiate an Anglo-German alliance.
18. 'If a war broke out with England...', letter of 1 December 1900.
19. On the Socialist Thomas Hodgkin (1902) and on *L'Angleterre et son Empire* (1905).
20. The first volume of the *Histoire* was to come out in 1912.

7
'Breaking the Banque': the Great Crisis in Franco-British Central Bank Relations between the Wars

Robert Boyce

With the world's financial markets always on the eve of going into turmoil, the press today is full of worried comment about the consequences of globalization, the fear that regulatory institutions are no longer adequate to their task and – almost for the first time – references to the Great Crash of 1929. This essay does not attempt a comparison of the interwar crisis and the situation today. However, it may be of some contemporary interest in so far as it surveys relations between two of the chief regulatory agencies in the earlier period, the Bank of France and the Bank of England. The survey is deliberately non-technical, its purpose being to put into political perspective the obstacles to co-operation between the two banks.

President Wilson's decision personally to represent America at the Paris Peace Conference encouraged hopes in Europe that the United States would contribute substantially to Europe's economic reconstruction and enable an early revival of international trade. In the event, however, Wilson found his position undermined by a hostile Senate. Not only did the American government withdraw into isolationism, but American bankers and financiers avoided Europe for fully six years after the Armistice. In the circumstances, the only power able and willing to provide leadership in the reconstruction of the international economic system was Britain. Britain, in contrast to the United States, had long experience of leadership, the personnel and institutions required, and the motive to act. Its empire, which stretched around the world, had been inflated further in the peace settlement, making it even more vulnerable to international conflict. Its economy depended upon commerce and finance, its population upon foodstuffs from overseas. At this time the City of London still far surpassed New York as the world's greatest concentration of markets – for gold, foreign exchange, commodities, stocks, bonds, bills of exchange, insurance and shipping. Leadership personnel was available from the Bank of England and other City institutions along with the Foreign Office, Treasury and Board of Trade.

From 1919 British businessmen and officials, directly or through one or another agencies of the League of Nations, worked to restore order to the international economy. Revolution in central Europe and the brief but severe post-war economic slump delayed recovery. Yet, within five years after the slump the first stage of reconstruction was almost completed, with the stabilization of all the world's major currencies. British authorities were instrumental in the stabilization of the Austrian and Hungarian currencies, on drawing in American financial interests to help end the hyperinflation in Germany, and in assisting stabilization in Greece, Estonia, Bulgaria, Belgium and Italy. In 1925 the pound itself was restored to the gold standard, and the next year France stabilized the franc de facto, although without external assistance.

Once currencies were stabilized, a start could be made on reversing the post-war rise in trade protection, and by 1928 some progress was made on this front as well. After the efforts of the International Chamber of Commerce, the World Economic Conference of 1927 and other initiatives under League of Nations auspices, quantitative trade controls were largely removed and tariff levels were at least stabilized. But the bilateral trade treaties which formed the legal framework of international trade were of much shorter duration than before the war. And reparations and war debts created an additional element of uncertainty. For these and other reasons the international trade and payments system remained very fragile, as Montagu Norman, Governor of the Bank of England, was acutely aware.

Norman, from his office in Threadneedle Street, worked behind the scenes for both currency stabilization and trade liberalization. He regarded it as his mission to create a global network of central banks, each independent of political controls and capable of taking the difficult decisions on interest rates necessary to maintain its currency in fixed relation to the other currencies of the world, as defined in terms of gold. Once realized, the banks could effectively constrain politicians who were tempted to 'bribe the electorate with their own money', and eliminate the need for 'artificial' constraints on trade, such as tariffs and quotas. Norman was not alone in this ambition. It was probably shared by every international banker, not least in France. Indeed, aside from second-order differences over the management of the gold standard, the bedrock principles on which the Bank of England and Bank of France operated were the same. Nevertheless, the course of events in the 1920s led each to regard the other as the source of many of its problems.

One reason was France's alleged protectionism and politicization of trade. British observers became increasingly outspoken at France's 'economic nationalism', because French import duties rose sharply after the war, and the bilateral trade balance which had favoured Britain before the war ran strongly in France's favour throughout the 1920s. In fact, taking import duties (by whatever name) as a percentage of total imports, France was not more protectionist than before the war, and indeed not substantially more protectionist than Britain. But France seemed to become more protectionist because its duties had been repeatedly raised in line with sharply rising price levels, while Britain seemed more liberal than it was because it resisted the introduction of a general tariff but introduced a range of specific duties including excise duties which if not specifically directed at foreign imports nevertheless restricted trade. And it was appearances that counted. So whereas British observers regarded the French as incorrigibly protectionist, they regarded themselves, with more than a little self-righteousness, as the beleaguered exemplars of free trade. Frustrations were intensified by the 1927 Franco-German commercial agreement which, seen from London, seemed to favour Germany at Britain's expense.[1]

The second reason for British complaints was France's handling of reparations and war debts. Britain had been as insistent as France on entering large claims against Germany during the Paris Peace Conference, but soon came round to the view that they were an obstacle to the revival of international trade. From 1922 therefore Britain sought to persuade the United States to abandon war debt demands and France, Belgium and Italy to accept the British policy of demanding from Germany only what was needed to pay their own war debts. French insistence upon higher payments, since it affected Germany's recovery and capacity to import, was treated as a blow to Britain as well as to Germany. As for war debts, the close attention historians have given to the US–European relationship has rather obscured the fact that the issue acutely divided Britain and France as well. Among other things, French observers criticized Britain for withholding the gold deposit on the 1916 loan in order to prop up sterling, while British observers criticized France for repaying loans in depreciated francs and delaying the consolidation of its short-term war debt.[2]

The third reason was the way that France had managed – or as Norman and colleagues believed, mismanaged – its post-war monetary and financial affairs. There was little separating British and French central bankers in principle. Both were impatient to restore the discipline of the gold standard and reopen their financial markets to international lending. But both were obliged to unpeg their currencies in 1919, and thereafter French central bankers were unable to keep inflation under control, which resulted in the franc falling to barely one-tenth of its pre-war value at the worst of the crisis in 1926. Then, having decided to stabilize the franc, French authorities chose an exchange rate which gave their exporters a substantial advantage over British competitors. To hold the franc at this rate, the Bank of France sold francs and accumulated foreign currency balances, but once the franc was restored to the gold standard in June 1928, it began to dispose of them. So large were its sterling balances that, had it acted precipitously, it would have driven the pound off the gold standard. Twice Norman was obliged to request the French governor, Emile Moreau, to show restraint.[3]

Norman evidently found it distasteful to have to acknowledge the weakness of his position, and particularly to the French. He had done everything he could to hasten a general return to the gold standard. Not least, he had accepted the resolution adopted at the Genoa Conference in 1922 inviting central banks to treat as reserve assets not only gold bullion but also foreign currencies which were themselves backed by gold; an innovation designed to increase the available resources for rebuilding the international monetary system. He was now helping British-led consortia to arrange currency stabilization loans to the Romanian and Yugoslav central banks. He sought influence over the latter's central banks mainly to ensure that they would play by what he regarded as the gold standard rules. But Moreau saw Norman's efforts as evidence of British imperialism, and demanded that French bankers take charge of the loan arrangements.[4] In turn, Norman probably interpreted Moreau's reaction as part of a plan to wreck the gold exchange standard by discouraging the use of sterling for reserve purposes, and evidence that France intended to use its recently rebuilt currency reserves as a political weapon. Since London always regarded France as narrowly nationalist, this seemed completely in character. The difficulty was that Norman was in no position to deal with the French challenge. He and his City friends had persuaded the British government to return to the gold standard in 1925, expecting that this would make sterling more attractive and draw foreign balances to London. In the event they gravely underestimated the difficulty of adjusting to the new exchange rate and the political reactions to further deflation.

The usual way of presenting Britain's return to gold is by reference to the approximately 10 per cent overvaluation of the pound in April 1925, based on purchasing power parity calculations.[5] From this it follows that had wages been just a little more flexible, adjustment to the new/old parity would have been rapid and relatively painless; unfortunately, the trade unions stood in the way and made serious trouble for all concerned. This is accurate so far as it goes, but the time frame creates a wholly misleading picture of events. First, Britain's return to gold coincided with the start of a global deflationary trend during which wholesale price levels declined every year from 1925 to 1933.[6] This greatly increased Britain's adjustment problems by putting additional pressure on wages. Second, British producers had already absorbed huge reductions of prices and wages *before* returning to gold. Elsewhere in Europe, countries had confronted post-war shortages and balance of payments problems by a combination of import restrictions and currency depreciation. Workers had to struggle to keep abreast of rising prices and real wages actually fell, but at least they did not fall in money terms. Not so in Britain. There, the decision to eschew trade protection and move quickly to restore the gold standard meant a period not of inflation but of severe deflation in which wages declined in both real and money terms. The deflation enabled Britain, alone of all the European belligerent powers, to return to the gold standard at the pre-war rate of exchange. This was a source of great pride to many Britons and a relief to those with savings or investments denominated in sterling. But it had required price deflation of fully 60 per cent over six years, with money wages forced down by a roughly similar amount. During the war, British soldiers and workers (like their counterparts elsewhere) had been encouraged to look forward to a better life after the victory, and large numbers had enrolled in trade unions after demobilization. The long deflation was a bruising experience for workers, their trade unions and their employers, which left them in no mood to face more deflationary pressure. Thus when sterling was restored to gold and Norman saw no alternative to a further rise in interest rates, there was an explosion of industrial unrest. A general strike, threatened in 1925, actually took place in May 1926. Albeit brief and relatively non-violent, it nevertheless highlighted the depth of frustration within the country. The Chancellor of the Exchequer constantly pressured Norman to forgo further deflationary action, threatening public criticism if he did so. Norman, aware of sterling's overvaluation, was thus constrained from taking the decisions he believed were necessary to restore equilibrium.

The difficulties confronting Britain and the rest of Europe in the latter part of the 1920s were largely, although of course not wholly, attributable to American irresponsibility. One aspect was the wildly erratic character of US foreign lending. Having shunned Europe after the war, US bankers lent freely to European borrowers once the German inflation was brought under control, then abruptly ceased almost all new lending in the latter half of 1927. A second aspect was the Republicans' decision to reverse the Democrats' policy of trade liberalization. The Fordney–McCumber Tariff of 1922 raised duties to a record level; Congress approved a general increase in duties in the spring of 1929 that raised the tariff substantially higher.

None of this might have mattered had America been smaller and Europe stronger. But Europe was still weak and the United States was now the world's leading exporter and enjoyed a huge balance of payments surplus with Europe and the rest of the world. Its behaviour was therefore profoundly destabilizing. Nevertheless, Norman and his British colleagues – almost alone among European leaders – refused to utter a word of criticism. One reason was that, almost without exception, British statesmen supported the principle of the 'special relationship', albeit a term not actually coined until later. When in 1928–29 Anglo-American antagonism over naval disarmament was allowed to reach alarming levels, they reacted strongly in favour of improved relations. They also hoped to persuade Washington of its interest in European stability. British statesmen tended to see America as a nation divided between enlightened internationalists and redneck nativists. This was not an unrealistic view. The error was in invariably expecting far too much from the internationalists, whose influence in Washington was always very limited.

Thus Norman cultivated relations with American central bankers, while making no complaint of US commercial and monetary policies. Instead, he directed his frustration against France. He took such personal affront at Moreau's actions in 1928 that he refused to meet him when he visited London for the first time.[7] Nor was Norman alone in his Francophobia. In 1928–29 British statesmen and Treasury officials displayed similar prejudice during negotiations to revise the Dawes reparations plan. The decision to revise the Dawes Plan had been taken because of growing fears that reparations were adding to Germany's already serious balance of payments problem. But by the summer of 1929, with sterling apparently once more under attack from Paris,[8]

British statesmen practically lost sight of the main purpose of reparations revision and treated it as a contest between Britain, which had already made heroic sacrifices for the sake of world prosperity, and France, which was still selfishly seeking to profit from reparations.[9] Philip Snowden, Chancellor in the new Labour government, led the British delegation to the diplomatic conference at The Hague, where the Young Plan was to be approved. Despite gaining negligible concessions, his decision to 'stand up to the French' was clearly popular in Britain, for on returning he was treated as a hero and was granted the freedom of the City of London.[10]

The Wall Street Crash two months later brought a welcome end to the frenzy of speculation and enabled Norman to reduce interest rates. But the general economic downturn had already begun, and by 1930 Germany, which had rebuilt its whole credit system on the basis of US and British loans after the hyperinflation, was in crisis. Behind the scenes, British central bankers supported by colleagues from the United States, Sweden and elsewhere had been searching for ways to shore up the international monetary system since 1928, and a few visionaries urged the creation of a new lender of last resort or source of drawing rights to cushion central banks from excessive deflationary pressures.[11] At its planning stage in 1929, Emile Francqui, Hjalmar Schacht and Sir Josiah Stamp, the British expert, had attempted to turn the Bank for International Settlements (BIS) into an effective agency.[12] But Norman himself was cool to any such experiments, and France raised objections to reparations being used in this way, and when it came into being in April 1930 the BIS lacked the resources to counter the worsening crisis.[13]

The Bank of France meanwhile faced an *embarras de richesses*. France continued to enjoy a competitive advantage from its new exchange parity. With tourist receipts still strong and foreign investment opportunities declining, gold and foreign currency balances both grew. Moreau and Clément Moret who succeeded him in September 1930 were both keen to replace the foreign currency balances with gold. The opportunity arose in the second half of 1930 when, with sterling already weak, gold bullion was shipped almost daily from London to Paris. This attracted notice in the British press and provoked increasingly angry criticism of French policy.

British expert opinion was divided on French motives for drawing gold from London. Some suspected that it was politically motivated: to weaken Britain so that France might dictate policy to Germany and in Napoleonic fashion extend its writ across the whole continent. Others doubted that it was politically inspired, ascribing it instead largely to an ultraconservative approach to the gold standard and an undeveloped banking system which required to a large amount of cash in circulation. But in either case, French central bank policy seemed highly dangerous, since it meant sterilizing gold which could be used to expand credit and revive the world economy, forcing up interest rates elsewhere, and ultimately threatening to destroy the gold standard altogether.[14]

In December 1930 British Treasury officials took advantage of French discomfort at the mounting criticism by seizing the opportunity for conversations on the gold/foreign exchange problem.[15] Officials at the Rue de Rivoli responded nervously, and suggested parallel talks between their respective central banks. Moret agreed, but Norman was unwilling to acknowledge sterling's weakness by accepting talks with a Frenchman. In any case, he wished to maintain the spotlight on the Labour government which faced mounting criticism to bring unemployment spending under control.[16] In the event, the Treasury conversations proved inconclusive.[17] But coincidentally pressure on sterling had eased, and the spotlight turned elsewhere.

Following the revelation on 20 March 1931 that Germany and Austria were planning to form a customs union, the Austrian schilling came under severe pressure. In June it was the turn of the German mark, which soon led to a temporary closing of the banks and the introduction of exchange controls. Only in July did sterling again come under pressure on the exchanges. The suddenness of the selling pressure appears to have caught everyone by surprise. Norman, asked to explain it, admitted that he was mystified.[18] However, the fact that it began on 15 July, when the Paris market reopened after the Bastille Day holiday, convinced most of the City that it was a politically inspired French attack.[19] After the Franco-British dispute over assisting Austria, when British statesmen lent official encouragement to the belief that France was throwing its weight about in order to get its way on the diplomatic front, it seemed not improbable that France was now deliberately selling sterling as a way to deter Britain from further shielding Germany from French demands. Similarly the recent dispute over the Hoover moratorium on intergovernmental debts, when Norman and the City were horrified that France would hold up implementation and risk the collapse of Germany and capitalism itself simply to obtain extra assurances for French reparation claims.[20]

The truth was altogether different. Moret and his colleagues in Paris regretted Britain's ambiguous attitude towards the Austro-German customs union project and its perpetual readiness to turn a blind eye to Germany's evasion of its obligations under the treaty of Versailles. But allegations of a deliberate French attack on the pound were wide of the mark. French bankers fully recognized the central importance of the Bank of England to the international monetary system and the value of co-operation. Their quarrel was not with the Bank of England's power or influence, but with its reserve policy and support for what seemed to them reckless foreign overlending. As seen from the Rue de la Vrillière, the British-backed gold exchange standard had resulted in a vast over-expansion of credit. Prices, far too high after the Armistice, had been kept inflated. Now that the business cycle had run its course, the inevitable consequence of this financial pyramiding was occurring. Countries that had borrowed dollars or pounds to expand their credit systems, now had savagely to contract credit to avoid seeing their monetary systems collapse altogether.

In the circumstances, Moret and colleagues were more than a little frustrated by London's constant efforts to mobilize other central banks against a policy of rigour and to provoke popular hostility towards the Bank of France. London had been the prime mover in setting up the League-sponsored Gold Delegation in early 1929 whose main purpose seemed to be to put the Bank of France on the spot over its large gold reserves. French authorities had had to bend all their efforts to restrict its proceedings and ensure that its reports were heavily qualified.[21] They had to face the Royal Institute of International Affairs' widely reported enquiry into the 'gold problem' in 1929–30, the British Treasury support for bilateral conversations in 1930, and the almost ceaseless criticism of French gold hoarding in the British press. With the Bank of France in an apparently unassailable position and the Bank of England on the ropes, it seemed almost self-evident to them who had won the argument. But just as they had recently helped other central banks, so they were prepared to help the Bank of England.[22] And so, when Norman approached them on 24 July, they immediately arranged a £25 million credit matched by a similar credit from the Federal Reserve Bank of New York.[23] This was made available to the Bank of England, without conditions, for the start of trading on 1 August.

In the event, the Bank of England squandered much of the credit. Norman, convinced that sterling's salvation required massive reductions in public spending to balance the national budget, chose this moment to turn the screws on the government. Instead of using the credits to counter speculation against the pound, he ordered the Bank's foreign exchange dealers to fold their arms and do nothing, so as to give the government a fright. Given the acute nervousness of the market, this was an extraordinary decision. Word immediately circulated that the

Bank would no longer defend sterling. Selling sharply increased, and the Bank belatedly mobilized most of the credit to stem the tide.[24]

By mid-August the central bank credit was on the way to exhaustion and the pressure was beginning to tell. Norman presently suffered a breakdown and sailed for Quebec City to recuperate. The second Labour government found it impossible to agree on sufficient economies to balance the budget, and was swept away on 24 August. In desperation, party government was set aside for the first and only time outside of war. A second credit was almost immediately secured in Paris and New York, this time for £40 million each, and to the British government itself. These were enormous credits: as a basis for comparison, the Bank of England's reserves at their strongest never exceeded £165 million during the 1920s, and only a small fraction of this total could be used for market operations. Yet, despite this ammunition, the Bank's foreign exchange dealers could not discourage sterling selling. French political leaders and central bank officials continued to proffer assistance. Moret urged the British government to seek a long-term loan, and large enough to convince everyone of sterling's strength. French bankers had become extremely nervous about foreign lending, he said, but this was one operation they would willingly support.[25] HMG was however reluctant to take on new liabilities, and talks on a third credit were still at a preliminary stage on 21 September when sterling was forced off the gold standard.

French officials regretted Britain's departure from the gold standard, but accepted British government assertions that it was a purely temporary suspension. Having repeatedly extended their support, and having promised to co-operate in minimizing reactions on the markets when they reopened after the twenty-first, they found it impossible to believe that Franco-British relations would be seriously affected. The Laval government invited Lord Reading, Foreign Secretary in the new National government, for talks. It was during this meeting, on 7 October, that the central bank conflict reached its climax.

Having held off further sterling sales in 1931 while the pound was weak, and having taken responsibility for the two large credits in the summer, the Bank of France's sterling balances amounted to £100 million (12.2 milliard francs). By October, with the pound depreciated 8 per cent, the Bank's losses amounted to almost 1 milliard francs; by mid-December, with the pound down to $3.28\frac{1}{2}$, they were to reach 3.15 milliards, two-thirds of this from the credits extended in the summer.[26] The Bank held huge gold reserves, second only to the Federal Reserve System, but it was also a commercial firm with limited capital and shareholder obligations. Since the sterling losses amounted to seven times its capital and reserves, it was technically bankrupt. There was no question of the Bank actually being wound up, but it did mean suspending dividends for some time and, if something were not done quickly to improve its accounts, an extremely severe blow to its prestige.[27] Moret sought compensation from the Bank of England, and when this was refused he turned to Reading and the British Treasury officials accompanying him. As he remarked, France had unhesitatingly responded to Britain's request for help during the crisis; the losses were incurred for Britain's, not France's sake. The British representatives, however, were still furious at the humiliation of being forced off gold, which they blamed chiefly on the French. They would not consider compensation; they would not even express regret for the Bank's losses. Moret was shocked. He was undoubtedly aware of increased Francophobia in London, but he clearly did not expect British officials to react this way. Dismayed and furious, he warned that if this was their view, he would dispose of his remaining sterling balances there and then. Given their size, this amounted to a threat of driving sterling through the floor.[28]

The immediate repercussions of this confrontation were far less severe than seemed likely at the time. Moret disposed of sterling, but did so cautiously without disrupting the foreign exchange markets. In October he and the regents agreed to a three-month renewal of the 31 July credit.[29] In turn, the French government agreed to indemnify the Bank of France for its losses, and overrode criticism of the Bank from Left and Right to secure the passage of a bill in December, just in time for its quarterly report.[30] That said, the conflict between the central banks undoubtedly intensified mutual animosities at the national level. Since the economic crisis largely overshadowed the political agenda, it is reasonable to assume that it affected diplomatic relations between France and Britain and intensified their mutual alienation.

The tragedy is that the conflict was over essentially secondary issues. The two banks entered the era with closely similar policies. Both sought independence from political interference to be free to regulate domestic credit in the interests of price stability; both sought to return to the gold standard, if possible at the pre-war rate of exchange.[31] Both regarded it as essential that their governments should contribute by restricting spending and balancing their budgets. Keynes and other British experts might deride the reactionary character of French financial and monetary policy. Not so Norman, for the simple reason that with only minor differences it was his policy, too.

The source of their differences was not matters of principle, but their radically different post-war experiences. In France the decade was marked by inflation, which threatened briefly to become hyperinflation. It was therefore natural for French bankers to seek a restriction of credit so as to deflate prices, and to avoid monetary experiments that threatened to release new inflation. In Britain, the same period was dominated by deflation. If British central bankers were prepared to support a gold exchange standard, it was because this seemed to be the only way to secure a general stabilization of currencies without provoking a scramble for gold and further deflationary pressures. Thus, throughout the 1920s French and British bankers saw the world as if through opposite ends of a telescope. Each attempt by the one group to escape their predicament, made the other's predicament worse. So consistent was the opposition that each imagined the other to be ill-intentioned and perhaps politically motivated. As each blamed the other for many of their economic problems, which persisted through much of the decade, so the conflict damaged relations during the crucial period leading to the Second World War.

Notes

1. The trade issues are developed in R. W. D. Boyce, *British Capitalism at the Crossroads, 1919–1932: a Study in Politics, Economics and International Relations* (Cambridge, 1987), pp. 99–100, 127–30.
2. On the 1916 loan controversy, see *Le Matin*, 29 Mar. 1927; *Le Petit Journal*, 31 Mar. 1927; *L'Agence Economique et Financière*, 2 Apr. 1927; *Petit Bleu*, 3/4 Apr. 1927; *Aux Ecoutes*, 10 Apr. 1927; Pouyanne to Poincaré, no. 47 159, 8 Apr. 1927, Ministère des Finances (hereafter MF) B12607. On the depreciated war loans, see Pouyanne to Poincaré, no. 47 443, 16 May 1927, MF B12607; de Chalendar to Chéron, 10 Jan. 1929, MF B12611.
3. On British reactions to the French sterling operations, see Pouyanne to Poincaré, no.47 503, 24 May 1927, MF B12607; also no. 47 534, 27 May 1927 and no. 47 542, 27 May 1927, no. 47 597, 11 June 1927, MF B12607.; Niemeyer to Seydoux, 28 May 1927, Ministère des Affaires Étrangères (hereafter MAE) 261, Papiers Seydoux 42; de Fleuriau to Seydoux, 11 June 1927, MAE 261, Papiers Seydoux 39; statement by Winston Churchill to House of Commons, Hansard, 28 June 1927.
4. E. Moreau, *Souvenirs d'un Gouverneur de la Banque de France* (Paris, 1954), pp. 506–9; Charles Addis diary, 28 Feb. 1928. The confrontation appears to have been encouraged by Joseph Avenol of the Quai d'Orsay, see Avenol to Quesnay, 17 Feb. 1928, MAE 006, Papiers Avenol 37.
5. This is the basis of analysis in D. E. Moggridge, *British Monetary Policy, 1924–1931: the Norman Conquest of $4.86* (Cambridge, 1972), the standard work on the subject.

6. B. R. Mitchell and P. Deane, *Abstract of British Historical Statistics* (Cambridge, 1962), p. 477; for wages pp. 352–3.

7. Boyce, *British Capitalism at the Crossroads*, p. 164.

8. De Chalendar to Farnier, 26 July 1929, MF B31727; statement by Moreau, Séance 1 Aug. 1929, Banque de France, Délibérations du Conseil Général (hereafter BqFr CG).

9. The banker Sir Charles Addis described it as a pyrrhic victory, yielding modest concessions all from the wrong people, dressed up to look like a great victory. Addis to Sir Josiah Stamp, n.d. (?30 Aug. 1929), Stamp papers. But other City bankers were taken in, see de Chalendar to Chéron, 3 Oct. 1929, MF B25452.

10. Boyce, *British Capitalism at the Crossroads*, pp. 207–12.

11. Ibid., pp. 166–85.

12. Ibid., pp. 193–7, 212–16.

13. Norman also lined up with Moreau against the creation of the Gold Delegation; see Moreau to Norman, 28 Dec. 1928, boîte 17, BqFr. Later, Norman appears to have worked as hard as the French to discourage progress by the Delegation; see Strakosch to Niemeyer, 1 Sept. 1930, Bank of England (BoE), OV9/264; Norman to G. Harrison and O. D. Young, 6 Sept. 1930, no. 181/30, Federal Reserve Bank of New York, C798.

14. Rueff to Reynaud and Farnier, no. 56 743, 29 July 1930, MF B12613.

15. F. Leith Ross minute to Sir R. Hopkins, 17 Nov. 1930, British Treasury T160/430, F12317/1; Leith Ross minute to Hopkins and F. Pethwick-Lawrence, 2 Dec. 1930, T160/430, F12317/1.

16. Ibid.; Leith Ross minute to Sir R. Vansittart, 2 Dec. 1931, Foreign Office (hereafter FO) 371/15640, W56/56/17; Séance 5 Dec. 1930, BqFr CG; minute by Waley, 30 Jan. 1931, T160/430, F12317/2; Leith-Ross to Fergusson, 17 February 1931, T160/430, F12317/2; Sir H. Clay, *Lord Norman*, (London, 1957), pp. 370–1.

17. The conversations are summarized in K. Mouré, *Managing the Franc Poincaré: Economic Understanding and Political Constraint in French Monetary Policy, 1928–1936* (Cambridge, 1991), pp. 58–65 ; Boyce, *British Capitalism at the Crossroads*, pp. 294–9.

18. Clay, *Lord Norman*, p. 384.

19. Dalton diaries, 16–17, 19 July 1931.

20. Memorandum by Thompson-McCausland, n.d. BoE, ATM 14/10; 'Germany and Europe in Suspense', *Financial Times*, 15 July 1931; 'France's Menace is – France', and 'Finance and Industry', *Daily Herald*, 21 July 1931.

21. See for instance 'Note de M. de Chalendar au sujet de la 40ème Session du Comité Financier de la S.D.N.', 22 Jan. 1931, MAE, SdN, IJ-QEF 1167.

22. In 1931 the Bank of France extended credits to the central banks of Austria, Germany, Hungary, Spain, Yugoslavia, Czechoslovakia, Romania, Finland and Sweden. Séances 1931–32, BqFr CG.

23. Séance extraordinaire, 27 July 1931, BqFr CG.

24. Séances 6, 13 Aug. 1931, BqFr CG; memorandum by Thompson-McCausland, 17–18, n.d. BoE ATM 14/10; minute by G. Harrison, 8 Aug. 1931, Federal Reserve Bank of New York, Harrison papers, 3125.2.

25. R. Campbell to Lord Reading, 22 Sept. 1931, FO 371/15681, W11075/10755/50; Leith Ross to Hopkins and Waley, 23 Sept. 1931, T188/286.

26. Séance 29 Oct. 1931, BqFr CG; statement for Agence Havas, 18 Nov. 1931, MF B12625; letter from Moret to Flandin in Séance extraordinaire, 5 Dec. 1931, BqFr CG; Convention du 7 décembre 1931, BqFr 1931 boîte 22.

27. 'The Dilemma of the Bank of France', *Financial News*, 30 Nov. 1931.

28. Séance 8 Oct. 1931, BqFr CG; Sir F. Leith Ross minute to Sir R. Vansittart, 9 Oct. 1931, FO 371/15682, W12411/10755/50.

29. Séances 22, 29 Oct. 1931, BqFr CG.

30. *Le Quotidien*, 9, 15 Dec., *L'Humanité*, 11 Dec., *Le Populaire*, 11, 16 Dec., *Le Temps*, *Petit Parisien*, 23 Dec., *La Dépêche*, 24 Dec. 1931.

31. See for instance Moreau's statement to the regents at the time the franc was restored to gold, Séance extraordinaire, 23 June 1928, BqFr CG.

8
British Official Perceptions of France and the French, 1936–1940*

Michael Dockrill

British official opinion of France and the French in the early 1920s was probably best summed up by Sir Warren Fisher, the Permanent Secretary to the Treasury, in July 1923: 'while I admit that the French between 1870 and 1914 had their tails well down and therefore assumed a veneer of moderation, during the rest of their centuries-old existence, they have played the part of bullies...and they are doing so now'.[1] The papers of British politicians, officials and military leaders were full of comments of this kind about the French. Nor did the early 1930s bring any change in the British attitude towards France and the French. In 1935 relations between the two countries reached their nadir over their different responses to Mussolini's invasion of Ethiopia, where French reluctance to support the half-hearted League sanctions against Italy promoted by Britain created serious tensions within the Entente. The Permanent Under-Secretary at the Foreign Office, Sir Robert Vansittart, described French behaviour in November 1935 as 'disloyalty and treachery in its dirtiest and blackest form'.[2] The debacle of the subsequent Hoare–Laval pact, which gave Mussolini the bulk of his territorial demands in Ethiopia, and which was leaked to the press, outraging British press and parliamentary opinion, worsened the atmosphere between the two countries. Sir Samuel Hoare, who was forced to resign as Foreign Secretary, blamed the French for the press revelation of the existence of the pact, while the French right wing blamed British intransigence over sanctions for the loss of the alliance with Italy which France had forged in 1935.

There was considerable relief in Whitehall at the end of January 1936 when Pierre Laval resigned as French Prime Minister. Laval was widely disliked and distrusted in British official circles, especially after what was regarded as his treacherous behaviour over Ethiopia. Sir Horace Rum-

bold, the former British ambassador to Germany, wrote that 'the only
white thing about Laval was his tie and even that was only washed
occasionally'.[3] Nor were Anglo-French relations improved by their subsequent disputes about the Entente's response – or lack of response – to
Hitler's remilitarization of the Rhineland on 7 March 1936. Britain
refused to contemplate any military action to eject the German troops
from the Rhineland. Not that the French were prepared to do anything
either, and certainly not without British support. The new Foreign
Secretary, Anthony Eden, feared that 'between military action on the
one hand and friendly action on the other, there lies a policy of sulking
and passive obstruction, and it is this policy to which the French Government in their weakness, will be inclined to have recourse, and out of
which we shall have to persuade them'.[4] However, the French were able
to prise one concession from the British as a result of the crisis, the
opening of Anglo-French-Belgian staff conversations and the reaffirm-
ation of their Locarno obligations by the three powers. This agreement
was deeply unpopular with the bulk of British ministers, who insisted
that the conversations be strictly limited to technical matters, and
should not involve joint war planning. The French were also informed
that the talks did not bind Great Britain to go to war on the side of
France. Indeed given Britain's military unpreparedness – only two ill-
equipped divisions could be spared for France – and the suspicions of
many ministers that the staff talks were a French manoeuvre to inveigle
Britain into war with Germany – this outcome was hardly surprising.
Vansittart protested in vain at the limited nature of the conversations –
'No Frenchman nor Belgian would ever accept the proposition that they
could do the land fighting and we would, for our own convenience,
limit ourselves to air and sea....'[5] Colonel H. R. Pownall, the military
assistant secretary to the Committee of Imperial Defence, confided to
his diary that the conversations were 'more of a political gesture to
please France than of any real practical value'. He added: 'It's high
time the French were "told where to get off"'.... It's time we ceased
being tied to their leading strings, and a rare lot of people in this country
think so too.'[6]

The advent of Léon Blum's Popular Front government on 1 June 1936
gave further impetus to anti-French feelings in Whitehall and Westmin-
ster, particularly among British right wingers who believed that Blum's
government was a front for the communists. Blum soon began to irritate
Vansittart and the Foreign Office by appealing for new disarmament
negotiations with Germany, since Blum's gesture contradicted the British policy of waiting for approaches from Hitler for a European security

pact to replace Locarno. When Blum told Sir George Clerk, the British ambassador to France, later in June that 'Hitler might...be a genuine idealist', Vansittart described Blum as 'naif and weak'.[7] The Foreign Office was relieved when Blum rejected any French involvement, in the form of military supplies to the Spanish Republican government, in the Spanish Civil War which broke out on 18 July 1936, and by the French Prime Minister's promotion of the so-called non-intervention agreement.

By the summer of 1936, the French economy seemed to be in terminal decline, with country-wide industrial disturbances and factory occupations by striking workers. Foreign Office officials feared that, as a result of this turmoil, the Republic might collapse altogether. The British Minister in Paris, Hugh Lloyd-Thomas, thought that 'the French Government as a fighting force has ceased to exist',[8] and these and similar apprehensions provoked an astonishing outburst from Eden:

> I find it impossible to resist a growing conviction that this Spanish horror is going to have repercussions so wide as perhaps to modify the present alignment of European powers. To read this [Clerk's] despatch is to feel France growing more 'red'. The French, we have comforted ourselves, could never be communist, their whole mode of life will not permit of it. But it is the mode of life that is changing. The standard of life of a large lower middle class that is being reduced until (is it possible?) France represents in her own midst the condition of Spain, or at least conditions approximating thereto.[9]

However, more perceptive officials in the Foreign Office Central Department, like the assistant under-secretary, Orme Sargent, did not put any trust in the alarmist talk which Clerk and his embassy was being fed by right-wing anti-Popular Front politicians in Paris. His main fear was that Blum's efforts to satisfy French working-class demands by sweeping concessions would undermine France's already feeble rearmament efforts, particularly in the air.

By the autumn the situation in France appeared to have stabilized. Eden admitted that 'our relations with France are now so much closer than they were in Barthou's prickly days...'.[10] Nevertheless there remained many in Whitehall who were convinced that, as the Cabinet secretary, Sir Maurice Hankey, put it, France 'in her present state...is not a very desirable ally'.[11] Sir Ernle Chatfield, the First Sea Lord, complained that 'France, our only real support, is...unreliable politically and militarily...'.[12]

During 1937, the Cabinet, the Chiefs of Staff and the Committee of Imperial Defence argued about the size of the British Expeditionary Force which would be despatched to France in the event of war. Neville Chamberlain, the Chancellor of the Exchequer, had long been anxious to reduce the size of the expeditionary force, since he was convinced that the expansion of the Royal Air Force would be a more effective and cheaper deterrent to Germany than the deployment of the British army in Europe, and would also enable Britain to avoid a repetition of the bitter trench attrition of the Great War. When he became Prime Minister in 1937 he could impose his will on the Cabinet and on 22 December 1937 he and the Minister for Co-ordination of Defence, Sir Thomas Inskip, secured Cabinet agreement to abandon the despatch of the expeditionary force to the continent altogether. In future it was to be equipped only for 'a colonial theatre'. It is difficult to see how this decision could be reconciled with the chiefs of staffs' warning at the end of 1937 that they 'regard the present internal conditions in France and Russia, and the consequent effects on the military strengths of these countries, as factors which increase the dangers of war'.[13] Chamberlain, Inskip and Leslie Hore-Belisha, the Secretary of State for War, suggested that France could defend the Maginot Line without British assistance. Eden did not accept this assumption and demanded the reopening of the 1936 staff conversations with the French as a means of reassuring them that, despite the downgrading of the expeditionary force, Britain would stand by them in a crisis. The Chiefs of Staff rejected this on the grounds that France would turn 'staff conversations to their own political advantage' by leaking them to the press 'to flaunt an Anglo-French accord in the face of Germany', which would wreck Chamberlain's hope of reaching 'a detente with Germany'.[14]

In any case, continuing French economic and financial instability during 1937 convinced many British conservatives that little was to be achieved by close co-operation with an unreliable and unstable France, and that it would be to Britain's advantage to reach a comprehensive agreement with Germany to preserve European peace. As the franc continued to depreciate during the year both the Foreign Office and the Treasury looked on helplessly as French financial instability threatened to 'constitute an invitation to aggressors to take advantage of her disorganised state'.[15] General Edmund Ironside, General Officer Commanding Eastern Command and future Chief of the Imperial General Staff, summed up the prevailing British attitude towards France in December 1937: 'Out of sight out of mind is particularly applicable to a people come to such straits as France today.'[16]

With the transfer of Vansittart to the ornamental post of Chief Diplomatic Adviser on 1 January 1938 and Eden's resignation on 20 February
after quarrelling with Chamberlain over British policy towards Italy, the
Francophobe tendency in the Cabinet was now in the ascendant. Chamberlain complained that France 'has been in a terribly weak condition
being continually subject to attacks on the franc & flight of capital
together with industrial troubles & discontent which seriously affects
her production of all kinds & particularly of arms & equipment'.[17] All
the more reason, therefore, to try to strive for a comprehensive settlement with Germany. The new Foreign Secretary, Lord Halifax, was a
safer pair of hands than Eden, fully behind Chamberlain's 'appeasement' policy. At this time the Foreign Office Central Department and
Sir Eric Phipps, the British ambassador to France since 1937, began to
interfere in France's internal political affairs to an extent which had not
been evident since before 1914. The Central Department wanted to see
the end of the Popular Front government, now led by Camille Chautemps, and its replacement by a National government which excluded
socialist pro-leaguers and supporters of the Franco-Czechoslovak alliance like Yvon Delbos, the current French Foreign Minister, and his
successor in March, Joseph Paul-Boncour. The Foreign Office wanted
to encourage the weakening of the ties between France and Czechoslovakia, while Chamberlain had little time for, or patience with, Geneva.
They were horrified when Blum became Prime Minister again on 13
March, fearing that this would result in further economically debilitat-
ing social reform measures and a greater determination to stand by
Czechoslovakia than Chautemps had demonstrated. As a result, Sargent
urged Phipps to do all he could 'to embarrass and weaken the present
French government', in the hope that this pressure would cause its
collapse and replacement by 'a gouvernement de concentration nationale'. Later Sargent wrote 'unofficially' to Phipps: 'In fact I would go as
far to say that anything we can do to weaken the present French Government and precipitate its fall would be in the British interest.'[18] In
April Édouard Daladier formed a government composed mostly of radical socialists and the Popular Front was finally extinguished, but it was
doubtful that this outcome owed much to Phipps's machinations.
Chamberlain was 'glad to see the French are pulling themselves together
again'.[19]

After Germany's annexation of Austria on 11 March 1938, the Chamberlain administration was preoccupied by the future of the Sudetenland, whose claims for autonomy were now being vigorously
championed by Hitler. Chamberlain and Halifax wanted to warn France

that Britain would not necessarily come to its assistance if France went to war with Germany to fulfil its obligations under the Franco-Czecho-slovak alliance. French passivity would enable Britain to mediate a settlement of the Sudeten issue favourable to the Sudetenlanders, and, it was hoped, acceptable to Berlin. At a meeting of the Cabinet foreign policy committee on 21 March to discuss the proposed note informing France that Britain might not intervene in Franco-German war over the Sudetenland, the Dominions Secretary, Malcolm MacDonald, protested that Britain's refusal to intervene would be 'a terrible blow to France'. Halifax displayed a characteristic lack of concern for French suscepti-bilities in responding that 'no doubt France would be shocked, but he could not see how in this case this could be avoided. Because France would be shocked was no reason why we should refrain from pursuing a policy the correctness of which we are fully satisfied.' The Foreign Secretary complained that 'the French are never ready to face up to realities, they delighted in vain words and protestations'. MacDonald pointed out that the contents of the proposed Foreign Office note to France 'sadly lacked the warmth and friendly sentiments which might in all circumstances have been expected. In particular it might well have referred in warmer and more friendly terms to our existing commit-ments to France.' It was eventually agreed that Phipps should communi-cate the note in 'warmer and more friendly terms' than had previously been proposed. Chamberlain said he did not 'at the present juncture, wish to offend France beyond what was absolutely essential'.[20] Never-theless the essence of the original draft note, that France should 'not assume that His Majesty's Government would at once take joint military action with them to preserve Czechoslovakia against German aggres-sion', remained unchanged.[21]

In an effort to mollify the French, and to satisfy them that Britain remained committed to their security in western Europe, especially after the shock of the *Anschluss*, a reluctant Chamberlain, after much Foreign Office pressure and an intervention by Halifax, was persuaded to agree in April to the reopening of limited air, naval and army staff conversa-tions during the summer. Halifax hoped that this concession would 'induce in the French a most collaborative disposition' with British policy towards Czechoslovakia.[22] This decision was only taken after long arguments in the Cabinet, where the majority of ministers remained opposed to such talks. As a result, this concession, if it could be thus described, was offered to the French in an extremely grudging spirit. The Air Ministry and the Admiralty insisted that the talks should be restricted to technical matters and refused to allow them to discuss joint strategic planning. As the Air Ministry's director of plans, Group Captain John Slessor, put it in June: 'A nation cannot undertake the discussion of war plans with a potential ally without in fact incurring a moral commitment, no matter what disclaimers of liability and responsibility are stipulated as basis of the conversations.'[23]

During the summer relations between Britain and France soured over disagreements over Italy and the Sudeten issue. In August, Ronald Campbell, the British Minister in Paris, complained to the Foreign Office that 'in the last week or two I have felt that the atmosphere of Anglo-French relations has lost something in mutual confidence'. The French suspected that there had been negotiations between Britain and Germany of which they had not been informed. Campbell warned the Foreign Office that if the French were taken into the fullest confidence about such matters 'we are more likely to keep them on what we consider the straight path, and also prevent them taking initiatives which interest us without our knowledge...'. However, Sargent replied that the Central Department suspected that the French would leak sensitive information given to them about Anglo-German relations to the press, and he could not therefore promise to keep France fully informed about any negotiations that might take place.[24]

In August and September, as tension over the Sudetenland increased, the British became even more determined to force the French to abandon their commitments to Czechoslovakia, especially given the parlous state of the French air force and the ongoing financial crisis in Paris. Whitehall was assisted in this endeavour when, in September, Phipps reported that most of the ministers in the French government, including Daladier, were now anxious to avoid war at any cost. Phipps's despatches on this subject were used by Chamberlain in the Cabinet to demonstrate that France had no intention of fighting for Czechoslovakia, and that in consequence there was no alternative but to accept Hitler's demands for a German takeover of the Sudetenland. However, Phipps relied almost exclusively on the opinions of defeatist French ministers and politicians, and especially on Georges Bonnet, who was petrified at the prospect of war. Phipps's campaign of misinformation which stemmed from his own conviction that France would be defeated in a war with Germany, culminated in a telegram in which he stated that 'All that is best in France is against war, *almost* at any price', and attributed support for war to a 'noisy and corrupt war group here'. Chamberlain read this telegram to the Cabinet on 24 September.[25]

The enthusiastic support with which press and parliamentary opinion greeted the Munich agreement soon began to fade as Hitler failed to follow up the settlement, as Chamberlain had anticipated, by making any proposals for a general European settlement. The Führer also caused considerable resentment in Britain by his attacks on British politicians like Churchill and Duff Cooper for their anti-German stand in September, and by the anti-Jewish pogrom – *Kristallnacht* – on 10 November, which outraged British and American opinion, even in those circles which had hitherto been sympathetic to Germany. This swing against Germany was echoed in the Cabinet by former 'appeasers' like Halifax and Hore-Belisha who began to urge a reluctant Chamberlain to accelerate British rearmament in the face of increasing German hostility. Halifax now feared that France, humiliated by Munich, might become so totally demoralized that it 'may in certain political circumstances turn so defeatist as to give up the struggle of maintaining adequate defence even for the safety of metropolitan France', with the result that 'we might have to face alone the weight of military power in the West'. Halifax wanted Britain to do all it could to encourage the French to rearm as quickly as possible.[26] The French took advantage of Britain's growing fears about Hitler's intentions by mounting a concerted campaign to convince British ministers and military leaders that if they failed to increase the size and efficiency of the British Expeditionary Force and promise to expedite its despatch to France in the event of war, French defeatists inside and outside the French Cabinet would succumb to a German offer of a non-aggression pact. Pro-Entente French ministers and generals correctly pointed out that German propaganda directed at France was inciting the French people to believe that Britain would leave French soldiers to do all the fighting in a war with Germany. This campaign made no impression on Chamberlain, who was reported to have said, before leaving for a meeting with French ministers in Paris at the end of November, that he would not give the French more troops 'than he had promised' and that 'as our Army is so small was it worth worrying whether it was ready or not?'[27] This did not appeal to Halifax and those other British ministers who were becoming increasingly concerned about the paucity of British land support for France and the depressing effect this was having on French opinion. In a memorandum for the ministerial conversations in Paris, Sargent pointed out that the collapse of France's security system in the east after the Munich agreement had demoralized the French, and he referred to 'the almost universal pacifist sentiment' in France which 'in its extreme form refuses to contemplate military action except in defence of an actual invasion of French soil'. If Germany attacked Britain alone, Britain might have to face the reality of France offering only benevolent neutrality on the grounds that its territory was surrounded on three fronts by hostile powers, that the French air force was unable to defend French cities from a German aerial offensive and that French morale would not withstand the strains of war.[28] At the meeting in Paris on 24 November 1938, despite a fervent appeal by Daladier for more British land support, Chamberlain refused to agree to send more than two divisions to France and dwelt on the necessity for Britain to devote its expenditure to anti-aircraft defence in view of the threat of a German aerial assault on London.[29] Halifax, who accompanied the Prime Minister, came away from Paris depressed by the demoralization he had witnessed in the Parisian populace, and determined to secure a more effective continental commitment to prevent France from abandoning the Entente. As a result of Halifax's pressure, supported by other ministers, there ensued, during the next two months, agitated meetings of the Chiefs of Staff, the Committee of Imperial Defence and the Cabinet, during which there were repeated interventions by Halifax, Hore-Belisha, the Chief of the General Staff and the First Sea Lord calling, in General Gort's words, for the formation of 'an efficient and well-equipped expeditionary force' which 'might again play a decisive part in stabilizing the situation'.[30] Sir Samuel Hoare, the Home Secretary, rejected fears that, without such an assurance, France might abandon Britain in the event of war: 'whatever the French might think, their interests were so bound up with ours that they could not afford to stand aloof from us'. Vansittart countered that 'there are just as many Anglophobes in France as there are Francophobes in England. Indeed perhaps there are more', and he wanted Britain to raise at least 20 divisions for service in France to prevent the French Anglophobes from succeeding in destroying the Entente.

It was, however, a rumour, probably emanating from anti-Nazi sources in Germany, early in the New Year, that Germany was planning a sudden descent on Holland which galvanized the British into making more strenuous efforts to improve their military preparations. The Cabinet foreign policy committee, meeting on 23 January 1939, agreed that Britain would be forced to intervene if Germany attacked Holland or Switzerland. It was essential, if these countries were to be successfully defended, that France supported Britain, and to achieve this would require not only an expanded British army, but Anglo-French staff talks to determine their strategic plans. Former appeasers like the Air Minister, Sir Kingsley Wood, and Hore-Belisha told the foreign policy committee that it was 'essential to get into as close an intimate relationship as possible with the only country which was in a position to render us assistance at the present time'. With the weight of Cabinet and military opinion now insisting on an expanded British military effort, and with mounting unease about the Axis threat on the Conservative back benches, Chamberlain and Sir John Simon, the Chancellor of the Exchequer, were both forced reluctantly to agree, at a subsequent Cabinet meeting, to the opening of 'regular and wide ranging staff conversations with France and Belgium'.[31] They were also persuaded to approve the provision of equipment and reserves for continental warfare for four divisions of the British expeditionary force and to agree that its embarkation dates for France should be brought forward.[32] Military, naval and air staff conversations, which dealt comprehensively with joint Anglo-French plans for war, began in the spring and were completed by the early summer.

Germany's seizure of Bohemia on 15 March 1939 prompted the acceleration of Britain's military preparations, as mounting Cabinet and parliamentary anxiety forced Chamberlain to agree to the introduction of limited conscription at the end of April. Sir Maurice Hankey, who had retired as Cabinet secretary in 1938, complained that the French 'are over-doing the pressure about National Service. They are actually doing harm. Serious people are beginning to say "What right have these people to talk?" They have spent all their money in funkholes (the Maginot Lines), and grossly neglected the main offensive weapon, the Air Force.'[33] The Chancellor of the Exchequer was concerned about the massive expenditure which would be incurred as a result of the simultaneous expansion of the Royal Navy, the Royal Air Force and the Army,[34] pointing out that, as a result, Britain's gold reserves were dwindling to an extent which jeopardized Britain's ability to sustain a long war. British planners had similar worries about the capacity of the weak French economy to survive an extended conflict. The Industrial Intelligence Centre (IIC) produced a memorandum earlier in the year which itemized France's inadequate material resources and industrial capacity. It questioned whether a French population of 41 millions, which included 2 million foreigners, was sufficient to provide simultaneously for the expansion of the country's fighting forces and the maintenance of its industrial and agricultural production (in which a third of its population was involved). The bulk of France's heavy industries and mineral resources lay in the highly vulnerable area between the German and Belgian frontiers and the Seine. France was already deficient in coal and if it lost its northern departments and Lorraine to the enemy, it would then become totally dependent upon Britain and the United States for its coal supplies, since its peacetime imports from Germany and Poland would be cut off. Given these gloomy statistics, and shortages of machine and precision tools and French dependence on seaborne trade for its vital raw materials, the IIC doubted that French industry would be able to sustain for long the large army it planned to raise at the outset of hostilities.[35]

The Foreign Office and the Board of Trade were, however, optimistic that Britain would be able to meet France's wartime deficiencies in coal and raw materials. By August 1939 a comprehensive system of Anglo-French co-ordinating boards and joint purchasing mission had been set up and the Anglo-French military, naval and air staffs had reached broad agreement on their contingency plans in the event of war. Moreover, during the spring and early summer there were encouraging signs of a French economic revival, attributed to the introduction, in January and April 1939, of sweeping economic and financial reforms by Paul Reynaud, the French Finance Minister.

Despite the embarrassing delay in declaring war on Germany in early September by Britain and France, which was not an auspicious beginning for the wartime relationship between the two countries, the four divisions of the British Expeditionary Force had crossed to northern France by the end of September, although it was inadequately trained, deficient in tanks, trench mortar and artillery. During the 'Phoney War' the two countries forged a relatively successful co-operation in financial, economic and trade relations, although their military and strategic co-ordination was less than adequate, reflecting of course the disparity between the size of the British army on the one hand and that of the French army on the other. For instance, the decision by the French Chief of the General Staff, Maurice Gamelin, in November to despatch Anglo-French forces to the River Dyle if Germany invaded Belgium, whereas he had previously planned to retain them close to the Franco-Belgian frontier, was reached after little consultation with the British General Staff, many of whom had serious misgivings about this manoeuvre. General Sir Alan Brooke, the commander of II Corps, commented, accurately as it turned out, that 'by trying to save the whole of Belgium, instead of half, not only would be lose the whole of Belgium but probably the war as well'.

The Foreign Office, reflecting the fragility of the Anglo-French connection after so many years of bickering and misunderstanding, was nervous about the likely influence of French defeatists on French opinion, especially if German propaganda's portrayal of Britain's war effort as inadequate and self-serving should prove to be effective. Observant British army officers in France like General Sir John Dill, the commander of I Corps of the British Expeditionary Force, feared that if these suspicions took hold in the French mind, the will of the French people to continue the struggle might eventually weaken. Every effort was made by British propaganda organs to convince the French that Britain was making positive efforts to support them. Anthony Eden, now Dominions Secretary, discounted reports of increasing Anglophobia and defeatism in many parts of France in January 1940: 'Personally I have never taken the view that the French temperament is flighty and ours is stoic. I am not sure that it wouldn't be nearer to the truth to say that the French is tenacious and ours sentimental. . . . It is clearly our duty to do everything we can to encourage the French and keep heart in them.'[36] However British generals now stationed in France became increasingly depressed by what they saw of the poor state and morale of the French army, although they tended to keep their doubts to themselves – 'team spirit' and the fear of being thought defeatist no doubt explained this.

There were of course numerous sources of discord in the Anglo-French relationship – over French demands for a full statement of Allied war aims, which, the British feared, would entail the imposition of a harsh peace on Germany, over British restrictions on the importation of luxury goods into Britain as a means of saving foreign exchange – the French protested this would hit French silk, textile, wine and liqueur producers and harm the alliance – and British restrictions on visas and foreign exchange, which inhibited French efforts to revive its tourist industry in the French Riviera and winter sports centres outside the war zone. These problems were settled more or less amicably, but at the end of December the Foreign Office concluded that only by forging an Anglo-French union could such potentially divisive issues between the two countries be removed. The Foreign Office and the Board of Education called for a publicity campaign to alert the British public to the advantages of such a union, with cultural exchanges, the compulsory teaching of French and English in each other's schools and the rewriting of French and British school textbooks to stress the historical co-operation, rather than the rivalry, between the two countries.

An interdepartmental committee was set up under Lord Hankey, who had been appointed Minister without Portfolio in Chamberlain's War Cabinet, to explore the administrative and procedural aspects of closer union, by converting the wartime supreme council into a peacetime institution which would pursue common policies in foreign affairs, defence, economic and financial relations and by establishing common Anglo-French nationality. After two meetings in May the more far-reaching proposals were emasculated in the committee. As a result of its deliberations, the supreme council was to become merely a co-ordinating body, while a customs union and a common currency were ruled out on constitutional, political and administrative grounds. The proposed association would become an extension into peacetime of the wartime military alliance. In June, of course, even this limited scheme had been abandoned, apart from Winston Churchill's brief and unsuccessful flirtation with an Anglo-French union on the eve of France's defeat: this was a council of desperation and in any case Churchill paid no attention to the practical difficulties which had been raised by Hankey's committee – it was unlikely that he even saw the committee's reports.

With the defeat of France, France's detractors in British official circles felt free to indulge in the recriminations against that country which had been muted since September 1939. Thus Hankey now complained that 'the more I reflect on the events of previous years the more I realise that the French have been our evil genius from the Paris Peace Conference until to-day, inclusive'.[37] The British reverted to the neo-isolationism which had characterized their attitude towards France before 1939. Neville Chamberlain was relieved that 'we are at any rate free of our obligations to France, who have been nothing but a liability to us'.[38] The Parliamentary Under-Secretary to the Foreign Office, the intensely Francophobe Henry Channon, welcomed the French collapse, writing on 10 July 1940 that 'the French Republic has ceased to exist and I don't care; it was graft ridden, ugly incompetent, Communistic and corrupt, and had long outlived its day.... The Old France is dead.'[39] The Foreign Office and the new Prime Minister, Winston Churchill, now turned to the United States as a possible partner to replace the lost alliance with France.

Between 1936 and 1938, when France appeared at times to be on the brink of political, social and economic chaos, and when it was fashionable to deride France in British establishment circles, even those who struggled to keep the Entente alive nursed secret doubts about its survivability. The question which many sympathetic British observers of France asked was whether the French were capable of pulling themselves together. In 1939 the question appeared to have been answered satisfactorily. The French economy had began to revive, and French armaments production was increasing, while Daladier was widely respected as a 'strong man', and his relatively lengthy term in office suggested that a degree of political stability had at last been established. The French were feeling more self-confident, and opinion polls after March 1939 produced large majorities who were prepared to stand up to Hitler.[40] This was a great relief to British officials like Vansittart who had long supported the maintenance of the Entente, particularly at a time when Hitler was showing himself to be increasingly aggressive. Unfortunately France's renaissance proved to be relatively short-lived. The collapse of the Third Republic in the summer of 1940 provided British Franco-phobes with all the evidence they needed to demonstrate the accuracy of their long-held opinion that France was rotten to the core and that Britain had made a disastrous error of judgement in allying itself with that country in 1939.

Notes

*This article is based on my book *British Establishment Perspectives on France, 1936–40* (Basingstoke: Macmillan – now Palgrave, 1999).

1. Quoted in John Robert Ferris, *The Evolution of British Strategic Policy, 1919–26* (Basingstoke: Macmillan – now Palgrave, 1989), p. 128.
2. Quoted in Nicholas Rostow, *Anglo-French Relations, 1934–36* (Basingstoke: Macmillan – now Palgrave, 1984), pp. 224–5.
3. Rumbold to Dawson, 13 December 1935, Dawson MSS, Bodleian Library, Oxford, Box 78, ff. 138–9.
4. Eden to Clerk, Paris, tel 42, 7 Mar. 1936, in *Documents on British Foreign Policy* (London: HMSO, 1977) second series, vol. XVI, no. 37.
5. Vansittart to Eden, 31 March 1936, *DBFP*, 2, XVI, no. 189.
6. B. J. Bond, *Chief of Staff: the Diaries of Sir Henry Pownall*, 2 vols (London: Leo Cooper, 1972), I, 30 March 1936, pp. 107–8.
7. Vansittart minute, 17 June 1936, FO 371/19857, Public Record Office, Kew.
8. Lloyd-Thomas to Vansittart, 11 June 1936, FO 371/19857.
9. Eden minute, 20 August 1936, on Clerk despatch, 1058, 17 August 1936, FO 371/ 19859.
10. Eden minute, 27 October 1936, FO 371/19879
11. Hankey minute, 21 December 1936, CAB 63/51.
12. Quoted in Martin Thomas, *Britain, France and Appeasement: Anglo-French Relations in the Popular Front Era* (Oxford: Clarendon Press), p. 21.
13. Chief of Staff report, 'Comparison of the Strength of Great Britain with that of Certain Other Parties as at January 1938', 12 November 1937, CAB 53/34.
14. 'Memorandum by the Chiefs of Staff Sub-Committee of the Committee of Imperial Defence on Staff Conversations with France and Belgium', 1 February 1938, *DBFP*, 2 , XIX, no. 491.
15. Foreign Office memorandum, 29 September 1937, FO 371/ 20691.
16. Colonel Roderick Macleod and Dennis Kelly (eds), *The Ironside Diaries, 1937–1940* (London: Constable, 1962), 28 December 1937, pp. 65–6.
17. Neville Chamberlain Diary, 19 February 1938, Chamberlain MSS, NC2 /24A, University of Birmingham.
18. Sargent to Phipps, 17 March 1938, enclosing minute by Sargent, Phipps MSS, PHPP 2/10, Churchill College Archives.
19. Chamberlain to Ida Chamberlain, 16 April 1938, Chamberlain MSS., NC 18/ 1/1047.

20. Cabinet committee on foreign policy, 27th meeting, 21 March 1938, CAB 27/ 623.
21. 'Draft Memorandum for French Government on Czechoslovakia Circulated to Foreign Policy Committee by Lord Halifax, 21 March 1938', CAB 27/625.
22. Cabinet conclusions, 19 (38), 27 April 1938, CAB23/93.
23. Minute by Group Captain J. G. Slessor, 17 June 1938, AIR 9/78, Public Record Office.
24. Ronald Campbell to Sargent, 11 and 12 August 1938; Sargent to Campbell, 20 August 1938, FO 371/21592.
25. For details see John Herman, 'The Paris Embassy of Sir Eric Phipps, 1937– 1939,' unpublished Ph.D. thesis, London School of Economics, April 1996, pp. 201–16.
26. Halifax to Phipps, 1 November 1938, *DBFP*, 3, III, no. 285.
27. *Pownall Diaries*, 7, 14, 21, 28 November 1938, pp. 165–72.
28. Memorandum by Sargent, 16 November 1938, FO 371/ 21591.
29. 'Record of Anglo-French conversations held at the Quai d'Orsay on November 24th, 1938', *DBFP*, 3, III, no. 325.
30. 'Memorandum by the Chief of the Imperial General Staff: Present Policy in the light of Recent Developments,' 2 December 1938, CAB 53/43.
31. Cabinet foreign policy committee, 35th Meeting, 23 January 1939, CAB 27/ 624; Cabinet conclusions, 6(39), 8 February 1939, FO 371/22922.
32. Peter Dennis, *Decision by Default: Peacetime Conscription and British Defence, 1919–1939* (London: Routledge and Kegan Paul, 1972), pp. 170–1.
33. Quoted in ibid., pp. 220–1.
34. Simon to Chamberlain, 17 April 1939, PREM 1/308.
35. Desmond Morton, Industrial Intelligence Centre, to J.W. Nicholls, Foreign Office, 6 March 1939, enclosing memorandum of 16 January 1939, FO 371/ 22916,
36. Eden to Captain Mountbatten, 8 February 1940, Avon MSS, AP 20/8/284. Birmingham University Library.
37. Hankey to Simon, 17 June 1940, Simon MSS, Box 16, The Bodleian Library, Oxford.
38. Quoted in J. D. Charmley, *Chamberlain and the Lost Peace* (London: Hodder & Stoughton, 1989), p. 449.
39. *Channon Diaries*, 10 July 1940, p. 261.
40. Robert J. Young, 'A. J. P. Taylor and the Problem with France' in Gordon Martel (ed.), *The Origins of the Second World War Reconsidered: the A. J. P. Taylor Debate after Twenty Five Years* (London: Allen and Unwin, 1986), pp. 110–14.

9

The Supreme War Council and the Allied War Effort, 1939–1940

William Philpott

On 13 December 1939, three months after the outbreak of war with Germany, the British Minister for Co-ordination of Defence, Admiral of the Fleet Lord Chatfield, addressed the National Defence Public Interest Committee. He was able to reassure his listeners:

> Further, we have the closest cooperation with *our great Ally.* Here again in the months before the war was organised the closest and most complete understanding. Not only had we at the outbreak of war a Supreme War Council, but Anglo-French staffs in all sections are completely organised and sit together daily to study the problems of war. It is true to say that never have allies started fighting with such a complete mechanism, such complete plans and such identity of spirit.[1]

While strictly accurate, Chatfield's statement, as might be expected in a ministerial address intended for public consumption, is disingenuous. The establishment of the allied Supreme War Council was a hasty response to the rapid deterioration of the international situation in the summer of 1939. The organization existed on paper by August 1939, but the actual machinery had to be rather hurriedly improvised on the outbreak of war. While it cannot be denied that this was a considerable improvement on the situation in the First World War, in which the allies spent three years, against a background of strategic rivalry and personal mistrust, evolving an effective co-ordination machinery,[2] in 1939 there was no opportunity for the new inter-allied machinery to function in peacetime, as had been the intention, to iron out any teething troubles in the machinery and to accustom the higher personalities of the alliance to working together.

The circumstances of the creation of the Supreme War Council are indicative of the allies' half-hearted approach to the coming war. Britain and France were only in earnest about preparing together for another general European conflict after Hitler's dismemberment of Czechoslovakia in March 1939. Only then were staff talks between the two countries' armed forces formalized and political and military contacts increased. It was one thing to plan together for another war, quite another to set up the inter-allied institutions for fighting it before it started. In this the pre-1914 situation, when Britain had been determined to retain a completely free hand until war broke out, set an unfortunate precedent. For the French the acceptance by Britain of a part in joint political and military organizations, which had been out of the question before 1914, would be an indication of Britain's commitment to a joint military effort. There were those in Britain, where the prevailing interwar attitude to continental war was 'no more Sommes', who resisted such a commitment for that very reason.[3] Joint planning implied a willingness to prepare for a war but, unlike the creation of joint directing machinery, did not involve any obligation to participate in it. Fortunately for the allies, there were also some valuable precedents from the Great War which could be drawn upon when establishing joint directing machinery. The allied Supreme War Council established at Versailles in November 1917 and developed over the following year could provide both a model for the institution and valuable experience of its operation which could be drawn on in 1939. It is certainly true that the 1917–18 model was closely studied and replicated in many of its features, although it is evident that not all the mistakes made in the first war were avoided in the second.

General Maurice Gamelin, Chief of the French Defence Staff, was the first to identify the need for an inter-allied body to co-ordinate strategic plans and military activity, during the first Czechoslovakian crisis. His dealings with the British during the crisis convinced him that the best way to ensure co-ordination between the British and French service staffs was by means of

> un *haut comité militaire franco-anglais* (tout au moins, pour débuter, une réunion des personalités interessées – civils et militiaires) leur donne les directives nécessaires et assume la charge de coordonner la préparation des actions à prévoir pour l'ensemble des forces terrestres, maritimes et aériennes des deux pays.[4]

The Conseil Supérieur de la Défense Nationale (CSDN), France's central defence committee, had already considered the problem of Anglo-French co-operation in April 1938, suggesting that the effective direction of a coalition war required an inter-allied body of responsible statesmen and military commanders. Moreover, it was appropriate to establish such an organization in peacetime to make the necessary joint diplomatic, economic and strategic preparations for war.[5] Nevertheless, this all remained academic while the British were reluctant to commit themselves formally to military and economic co-operation. The initiative by the French Premier, Edouard Daladier, to raise the issue of close political and military co-operation during talks in London in November 1938 fell on deaf ears.[6]

The formalization of military staff talks in the spring of 1939 presented the first realistic opportunity to consider the higher directing machinery of the alliance. If the establishment of a Supreme War Council (SWC) could not be addressed during the first round of talks, the French hoped at least to discuss the preliminary step of creating a higher military committee of allied commanders-in-chief.[7] It seemed that British political and public opinion was coming to accept the prospect of a war with Hitler, and to recognize the need to be prepared. In February 1939 a member of the House of Commons and expert on Anglo-French relations, Brigadier-General Sir Edward Spears,[8] called for the creation of an allied war council in the press.[9] Although not raised during the first stage of the talks in March, the French delegation considered that the talks had been conducted in a mood of such openness and cordiality that the matter could be placed on the agenda for the second phase of the talks in late April.[10]

The initiative for this approach lay with Gamelin, who was particularly anxious to sort out the arrangements for joint military command in time of war, which were inseparable from the question of higher co-ordination.[11] Gamelin proposed to go beyond the 1918 arrangements and establish what amounted effectively to an executive inter-allied politico-military organization. At the top of the executive pyramid would sit an allied 'Comité de Guerre' or 'Conseil Supérieur' of political and military representatives (composed of prime ministers, defence ministers and chiefs of staff) to co-ordinate alliance policy. There would also be a 'Haut Comité Militaire' of the chiefs of staff and commanders-in-chief, for determining allied strategy and directing military operations, with authority over four subordinate military committees, one for each of the three services, and one for the colonies. The latter arrangement would address the problem of co-ordinating the military operations of the allies in the field which had proved so difficult in the earlier conflict; a difficulty of which Gamelin had had first-hand experience while serving on General Joffre's staff between 1914 and 1916. Although this experience suggested to him that it would be impossible to appoint a single allied supreme commander who had the confidence of all the allied armies on the outbreak of hostilities, Gamelin envisaged that the president of the allied military committee would gain the trust of his allied collaborators and in time be able to give orders to the other forces of the coalition, as the generalissimo General Foch had been able to do in 1918.[12] Of course Gamelin also had every expectation that as the senior military official of the leading military power of the coalition he would be president of the allied military committee. Leaving aside this personal ambition, Gamelin's organization did go some way towards addressing some of the weaknesses of the executive organization of the previous war, in which relations between the SWC and the allied commanders in chiefs had been ill-defined and fractious before Foch's appointment.[13] It might be speculated that his proposed military committee might have had a dynamic input into the strategic direction of the war; the analogous Anglo-American Joint Chiefs of Staff Committee created later in the war certainly fulfilled this role. It would certainly have defined more clearly the relationship between the allies' political and military leaders, although in practice it would have increased military influence considerably. Without such a committee tensions in civil–military relations, particularly rivalry between Gamelin and Daladier for control of French military policy in the early months of the war, were to compromise the cohesion and dynamism of allied policy-making as they had done in the previous war.

Although raised during the staff talks in the spring of 1939, the issue of higher allied direction, and with it the linked question of the higher command of the British Field Force deployed in France, could not be settled by the junior officers delegated to conduct the talks. In Britain the matter was passed to Committee of Imperial Defence (CID) for consideration. Chatfield took it upon himself to prepare a paper for the CID,[14] which was ultimately delivered and approved in mid-July.[15] Although submitted under the Minister for Co-ordination of Defence's signature, it is evident that much of the work behind this submission was carried out by the secretary of the CID, Major-General Hastings Ismay. Ismay's conclusion was that 'we could do no better than repeat the arrangements which were made towards the end of the 1914–18 war'.[16] Consequently the letter sent by the British Prime Minister, Neville Chamberlain, to Daladier at the end of the month proposed a non-executive council exactly like that which had existed at the end of the last war. Only the Premier and one other minister from each country were to be permanent members of the council, other ministers, officials and service chiefs being summoned when required. The council was to be advised by a staff of permanent military representatives drawn from the three services of each country. Ismay was to follow Chamberlain's letter to Paris, where he was to meet Gamelin and other French officials to discuss the implementation of the scheme.[17]

It is evident that the CID made no real attempt to evaluate the effectiveness of the earlier SWC. Chamberlain, notorious as a peacemaker, showed no real interest in organization for war, and left this important task to his deputy on the CID and his permanent officials. As is often the way with civil servants, the latter looked to precedents from the past. Over the whole process hung the spectral presence of Lord Hankey, the architect of the CID system and the British official who had overseen the smooth running of the Versailles SWC in the absence of a permanent secretariat. As Ismay's mentor,[18] Hankey's methods had a powerful influence over his successor as CID secretary, and his written recollections of the earlier SWC were drawn on heavily in Ismay's work.[19] Yet there is no evidence that Hankey was approached in person for his thoughts on the strengths and weaknesses of the earlier organization. Nor was the former Prime Minister, David Lloyd George, who had been a permanent member of the first SWC for its whole existence, approached.[20] In extenuation of this rather perfunctory approach, it was still thought while this examination was going on that war was some way off and there would be time to test the new inter-allied institutions in the less demanding circumstances of peacetime.[21]

The French were naturally receptive to the British approach. Gamelin himself had been apprised of the trend of British thought on the matter when he visited London in early June. He had talks with both Chatfield and Ismay, the latter briefing him on his proposals for a war council along the lines of that of the Great War and suggesting the possibility of setting up a peacetime inter-allied body.[22] Immediately on his return to Paris Gamelin had taken up the matter, recirculating his earlier memorandum.[23] No action was taken until Chamberlain's letter arrived in late July, although then Gamelin and his staff set about preparing a reply to the British proposals. While raising no objection to the principle of an inter-allied council – indeed going further and suggesting that the council as well as the permanent military staff should start to function in peacetime[24] – Gamelin sought to create an organization in which the allied commanders-in-chief had greater influence. He still argued for a

'Haut Comité Militaire Interallié' in addition to the 'Conseil Supreme', which should be constituted once war broke out. As far as the relations between the military and political councils were concerned, it was expected that the allied commanders-in-chief and chiefs of staff would, as in the last war, be seconded to the SWC in a consultative role, while not being permanent members of it. Gamelin also hoped to restrict the role of the permanent military representatives, who he feared might come to rival the commanders and military staffs in their role of advising ministers and executing policy. Gamelin was well aware of the mistakes made in the earlier conflict, firstly when the British had appointed Sir Henry Wilson to the Versailles SWC as an alternative source of strategic advice to the Chief of the Imperial General Staff, Sir William Robertson; and secondly, when the Versailles SWC had attempted to create an Executive War Board under Foch to restrict the operational independence of the allied field commanders, General Philippe Pétain and Field Marshal Sir Douglas Haig. Consequently Gamelin pressed for an advisory 'Comité d'Etudes Militaire Interallié' of officers subordinate to the allied military staffs, rather than an independent permanent staff organization. These officers would examine common problems in peacetime, laying the groundwork for the expansion of the allied organization in wartime, when they would function as the secretariat of the 'Haut Comité Militaire Interallié'. It was in these terms that Daladier replied to Chamberlain's letter on 3 August.[25]

Another contentious issue was the location of the inter-allied organization,[26] indicative of deep-rooted *amour-propre* on both sides of the Channel. Chamberlain had suggested that it should be based in London;[27] but Ismay's rationale for this, that the British capital was more secure from air attack, and that questions of mercantile shipping would be of vital importance in the next war and Britain was the principal mercantile power of the alliance, seems rather lame.[28] The French naturally wished it to sit in Paris, although they were prepared to accept that it should meet alternately in the two capitals.[29]

On 17 August Chamberlain replied to Daladier's letter, indicating his complete agreement with the French proposals.[30] This was not quite the case. Chamberlain accepted the proposed arrangements for the attendance of military chiefs at the council, but made no mention of the idea of setting up a separate 'Haut Comité Militaire' parallel to the 'Conseil Suprême'. It is not clear why the British rejected, or ignored, this proposal, but such a committee was not established after war broke out.[31] The French political authorities certainly voiced no objection to this omission.[32] The most likely explanation is that since the British government had accepted the Chiefs of Staff Committee's (COS) recommendation that the British Field Force sent to France should be placed under French military control, this perhaps obviated one of the main functions of the higher military committee, the co-ordination of allied field operations.[33] Similarly, Chamberlain made no mention of the venue for the inter-allied organization, although it seems that the principle that the SWC should meet alternately in Britain and France, as became the case after war broke out, was accepted by default. Administrative details, Chamberlain suggested, should be left to the appointed allied military representatives to work out.[34] The French concurred with this arrangement.[35]

Chamberlain had already referred the matter of the 'Comité d'Études' to the COS. After interviewing the French military attaché, Brigadier-General Albert Lelong, they recommended that a staff on the lines proposed by Gamelin be set up at once, so that the nominated British and French officers could get used to working together; and, equally importantly, so that if it came to war they would be united enough to force the Anglo-French point of view over the opinions of other members of the alliance.[36] Indeed, the question of how Anglo-French authority was to be imposed over lesser allies was one of the preoccupations of these negotiations. It was agreed, on Chatfield's recommendation, that in wartime other allies should be invited to send representatives to the SWC, and appoint officers to the 'Comité d'Études'. However, communications problems indicated that eastern European allies would only be able to nominate their ambassadors as members of the SWC, and that they would therefore have less influence over alliance business than the principal partners. This rather authoritarian arrangement satisfied both allies, who anticipated that on the outbreak of war Anglo-French military missions would be sent to lesser allies to

> assist in the co-ordination of allied effort by explaining and elaborating the recommendations of the Supreme War Council to the authorities of these countries, and by sending the Supreme War Council accurate information, which might not be otherwise available, of the situation in their respective theatres of war.[37]

The other outstanding issue referred to the COS was whether the organization should have a permanent secretariat, drawn from the secretariats of the CID and the CSDN, to manage SWC business. This had not been the case with the Versailles organization, and ultimately it was decided, again following the precedent of the earlier war, that rather than establishing a separate administrative body Ismay and the head of the CSDN secretariat, General Louis-Marie Jamet, should liaise over war council business through an Anglo-French liaison section drawn from their staffs.[38] The Inter-Allied Military Committee, as it became known, was to have its own secretariat drawn from the allied defence staffs, to ensure liaison between London and Paris.[39] The personnel of the new Inter-allied Military Committee were quickly chosen. The French appointed the officers who had represented the French service staffs during the recent round of staff talks, while the British appointed three new officers, chosen because they were not burdened with other responsibilities. This, the French military representative, Lelong, complained, would impede the rapid operation of the new body, since the new British officers were unacquainted with both allied business and their French counterparts. Nevertheless, the new organization was to meet on 28 August to discuss the most pressing strategic matters, principally aid to Poland and the impact of the Nazi–Soviet pact, which had been building up while these negotiations were in progress.[40] Their other task was to consider the nature and functions of inter-allied organizations.[41]

As the military committee's agenda makes clear, these negotiations had been overtaken by events. The allies were at war six days after the first meeting of the Inter-Allied Military Committee.[42] The intention to get this organization functioning effectively in peacetime at least, and to allow it to consider at leisure the expansion and functioning of inter-allied machinery, was not to be realized. It is to the allies' credit that, unlike in 1914, they did not ignore the question of co-ordinating machinery during peacetime, leaving it to be improvised by a lengthy process of trial and error against a background of military reverse and political disagreement. Nevertheless, in 1939 the new machinery, or more accurately the revived old machinery, was going to have to be constituted and to evolve against a background of conflict, rather than in the relative tranquillity of peacetime.

Luckily for the allies, on their shared western front at least, tranquillity reigned throughout the first eight months of the so-called 'phoney war'. It allowed some time for the inter-allied institutions to find their role and to iron out any teething troubles in inter-allied co-ordination. In an essay of this length it is impossible to review the functioning of the SWC in its entirety; instead some of the problems encountered at the organizational level will be analysed, to give some impression of the effectiveness of inter-allied co-ordinating machinery.

At the most basic level the allies had to fashion an effective means of communicating their ideas and settling their differences. While the armies mobilized the soldiers and diplomats communicated and organized and the allied liaison structure blossomed. Military and civilian missions were exchanged, and offices established, so that by the end of September there was a functioning, if somewhat complex and as yet untested, mechanism for communication between the allied governments and armies.[43] The SWC itself sat at the pinnacle of this elaborate network of liaison missions and subcommittees. Yet the creation of inter-allied links was one thing, their efficient operation quite another. As the British secretary of the Anglo-French Liaison Section remarked; 'Experience only can show what final organisation will best serve requirements.'[44]

While the allies were preoccupied with mobilization the new organization was given little thought. The Inter-Allied Military Committee found itself with nothing practical to do. During the first weeks of September it met daily, so that its members could get to know one another and exchange information; or rather the British could pass on information to the French, for as yet the French representatives had nothing to give. The committee hoped to start work on strategic problems thrown up by the expected defeat of Poland and the possibility of a German attack on the Low Countries.[45] Yet the committee had no authority to undertake work which had not been referred to it by higher allied authorities, and it therefore remained dependent for its livelihood on the effective functioning of the SWC. This too took time to develop effective procedures. The first meeting, called rather hurriedly on 12 September, had no formal agenda, and served more as a means of demonstrating allied solidarity in the face of German aggression than as a forum for effective decision making. In this, at least, 'it was a great success'.[46] Indeed it is perhaps indicative of the way the allied leaders viewed the organization that the first instruction issued by Daladier to Gamelin was that he should study the French war plan 'd'établir, en fonction des résultes de cette étude, un avant-projet des décisions à proposer au Conseil Suprême pour la conduite de la Guerre sur le Plan interallié'.[47] It was clearly envisaged, by the French at least, that the SWC would be used to put the allied rubber stamp on projects developed by the individual allies.

The first meeting exposed the administrative lacunae in the new organization. As well as the lack of a formal agenda, rectified for future sessions, the SWC had no formal procedures for taking minutes and drawing up resolutions. The problem of drawing up an effective record of the SWC's meetings preoccupied Ismay and Jamet over the ensuing months. It was not until January 1940 that administrative procedures were settled. Eventually a procedure similar to that of the previous war, whereby joint resolutions would be drawn up and agreed at the meeting, while separate Anglo-French minutes would be prepared afterwards, was adopted.[48] As well as perfecting administrative procedures, the organiza-tion itself expanded in the early months. Its responsibilities were extended from diplomatic and strategic questions to economic matters, an Anglo-French Co-ordinating Committee and six executive subcom-mittees analogous to those which had operated in the earlier war being set up in October to deal with the management of common economic questions.[49] It was contemplated that in time the organization would expand to cover other raw materials and commercial undertakings, the whole being overseen by a separate allied Supreme Economic Council.[50] By the end of 1939 a complex multi-levelled committee organization was up and running, and administrative procedures, if not perfect, were effective.

The SWC itself was not the dynamic flywheel of a well-co-ordinated war effort, being a consultative rather than an executive body.[51] It met only irregularly when one or other of the allied governments had some-thing for discussion. As in the First World War, as time went on the membership increased to such an extent that the organization became unwieldy and difficult to manage.[52] An indication of how the SWC worked can be gathered from the diary record of the meeting of 28 March 1940 made by the British Chief of the Imperial General Staff, General Sir Edmund Ironside:

> The Supreme War Council was far better than I expected. These old *rusés* politicians like Chamberlain have a strategy their own and he certainly had a good one this time. He started off with a ninety minutes' monologue upon the general situation, apologizing every now and then for taking so long. He took all the thunder out of Reynaud's mouth and left him gasping with no electric power left. All the 'projects' that Reynaud had to bring forward, Chamberlain took away. It was most masterly and very well done. Little Reynaud sat there with his head nodding in a sort of 'tik', understanding it all for he speaks English very well, and having to have it translated all over again for the benefit of others. He was for all the world like a little marmoset.

The new Air Minster, Laurent d'Eynac . . . and Vuillemin, his Service Chief, were asleep . . . Darlan, the French Admiral, smoked his pipe all the time and drew pictures on his bit of paper.

. . .The whole War Council took in all five and a half hours and it was conducted completely from beginning to end by Chamberlain and Reynaud. Nobody else said a single word. A battle of wits, and I am quite sure that Chamberlain won.[53]

The SWC's sessions were carefully managed by the allied prime ministers to produce a show of consensus and alliance solidarity to the nation and the world.[54] Potentially contentious issues, such as the general examination of the manpower and material resources of the two allied nations proposed by the chairman of the Anglo-French Co-ordinating Committee, Jean Monnet, would in general not be put on the agenda 'until the two Prime Ministers had had the opportunity for informal discussion on the matter'.[55] Most important business was discussed and settled between the relevant authorities before the SWC assembled. For example the decision to evacuate the allied landings around Trondheim in Norway, formally taken at the SWC on 27 April 1940, was the consequence of three days of shuttle diplomacy and tense negotiations between the allies' military and political authorities.[56] The real purpose of the institution might be surmised from the bland press releases put out after each session. After the third meeting on 17 November it was announced; 'Complete agreement was reached on the best method of combined employment of French and British forces for the most effective conduct of operations.'[57] But as one who was present later caustically commented, 'Quelle que soit la bonne volonté de ses membres, on ne conduit pas la guerre avec un conclave.'[58]

In time the pressure of business became too much for the existing structure.[59] When faced in the spring of 1940 with the likelihood that the war would soon become a real one, some thought was given to strengthening the SWC. The initiative was taken at the meeting on 28 March by the new French Premier, Paul Reynaud. Reynaud proposed more frequent and regular meetings and the creation of a permanent secretariat to drive the institution. While the British government agreed to the former, the vested interests of the British Cabinet secretariat prevented the latter, forgoing the last chance to strengthen the inter-allied organization before the war started in earnest.[60] The German attack on Norway in April presented the alliance with its first major military challenge, and exposed the inadequacies of the higher directive machinery.[61] It could not take rapid decisions, and therefore surrendered military initiative to the enemy. The institution all but collapsed after the German invasion of France in May, the last meetings of the SWC being hurriedly improvised and tense. While this might be expected in the circumstances, it is nevertheless a reflection on the lack of solidarity in the alliance, something which could not be compensated for by an institution which was primarily intended to present a united front to the world, while avoiding wherever possible differences of opinion.

Generals are often accused of fighting the last war, and this is said particularly of the French generals in 1939–40. Study of the SWC suggests that the same might be said of the politicians. The allies created an institution for the war that they planned to fight – one of static defence, attrition and economic blockade – rather than the one they found themselves fighting. The SWC ensured close allied liaison, but gave no real direction. Innovations which might have allowed a more dynamic prosecution of the joint war effort, such as a higher military committee and a permanent secretariat, were never tried, as they were not present in the 1917–18 organization, and they threatened vested interests. The machinery created functioned well enough in 'une guerre d'attente et inaction', but proved ill suited to the needs of modern lightning war. The historian of the SWC, François Bedarida, has suggested that this was not a fault of the institution itself, but of the mental attitudes of its members, pursuing a strategy 'paralysée par la passivité, l'attentisme et les illusions'.[62]

The alliance had to manage the war effort as best it could with the machinery at its disposal. But it could accomplish only so much in the face of traditional Anglo-French suspicion and mistrust. Spears, who had served at the heart of the Anglo-French liaison system in the Great War, commented prophetically on the eve of the war:

It is all too evident that centuries of peaceful intercourse will be needed to achieve what even the common suffering of the war failed to accomplish, a capacity to view a given situation from the point of view of the man of another nationality. To do so calls for a degree of education, knowledge and imagination that the men of the war generation did not possess.[63]

Nine months of warfare could not alleviate this problem. One commentator has suggested that there was no real camaraderie in the Anglo-French SWC.[64] Rivalries clearly bubbled under the surface. Sir Edward

Bridges, the British Cabinet secretary, minuted after discussing French proposals to develop the economic infrastructure of the allied co-ordinating machinery with Monnet: 'it seemed to me that it was better to seize the opportunity of getting the drafting of the document into our hands, rather than to leave it to them, in which case we might have found ourselves faced with something we did not like the look of at all'.[65] The SWC could do nothing to prevent such ingrained suspicions and tensions, which continued to bedevil Anglo-French relations. But without the SWC the tensions would no doubt have been greater, and more difficult to resolve. One only needs to look back at the First World War for an idea of what might have occurred if this apparatus had not been in place.

Notes

1. 'Speech to National Defence Public Interest Committee Lunch', 13 December 1939, Admiral of the Fleet Lord Chatfield papers, National Maritime Museum, Greenwich, CHT/6/4.
2. For the First World War see W. J. Philpott, *Anglo-French Relations and Strategy on the Western Front 1914–1918* (London: Macmillan – now Palgrave, 1996); W. J. Philpott, 'Squaring the Circle: the Higher Coordination of the Entente in the Winter of 1915–16', *English Historical Review* (forthcoming).
3. For the struggles over a continental military commitment between the wars see B. J. Bond, *British Military Policy between the Two World Wars* (Oxford: Clarendon Press, 1980).
4. 'Note sur la collaboration militaire franco-britannique', by Gamelin, 23 Nov. 1938 (Gamelin's emphasis), Service Historique de l'Armée de Terre, Vincennes (SHAT), 2N227/3.
5. 'Note sur la collaboration militaire franco-britannique', unattributed CSDN memorandum, 24 April 1938, SHAT, 2N227/2.
6. F. Bédarida, *La stratégie secrète de la drôle de guerre: la Conseil Suprême Interallié septembre 1939–avril 1940* (Paris: Presses de la Fondation Nationale des Sciences Politiques, 1979), p. 21.
7. 'Note sur la collaboration franco-britannique', 2 March 1939; 'Note sur les accords d'états-majors franco-anglais (directive pour la délégation envoyée à Londres)', c. 8 March 1939, SHAT, 5N579/2.
8. Spears had been active in Anglo-French liaison in the First World War and was to play a similar role in the Second. See M. Egremont, *Under Two Flags: the Life of Major-General Sir Edward Spears* (London: Weidenfeld, 1997).
9. 'Article du général Spears sur la solidarité franco-britannique', report by Lelong, 23 February 1939, SHAT, 7N2816.
10. 'Note sur diverses questions traitées au cours de la première phase des conversations franco-britanniques ou pouvant être traitées dans la 2ème phase', unsigned, 11 April 1939, SHAT, 2N229/1; 'Information du President: conversations d'état-major franco-britanniques', unsigned, 12 April 1939, SHAT, 5N579/2.

11. 'Analyse', by Gamelin for Daladier, 8 March 1939, SHAT, 5N579/2.
12. Ibid.; 'Note sur diverses questions traitées au cours de la première phase des conversations franco-britanniques ou pouvant être traitées dans la 2ème phase', unsigned, 11 April 1939; 'Note sur la préparation du haut commandement de la coalition', by Gamelin, 10 June 1939; 'Note sur la direction d'une guerre de coalition', by Gamelin, 10 June 1939, SHAT, 2N229/1.
13. Philpott, *Anglo-French Relations and Strategy*, pp. 150–3.
14. CID, minutes of the 355th meeting, 2 May 1939, Cabinet Office: Committee of Imperial Defence minutes, Public Record Office (PRO), Kew (CAB 2): CAB 2/8.
15. CID, minutes of the 364th and 365th meetings, 6 and 13 July 1939, CAB 2/9; 'Supreme Control in War', memorandum by the Minister for Co-ordination of Defence, 3 July 1939, Cabinet Office: Committee of Imperial Defence ad-hoc sub-committees of enquiry: proceedings and memoranda, PRO (CAB 16): CAB 16/183A/DP(p)64.
16. Lord Ismay, *The Memoirs of Lord Ismay* (London: Heinemann, 1960), p. 87. See also 'Supreme Control in War', unattributed memo, 3 July 1939, which was clearly the precursor of the memo of the same title submitted to the CID (see note 15), SHAT, 2N229/3.
17. Chamberlain to Daladier, 26 July 1939, SHAT, 2N229/3; Ismay, *Memoirs*, p. 87. See also CID, minutes of the 365th meeting, 13 July 1939, PRO, CAB 2/9; 'Supreme Control in War', memorandum by the Minister for Co-ordination of Defence, 3 July 1939, PRO, CAB 16/183A/DP(p)64.
18. Ismay, *Memoirs*, p. 44.
19. See 'Supreme Control in War', unattributed memo, 3 July 1939, SHAT, 2N229/3.
20. Ismay did draw on Lloyd George's war memoirs for his analysis of the earlier Supreme War Council. The French too seem not to have consulted former members of the earlier Supreme War Council for their recollections of its organization and efficiency. General Maxime Weygand, the French military representative in 1917, was still on the active list although inaccessible in the Middle East.
21. CID, minutes of the 365th meeting, 13 July 1939, PRO, CAB 2/9.
22. Lelong to Daladier, 13 June 1939, SHAT, 7N2816.
23. 'Note sur la préparation du haut commandement de la coalition', by Gamelin, 10 June 1939; 'Note sur la direction d'une guerre de coalition', by Gamelin, 10 June 1939, SHAT, 2N229/1.
24. 'Note of Major General H. L. Ismay's Conversations in Paris on the 29th July, 1939'; Ismay to Rucker, 31 July 1939, Prime Minister's papers, PRO (PREM 1): PREM 1/311.
25. Gamelin to Daladier, 2 August 1939, SHAT, 5N579/2; 'Signature du Président: project du réponse à Monsieur Chamberlain au sujet de l'organisation du commandement interallié', 2 August 1939, SHAT, 5N579/2; Daladier to Chamberlain, 3 August 1939, SHAT, 2N229/3. See also untitled note on the functioning of the Versailles Supreme War Council, [July 1939?], SHAT, 2N229/3.
26. 'Note of Major General H. L. Ismay's Conversations in Paris on the 29th July, 1939', PRO, PREM 1/311.
27. Chamberlain to Daladier, 26 July 1939, SHAT, 2N229/3.

28. 'Supreme Control in War', memorandum by the Minister for Co-ordination of Defence, 3 July 1939, PRO, CAB 16/183A/DP(p)64.
29. Gamelin to Daladier, 2 August 1939, SHAT, 5N579/2; Daladier to Chamberlain, 3 August 1939, SHAT, 2N229/3.
30. Chamberlain to Daladier, 17 August 1939, SHAT, 2N229/3.
31. In the wartime organization the service chiefs were called to the council 'whenever important decisions on military matters require [sic] to be taken, with a consultative voice and with not only the right but the duty to state their opinions on military matters'. 'Inter Allied Military Organisation', 22 November 1939, Cabinet Office: Registered Files, PRO (CAB 21): CAB 21/ 1377.
32. 'Je suis en particulier heureux de constater que notre point de vue est le même pour tout ce qui a trait à la responsabilité à laisser, au sein même du Conseil Suprême, aux hautes autorités militaires de nos deux Pays.' Daladier to Chamberlain, 28 August 1939, SHAT, 2N229/3.
33. CID minutes of the 368th meeting, 24 July 1939, PRO, CAB 2/9. Significantly, in his draft reply to Chamberlain's letter of 17 August Gamelin made no mention of the 'Haut Comité Militaire'. Gamelin to Daladier, 24 August 1939, SHAT, 5N579/2.
34. Chamberlain to Daladier, 17 August 1939, SHAT, 2N229/3.
35. Daladier to Chamberlain, 28 August 1939, SHAT, 2N229/3.
36. Lelong to Gamelin, 10 August 1939, SHAT, 7N2817.
37. 'Supreme Control in War', memorandum by the Minister for Co-ordination of Defence, 3 July 1939, PRO, CAB 16/183A/DP(p)64; Chamberlain to Daladier, 26 July 1939, SHAT, 2N229/3; Daladier to Chamberlain, 3 August 1939, SHAT, 2N229/3.
38. Lelong to Gamelin, 10 August 1939, SHAT, 7N2817. This solution had been suggested by Ismay when he visited Paris. 'Notes of Major General H. L. Ismay's conversations in Paris on the 29th July 1939', PRO, PREM 1/311.
39. Gamelin to Lelong, 19 August 1939, SHAT, 2N229/3.
40. CID, minutes of the 368th meeting, 24 July 1939, PRO, CAB 2/9; Lelong to Gamelin, 24 August 1939, SHAT, 7N2817.
41. Note for Gamelin, 25 August 1939, SHAT, 2N229/3.
42. In fact the Inter-allied Military Committee was not yet up and running, and this meeting was designated a further session of the inter-allied staff talks. *Procès-verbal* of the 14th meeting, 28 August 1939, SHAT, 2N229/2.
43. For the structure and personnel of these many missions see the organization tables, 'Liaisons franco-britanniques en France', SHAT, 27N189; 'Diagramme de la liaison franco-britannique sur les questions militaires et civils', SHAT, 2N229/3. For an example of the negotiations behind the creation and functions of this liaison structure see untitled memorandum of a meeting to organize Anglo-French liaison, c. 5 September 1939, SHAT, 2N231.
44. Secretary of the Anglo-French liaison section to Ismay, 1 September 1939, SHAT, 27N189.
45. Admiral Odend'hal to 'Mon Général' [Jamet?], 13 September 1939, SHAT, 2N231.
46. Ismay to Hankey, 12 September 1939, PRO, CAB 21/746; Halifax to Phipps, 8th September 1939, PRO, PREM 1/410; Note for the Prime Minister, no date, PRO, PREM 1/437; Bédarida, *La stratégie secrète de la drôle de guerre*, p. 33.

47. Daladier to Gamelin, 6 September 1939, SHAT, 5N580/3.
48. An account of the process can be found in Bédarida, *La stratégie secrète de la drôle de guerre*, pp. 35–40. Details of the negotiations are in PRO, CAB 21/764 and CAB 21/1377.
49. The committees covered air production and supply, armaments and raw materials, shipping, economic warfare, oil and food.
50. Monnet to Bridges, 1 October 1939, PRO, CAB 21/747; Daladier to Chamberlain, 18 October 1939; Chamberlain to Daladier, 22 October 1939, PRO, PREM 1/437.
51. Bedarida, *La Stratégie secrète de la drôle de guerre*, p. 29.
52. Ibid., pp. 30–1. There is evidence that various British ministers and officials attended on the off chance that the French would raise matters not on the formal agenda of the meeting. Bridges to Wilson, 15 November 1939, PRO, CAB 21/764.
53. R. Macleod and D. Kelly (eds), *The Ironside Diaries, 1937–40* (London: Constable, 1962), pp. 237–8.
54. Bedarida, *La stratégie secrète de la drôle de guerre*, pp. 32–3. See also Chamberlain's speech to the House of Commons, 8 February 1940, PRO, CAB 21/1377.
55. 'Explanatory note' by Bridges to Rucker, 27 March 1940, PRO, PREM 1/437.
56. 'Historique sommaire des journées des 26, 27 et 28 Avril 1940', SHAT 27N4/1.
57. Press communiqué on the 17 November 1939 meeting, PRO, CAB 21/1377.
58. Admiral Auphan, quoted in Bedarida, *La stratégie secrète de la drôle de guerre*, p. 33.
59. Ismay to Howard-Vyse, 26 March 1940, PRO, CAB 21/1377.
60. Bedarida, *La stratégie secrète de la drôle de guerre*, pp. 44–9.
61. Ibid., p. 34.
62. Ibid.
63. E. L. Spears, *Prelude to Victory* (London: Jonathan Cape, 1939), p. 81.
64. Marc Bloch, quoted in Bedarida, *La stratégie secrète de la drôle de guerre*, p. 34, n. 8.
65. Bridges to HJ, 30 September 1939, PRO, CAB 21/747.

10
France in Churchill's *The Second World War*

Antoine Capet

The similarities between Churchill and de Gaulle have already been examined in great detail, but another one could perhaps be added here. The celebrated opening sentence of the first volume of de Gaulle's *Mémoires de guerre*, 'Toute ma vie, je me suis fait une certaine idée de la France', could just as easily have been written by Churchill. Gordon Craig reminds us that Winston Churchill knew little about Germany and was only remotely interested in its great figures.[1] This is not the place to discuss Churchill's views on Germany, but Craig goes on with what appears to be a sweeping statement on Churchill's supposed lack of interest in foreign countries: 'this was, for the most part, true of his attitude towards other countries as well'.[2] In the same book, Craig's opinion is indeed immediately contradicted in the next chapter, 'Churchill and France', by Douglas Johnson:

> His knowledge of French history was considerable and was spread over a wide period. He yielded to no-one in his admiration for Joan of Arc, whom he described as 'the winner' (and he was always insistent that it was not the English who had burned her, but the Burgundians). His sense of humour sometimes misled others into thinking that he was ignorant of French history, as when he urged his compatriots to drink Veuve-Clicquot champagne, since it would support a worthy French woman who had been widowed in the First World War.[3]

And, though Churchill did not go to France until he was 17, in 1891, one can argue that his links with that country were almost consubstantial with his existence, since it is in Paris, in the British embassy's chapel, that his parents were married, on 15 April 1874; moreover, the date of

Presently Montgomery, who had left us some time before, drove up. Freyberg went out to salute him, and told him his place had been kept and that he was expected to luncheon. But 'Monty', as he was already called, had, it appeared, made it a rule not to accept hospitality from any of his subordinate commanders. So he sat outside in his car eating an austere sandwich and drinking his lemonade with all formalities. Napoleon also might have stood aloof in the interests of discipline. *Dur aux grands* was one his maxims. But he would certainly have had an excellent roast chicken, served him from his own *fourgon*.[12]

His other favourite Frenchman was Clemenceau. During the great victory celebrations of 11 November 1944 in Paris, his thoughts went to him.[13] Like him, Churchill the war leader liked to say 'je fais la guerre'. Like him, Churchill was removed from power after the war by an ungrateful people.[14] Churchill identified himself with Clemenceau as the arch-enemy of defeatism, and he used him as an authority during his discussions with Pétain at Briare on 11 June 1940: 'I also reminded him how Clemenceau had said: "I will fight in front of Paris, in Paris and behind Paris."'[15]

The real culprits in the fall of France

'Churchill's fondness and compassion for France', François Kersaudy argues,[16] were to lead to a grave misunderstanding between de Gaulle and Churchill, with de Gaulle interpreting this attitude in 1940 as an encouragement given to defeatism. Yet, in the chapter called 'The French Agony' in Volume II of *The Second World War*, nothing can be found to support even remotely the idea of a recognition of the position of the French '*capitulards*'.

In fact the arguments of realpolitik as found in the 1936 speech had completely disappeared by May–June 1940, and on the affair of the Anglo-French Union proposed on 15 and 16 June 1940, Churchill explains that his 'realistic' reservations were gradually eliminated by the 'idealistic' arguments which he heard:

My first reaction was unfavourable. I asked a number of questions of a critical character and was by no means convinced. However, at the end of our long Cabinet that afternoon [15 June 1940] the subject was raised. I was somewhat surprised to see the staid, stolid, experienced politicians of all parties engage themselves so passionately in an immense design whose implications and consequences were not in any way thought out. I did not resist, but yielded easily to these generous surges which carried our resolves to a very high level of unselfish and undaunted action.[17]

Incidentally, the reaction which he describes on the part of de Gaulle when he gave him the draft to be submitted to Paul Reynaud is equally curious: 'The General read it with an air of unwonted enthusiasm.'[18] The full dimension of this 'unthinkable'[19] idealistic conversion of the two great statesmen becomes apparent when one reads the two most important clauses of the 'Declaration of Union':

– The two Governments declare that France and Great Britain shall no longer be two nations, but one Franco-British Union.
– Every citizen of France will enjoy immediately citizenship of Great Britain; every British subject will become a citizen of France.[20]

In fact, there was very soon an essential point in common between Churchill and the man whom he calls 'the Constable of France'[21] on 16 June 1940, showing once more his profound knowledge of French history: both assert that the French population, if one omits the decayed elites, is fundamentally pro-British and anti-German. Churchill writes without any apparent qualms that the whole of the French nation rejoices at the news in the autumn of 1940 that the Germans, having lost the Battle of Britain, will not be able to invade Great Britain.[22]

Therefore, when he describes the crumbling of the French military machine in May–June 1940, Churchill can alas no longer say 'Thank God for the French Army', but, everything considered, the unsophisticated reader closes his 200 pages or so on the fall of France with the perfectly *'Gaullian'* feeling that this magnificent army was in fact betrayed by its defeatist leaders and the communists' subversive action. The underlying conclusion is that the 'real' France has saved its honour. But we know that these things are far more complicated, as the evolution of the war was to show, and as the Oran affair was immediately to demonstrate.

Oran (Mers el-Kébir)

Churchill, rightfully renowned for his pithy turns of phrase, describes the Oran incident in four words: 'It was Greek tragedy',[23] and in his narrative he resorts to a superlative which carries enormous weight

considering the length of his political career: 'This was a hateful decision, the most unnatural and painful in which I have ever been concerned.'[24] The inevitable historical references are interesting, with two
parallels dating from the Revolutionary and Napoleonic period: 'It
recalled the episode of the destruction of the Danish fleet at Copen-
hagen by Nelson in 1801.' And even more associated with French history: 'I thought of Danton in 1793: "The coalesced Kings threaten us,
and we hurl at their feet as a gage of battle the head of a King."'[25]

But, even though the reader can readily perceive the allusion to times
of extreme national peril, the link between the elimination of the King
of France by the French in 1793 and the elimination of the French fleet
by the British in 1940 is not self-evident. In fact, Churchill gives the
explanation a few pages later: 'It was made plain that the British War
Cabinet feared nothing and would stop at nothing. This was true.' In
other words, in his mind, the elimination of the French fleet was meant
to be a declaration of total war, and as such it was not primarily directed
against the French, but against the Germans, who continued to nurture
the illusion that Britain was about to yield. Once more, Churchill dis-
tinguishes between the real French people and its misguided leaders,
Admiral Darlan on this occasion. Adopting Ciceronian tones, he ex-
claims about the Admiral:

> How vain are human calculations of self-interest! Rarely has there
> been a more convincing example. Admiral Darlan had but to sail in
> any one of his ships to any port outside France to become the master
> of all French interests beyond German control. The whole French
> Empire would have rallied to him. Nothing could have prevented
> him from being the Liberator of France. The fame and power which
> he so ardently desired were in his grasp. Instead, he went forward
> through two years of worrying and ignominious office to a violent
> death, a dishonoured grave, and a name long to be execrated by the
> French Navy and the nation he had hitherto served so well.[26]

Admittedly, their relations had had an inauspicious start, if one is to
believe the anecdote which he gave a few lines earlier:

> When in December 1939 he had visited England we gave him an
> official dinner at the Admiralty. In response to the toast, he began by
> reminding us that his great-grandfather had been killed at the battle
> of Trafalgar. I therefore thought of him as one of those good French-
> men who hate England.[27]

What enables us to see in that episode another example of Churchill's distinction between the two Frances is the fact that he concludes his discussion by a glowing tribute to the 'real' France: 'The genius of France enabled her people to comprehend the whole significance of Oran, and in her agony to draw new hope and strength from this additional bitter pang.'[28] Moreover, he gives us to understand that the judgement of history is in his favour, since liberated France has approved de Gaulle and de Gaulle had approved Churchill's position in his speech on the BBC of 8 July 1940 – *ergo* the 'real' France was behind Churchill: 'General de Gaulle, whom I did not consult beforehand, was magnificent in his demeanour, and France liberated and restored has ratified his conduct.'[29] The reason is not far to see: the French who are 'worthy of the name', as de Gaulle calls them, are as a rule to be found not among sophisticated admirals, but among the unsophisticated 'real' people:

> In a village near Toulon dwelt two peasant families, each of whom had lost their sailor son by British fire at Oran. A funeral service was arranged to which all their neighbours sought to go. Both families requested that the Union Jack should lie upon the coffins side by side with the Tricolour, and their wishes were respectfully observed. In this we may see how the comprehending spirit of simple folk touches the sublime.[30]

But for Churchill the politician the matter was even more complicated, for when he went to the Commons on 4 July 1940 to announce that the operation had been successful, he almost unintentionally conquered a Conservative Party which had so far been rather lukewarm towards its leader:

> The House was very silent during the recital, but at the end there occurred a scene unique in my own experience. Everybody seemed to stand up all around, cheering, for what seemed a long time. Up till this moment, the Conservative Party had treated me with some reserve, and it was from the Labour benches that I received the warmest welcome when I entered the House or rose on serious occasions. But now all joined in solemn stentorian accord.[31]

In his narrative, Churchill insists that his speech was about 'sombre events' and 'a mournful episode': yet these facts, dismal in his eyes, resulted in his new impregnable position as party leader, which could only objectively satisfy him. All the difficulty – some would say all the ambiguity – of Churchill's position regarding defeated France is encapsulated in this dilemma: he pities the 'real' France, he respects it, he does everything in his power for it – except what could harm British political and military interests, and with them the prospect of final victory, which will anyway 'restore'[32] France. This had already been apparent when he refused to engage more British fighters in the Battle of France once he had become convinced that the battle was lost in any case in view of the absence of a political will to win it, and de Gaulle had supported this refusal, again in the name of the long-term perspectives of the war. On the correct attitude to adopt towards Vichy, however, Churchill and de Gaulle were in constant conflict, and in *The Second World War* Churchill of course seeks to explain and justify his point of view at the time.

The Vichy government

Churchill devotes a full chapter to the Dakar Expedition (23–25 September 1940). As usual, he gives the greatest possible strategic and tactical detail about the operation, with repeated references to military history, alluding successively to Nelson, the Dardanelles and Cromwell's order to conquer San Domingo in 1655,[33] which resulted in fact in the capture of Jamaica. Over the Dakar affair, he faced an uphill task, because he was criticized on all sides: by the Australian government, but also by the British press – but he bravely uses his book to defend his action. Of course, he writes, we failed at Dakar – but he immediately adds that the 'real' France gained immensely, because the operation put an end to Vichy hopes in Africa, and the reader now fully understands the historical allusion to San Domingo and Jamaica: in matters of high international politics as in ordinary life you sometimes lose on the swings only to gain on the roundabouts.

It will be remembered that following Oran, the Vichy government broke diplomatic relations with the United Kingdom and that, following Dakar, Vichy launched retaliation air raids on Gibraltar from French North Africa. Churchill was not overly disturbed by these attacks: 'The French aviators did not seem to have their hearts in the business, and most of the bombs fell in the sea.'[34] Here, we have again the central factor already underlined: Churchill was convinced, not only when he wrote his book, but also at the time, that the French did not follow the Vichy elites on the anti-British ground. A number of British people feared a declaration of war on the part of Vichy, but Churchill tells us that he never believed in the possibility, precisely for that reason:

There were times when the Admiralty were deeply concerned lest France should declare war upon us and thus add to our many cares. I always believed that once we had proved our resolve and ability to fight on indefinitely the spirit of the French people would never allow the Vichy Government to take so unnatural a step.[35]

This constant attitude finds a parallel in the extraordinary plea for leniency with which he opens his chapter on relations with Vichy in the autumn of 1940:

In spite of the Armistice and Oran and the ending of our diplomatic relations with Vichy, I never ceased to feel a unity with France. People who have not been subjected to the personal stresses which fell upon prominent Frenchmen in the awful ruin of their country should be careful in their judgments of individuals. It is beyond the scope of this story to enter the maze of French politics. But I felt sure that the French nation would do its best for the common cause according to the facts presented to it. When they were told that their only salvation lay in following the advice of the illustrious Marshal Pétain, and that England, which had given them so little help, would soon be conquered or give in, very little choice was offered to the masses. But I was sure they wanted us to win, and that nothing would give them more joy than to see us continue the struggle with vigour.[36]

What can therefore be concluded from his reflection dictated by wisdom over relations with Vichy: 'There is no room in war for pique, spite, or rancour. The main objective must dominate all secondary causes of vexation',[37] if not that it applied, antithetically and a posteriori, to his partner de Gaulle, who constantly reproached him with 'trying to placate Vichy'?[38]

Relations with de Gaulle

Disagreements with de Gaulle became obvious over Syria, 'reconquered' from Vichy in July 1941. But, whereas de Gaulle devotes many pages in his War Memoirs to the political rivalry between the British and the (Free) French during that episode, Churchill covers practically only the military aspect, with one of those famous maps of operations which recur through the book.[39] The question of the armistice with Vichy in Syria, so complex in de Gaulle's Memoirs, is briefly alluded to by Churchill in two sentences. One finds almost the same pattern in the chapter on Madagascar (autumn 1942), namely a long description of military operations, this time with two maps, which glosses over the political aspects which were nevertheless essential in the opinion of those whom he calls the 'de Gaullists'[40] on that occasion. But, with the United States' participation in the war after 1941, a new three-cornered relationship was established, and even though it has already been described many times, Churchill's personal contribution is not without interest, especially over the Normandy landings and the liberation of France.

Victory

Churchill begins his account of these events in a very candid way, explaining why he asked de Gaulle to leave Algiers for London on 4 June 1944: 'I felt that the history of our two countries required that the liberation of France must not be undertaken by the British and Americans without the French being informed.'[41] Then de Gaulle raised what was then the most contentious subject between the Allies: 'De Gaulle was anxious about who was to administer liberated France. This should have been arranged long ago, last September.'[42] And we have a description of the explosion:

> This remark made me speak bluntly. The United States and Great Britain were willing to risk the lives of scores of thousands of men to liberate France. About the administration of liberated French soil, if General de Gaulle wanted us to ask the President to give him the title-deeds of France the answer was 'No'. If he wanted us to ask the President to agree that the Committee was the principal body with whom he should deal in France the answer was 'Yes'. De Gaulle replied that he quite understood that if the U.S.A. and France disagreed Britain would side with the U.S.A. With this ungracious remark the interview ended.[43]

This was not the end of the story, as a few days later Churchill invited de Gaulle to go to Normandy on his own initiative: 'To the President I wrote on the same day about various questions, including the visit of de Gaulle to France, which I had arranged without consulting Roosevelt beforehand.'[44] De Gaulle's triumphant reunion with the population of liberated France was to take place in Bayeux on 14 June, but Churchill makes absolutely no mention of it, preferring to pass on directly to the liberation of Paris and the ceremony at Notre Dame, briefly described.[45]

Churchill in fact preceded de Gaulle in liberated Normandy, but they did not meet. Churchill's great reunion with the French – and de Gaulle – was to take place on the occasion of the ceremonies of Victory Day, 11 November 1944, in which the British Prime Minister was the guest of honour. Churchill, who never lost his sense of humour, mentions that his room at the Quai d'Orsay was that of Goering during the Occupation.[46] But, as usual in *The Second World War*, this jocular mood is followed by a more melancholy one: 'Everything was mounted and serviced magnificently, and inside the palace it was difficult to believe that my last meeting there, described in a previous volume, with Reynaud's Government and General Gamelin in May 1940 was anything but a bad dream.'[47]

He was undeniably touched by this welcome, and as early as 15 November, he sent a letter to Roosevelt in which he pleaded the French case, notably for a zone of occupation in Germany, with a concluding sentence which was far removed from the very harsh words which he had had on the eve of D-Day: 'I had a considerable feeling of stability in spite of Communist threats, and that we could safely take them [the French] more into our confidence. I hope you will not consider that I am putting on French clothes when I say this.'[48] It is also interesting to note that during the Yalta Conference, on 6 February 1945, Churchill resumes a very pro-French line of reasoning which is not dictated by sentimentality – it is in fact strongly reminiscent of the theme of 'Thank God for the French Army':

> To give France a zone of occupation was by no means the end of the matter. Germany would surely rise again, and while the Americans could always go home the French had to live next door to her. A strong France was vital not only to Europe but to Great Britain. She alone could deny the rocket sites on her Channel coast and build up an army to contain the Germans.[49]

From the point of view of British military interests, the wheel had turned full circle: 'freed and restored' France, whose rebirth Churchill the statesman had never ceased to promise since June 1940, had become again one of the pillars of British defence. But for Churchill the private citizen, victory and the return to the pre-war alliance had other blessings.

In order to take a rest from the tensions accumulated for five years at the helm without any break, Churchill went to Hendaye for a week on his

way to Potsdam. To relax, he took up a book whose title he unfortunately does not give:

> On July 7, two days after polling day, I flew to Bordeaux with Mrs.
> Churchill and Mary, and found myself agreeably installed at General
> Brutinel's villa near the Spanish frontier at Hendaye, with lovely
> bathing and beautiful surroundings. I spent most of the mornings
> in bed reading a very good account, by an excellent French writer, of
> the Bordeaux armistice and its tragic sequel at Oran. It was strange to
> revive my own memories of five years before and to learn of many
> things which I had not known at the time.

As another source of relaxation, he resumed his painting: 'In the
afternoons I even sallied forth with my elaborate painting outfit, and
found attractive subjects on the river Nive and the Bay of St. Jean de Luz.
I found a gifted companion of the brush in Mrs. Nairn, the wife of the
British Consul at Bordeaux.'[50]

Now this is typical of the human interest one finds in *The Second World
War*. This description of a holiday at Hendaye has no prima facie connection with the title taken literally. And yet, if one comes to think of it, the
connection is self-evident: the vast geostrategic problems which are dealt
with in the book are only fascinating, in his eyes, because they allow him
to explain why and how he can continue to go to Hendaye to do some
painting in 1945. One of Churchill's thinly disguised war aims was no
doubt being able to continue to enjoy the charm of French holidays. And
who would dare to argue that this was not a noble aspiration?

Notes

1. See Gordon Craig, 'Churchill and Germany', in Robert Blake and William
   Roger Louis (eds), *Churchill* (Oxford: University Press, 1993), p. 21.
2. Ibid.
3. Douglas Johnson, 'Churchill and France', in W. Blake and Louis (eds), *Churchill*, p. 45.
4. Winston Churchill, *The Second World War* (hereafter *SWW*), 6 vols (London:
   Cassell, 1948–54). Our notes refer to the Reprint Society edition, London,
   1950–55.
5. *SWW*, vol. 1, *The Gathering Storm*, p. 179.
6. *SWW*, vol. 2, *Their Finest Hour*, p. 456.
7. *SWW*, vol. 5, *Closing the Ring*, pp. 104 and 159.
8. *SWW*, vol. 4, *The Hinge of Fate*, p. 419.
9. *SWW*, vol. 2, *Their Finest Hour*, pp. 46–7.

10. Ibid., p. 484.
11. *SWW*, vol. 3, *The Grand Alliance*, p. 265.
12. *SWW*, vol. 4, *The Hinge of Fate*, p. 420.
13. 'I laid a wreath beneath the statue of Clemenceau, who was much in my thoughts on this moving occasion.' *SWW*, vol. 6, *Triumph and Tragedy*, p. 211.
14. *SWW*, vol. 1, *The Gathering Storm*, p. 28.
15. *SWW*, vol. 2, *Their Finest Hour*, p. 136.
16. 'L'affection et la compassion de Churchill pour la France'; François Kersaudy, *De Gaulle et Churchill* (Paris: Plon, 1982), p. 56.
17. *SWW*, vol. 2, pp. 176–7.
18. Ibid., p. 179.
19. 'Impensable' is the word used by Weygand in his Memoirs: Maxime Weygand, *Mémoires: Rappelé au service* (Paris: Flammarion, 1950), p. 234.
20. Full text reproduced in *SWW*, vol. 2, *Their Finest Hour*, p. 179.
21. Ibid., p. 184.
22. 'This was a new fact; and a fact at which the *whole* French nation rejoiced' (our emphasis). Ibid., p. 185.
23. Ibid., p. 198.
24. Ibid.
25. Ibid.
26. Ibid., p. 195.
27. Ibid., p. 194.
28. Ibid., p. 203.
29. Ibid.
30. Ibid.
31. Ibid., p. 202.
32. Churchill's vocabulary varies between 'freed and restored' and 'liberated and restored'. Ibid., p. 203.
33. Ibid., pp. 391 and 394.
34. Ibid., p. 393.
35. Ibid., p. 408.
36. Ibid., p. 404.
37. Ibid., p. 490.
38. Charles de Gaulle, *Mémoires de Guerre*, vol. 1, *L'Appel (1940–1942)* (Paris: Plon, 1954), p. 153.
39. *SWW*, vol. 3, *The Grand Alliance*, Chapter XVIII: 'Syria'.
40. 'I had always been favourable to the idea of installing the de Gaullists in Madagascar': *SWW*, vol. 4, *The Hinge of Fate*, p. 190.
41. *SWW*, vol. 5, *Closing the Ring*, p. 488.
42. Ibid., p. 489.
43. Ibid.
44. *SWW*, vol. 6, *Triumph and Tragedy*, p. 28.
45. Ibid., pp. 44–6.
46. Ibid., p. 211.
47. Ibid.
48. Ibid., p. 214.
49. Ibid., p. 291.
50. Ibid., p. 488.

11
The '*Mésentente Cordiale*': Economic Relations between France and Great Britain since 1945

Isabelle Lescent-Giles

Economic relations between Britain and France in the twentieth century attracted relatively little attention from politicians, academics and businessmen alike. The stormy relationship between de Gaulle and the successive British governments of the 1960s, or François Mitterrand's fascination with Margaret Thatcher's eyes and mouth have been more documented than the transfers of goods, capital and people between the two countries. In the business world itself, France has appeared to be more likely to take Germany or, to a lesser extent, the USA as role models. In the eyes of the average *énarque*, Britain is just a second fiddle in the great battles between France and the United States, at best America's – and more recently Japan's – Trojan horse. Conversely, France has not been a 'natural reference' for the British business community, compared to America, Japan or, in Europe, Germany.

Although to be deplored, this is easy to explain. Most comparisons focused on the 1600–1870 period, as Youssef Cassis reminded us in *Management and Business in Britain and in France*.[1] Then, Britain was the leading technological and industrial power in the world, and France its immediate follower. Although specific in many ways, French industrialization took British industry as its benchmark. In the twentieth century, both nations slipped in the hierarchy of nations and compared themselves with the leading powers of the day: first America, then Japan and Germany.

Economic comparisons between France and Britain did not become fashionable again until the 1980s. French economists, businessmen and journalists, belatedly followed by politicians, became fascinated by an 'English model' they rather superficially equated with Thatcherism. But this comparison has remained limited in scope, focusing mainly on productivity and unemployment figures. At least as interesting for the economic historian and much lesser known are the works of consultants, or sociologists and anthropologists, on cultural differences in business. The most prominent book on the subject is *Cultures and Organisations* by the Dutch academic, Geert Hofstede, which tries to determine the impact of such differences in the 1990s, in Europe, Asia and America. Historians can give this concept extra depth by studying how the French and the British have worked together in the world of business over the last 100 years.

Information is scarce and scattered: official publications are an important source of information throughout the period, although mainly statistical,[2] as well as the archives of the firms, even multinational ones, which had plants in both countries.[3] For the more recent period, interviews or questionnaires of French people working in the UK and vice versa are of valuable use. Some head-hunters specializing in international postings have conducted such inquiries, but the findings usually remain confidential. A fourth and final source comes in the shape of institutions such as the British Chamber of Commerce in Paris and the press.[4]

Offering conclusions would be premature, but we can summarize the extent of our knowledge on the exchanges of goods, technology, financial and human capital between France and the UK, before setting an agenda for further research. I shall start by surveying the main areas of economic co-operation between France and Britain in the twentieth century, before formulating a hypothesis for future research: that of a growing convergence in business culture between the two countries over that century, and especially since the Second World War. Yet friction points remained, most notably in attitudes to and of the state, education, corporate governance and the process of decision-making within the firm. Throughout this essay, the main unit for analysis will be the firm itself, as it provides a concrete example of the way the French and the British can – or cannot – work together.

One century of Franco-British economic relations

Converging structures and performance in the twentieth century

The twentieth century saw a gradual convergence in the economies of both countries, as France depended less on agriculture and Britain's share of industry declined. As shown in Table 11.1, by the 1980s both countries depended on services for half of the gross value added (GVA) created and for a fifth on manufacturing. Non-market services accounted for roughly 15 per cent of GVA. The only major differences were in energy and water supply, where North Sea oil gave Britain a 2 per cent advantage over France.[5]

However, major differences did appear in the manufacturing sector. By 1993, the two countries had a similar number of manufacturing units (about 27 000), of manufacturing workforce (3.73 million for the UK, 3.33 for France), of net capital expenditure (15 and 15.56 million ECU respectively) and GVA at factor cost (135.6 and 139.4 million ECU). Britain and France displayed more resemblance than any other European country.

Major differences still set them apart. Manufacturing labour costs came first: in 1993, in the UK, it was 21 960 ECU per head against 32 793 for France (in 1981: 66 869 against 73 977). The second difference was in production, much higher in France (464 311 million ECU) than in the UK (370 482), with the gap once again widening in the 1980s. These were consistent with higher GVA as a percentage of production in the UK (36.6 per cent vs 30.0 per cent in France and 38 per cent in Germany), lower unit wage costs (60.4 vs 78.3 per cent) and higher gross operating surplus (53.7 vs 30.3 million ECU). On the other hand, French

Table 11.1   Sectoral breakdown of gross value added as % of total

	1980		1991	
	UK	*France*	*UK*	*France*
Whole economy	100.0	100.0	100.0	100.0
Agriculture, forestry and fisheries	1.7	4.5	1.5	3.2
Energy and water supply	9.6	4.1	6.1	4.2
Total manufacturing	26.6	24.1	21.8	20.3
Chemicals, metal and mineral products[6]	6.1	6.9	4.9	5.6
Engineering	9.5	8.0	7.1	6.9
Other manufacturing	11.0	9.2	9.7	7.8
Construction	5.9	7.3	6.3	5.4
Total market services	40.4	43.2	48.5	50.5
Distributive trades	11.8	12.8	11.9	13.1
Hotels, restaurants and catering	1.7	2.2	2.8	2.9
Transport and communications	6.5	6.2	7.3	6.2
Banking and insurance	2.3	4.6	5.0	4.5
Other market services	18.1	17.5	21.6	23.8
Non-market services	15.8	16.8	15.8	16.5

From Eurostat.

productivity per head remained higher (36 100 vs 40 100 ECU) although Britain did regain some of the lost ground (1981: 30 300 and 22 900). The third difference was structural: although Britain exported a slightly bigger share of its production than France (37.6 and 35.8 per cent in 1993), representing a significant increase on 1981 (28.1 and 27.7 per cent), it also imported more manufactured goods from abroad, resulting in a 5.6 per cent deficit against France's 1.6 per cent surplus. How much of this trade happened between the two countries?

Franco-British trade

The history of exchanges of goods, capital and people between France and Britain has to be set within an international context. At the end of the nineteenth century, Britain was by far the world's leading exporter, with a share of exports varying from 45 per cent in 1885 to 31.8 per cent in 1913. France was one of Britain's main trading partners, first as an importer of basic industrial goods (e.g. pig-iron), then as an importer of more elaborate products (locomotives, structural steel, etc.). Up to the First World War and the move over to oil as a source of energy, it was also the major client for British coal. Nevertheless, from the 1860s onwards, France's role as a major market for British products diminished, until, between the wars, it was no longer considered a strategic market. From 1914 to the 1960s, the European market was of decreasing importance for British goods and capital (see Figure 11.1). Industrial production became home-centred, with the beginning of mass consumption, while industrial goods and capital were exported to America and the Commonwealth, much more than to Europe.

France was not the leading exporter of goods and capital throughout the twentieth century, but its role was important, although far behind Britain. Its share of world exports of manufactures never went above 15 per cent (1885) and thereafter oscillated between 6 per cent and 12 per cent, with high points in the late 1920s and the early 1970s, and low points at the end of the 1930s and in the mid-1960s. France's share of foreign direct investment was comparable to its share of goods exported: around 12 per cent in 1914, 9.5 per cent in 1938, 6 per cent in 1960 and 5 per cent in 1983. Britain was also a major destination for French products. In fact, both countries were complementary. British exports were mainly coal, cotton and iron wares. Unlike Britain or the Netherlands, France never featured prominently in the re-export trade of colonial produce. It specialized in high added value products, especially luxury goods, exported to an affluent British clientele. French silks and wools were to be found not only in London, but all over the

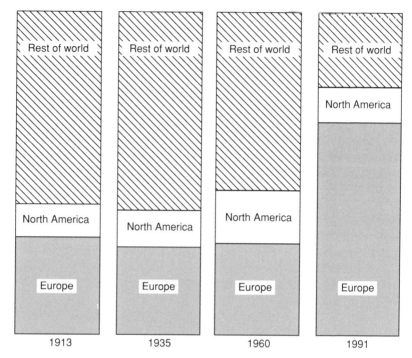

1913   1935   1960   1991

Figure 11.1   UK exports (percentage distribution by destination), selected years
1913–91

Sources: *Abstract of British Historical Statistics*, B. R. Mitchell and P. Deane (Cambridge)

country. And while Britain diversified its markets between 1870 and
1914, France did not: it still exported 70 per cent of its products to
Europe by 1910. On the other hand, its capital exports did change in
geographical distribution, the priority between 1890 and 1914 being
given to eastern Europe, particularly Russia (25 per cent of French
investment in 1914), and an increase in investment outside Europe:
from 90 per cent in 1881, the latter fell to just over half by 1914. Britain
was not a major area of investment for French companies throughout
the nineteenth century, and it remained so until the 1960s.

It is only since the 1950s that Continental Europe has regained its
importance as a major market for Britain. Britain's first application to
the Common Market, in 1961, can be seen as the recognition that
Europe, not the Commonwealth, was the main trading partner. In
1960, one-quarter of UK exports went to Europe. This was reinforced
from 1973 onwards with the integration of Britain within the EEC. By

1984, exports of goods to EEC countries represented just under half of all British exports, rising to 53 per cent in 1993.[7] In 1984, France represented 16.3 per cent of the UK imports from its EU partners, while France took 21.5 per cent of UK exports to EU countries. By 1992, imports from France had climbed to 18.9 per cent and exports fallen to 19.8 per cent, with a 2.2 billion ECU trade surplus turning into a small 0.54 billion ECU deficit.[8] By then, France had become Britain's second market for exports after Germany, and sent about 15 per cent of its exports to Britain (see Figures 11.2 and 11.3).

France's trade deficit with Britain throughout the 1960s became a surplus in the 1970s, with a ratio of exports to imports of 145 per cent in 1986 (Table 11.2). Then, France retained a trade deficit with the UK for organic chemistry, hosiery, diamonds, some non-ferrous metals, some articles of ironmongery, machine tools, TV sets, electrical cables, aeroplane parts, sports clothes and toys. France had the advantage in, unsurprisingly, luxury goods, glass, furniture, but also in plastics, rubber, paper, textile thread and manufactured metal goods, especially steel tubes and motor cars. Trade in services between the two countries was much lower. Britain still focused on non-European partners, with only a quarter of British exports of services going to EU countries in 1981–83 and still under a third in 1991–93.[9]

Exports of capital followed a similar pattern. Increased globalization and international competition, as well as integration within the

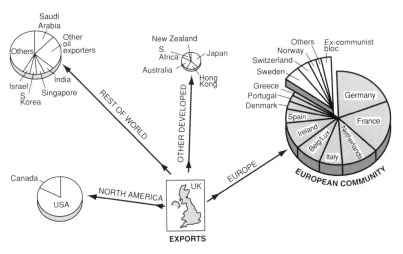

Figure 11.2   UK exports by destination 1991.

Source: *Annual Abstract of Statistics*

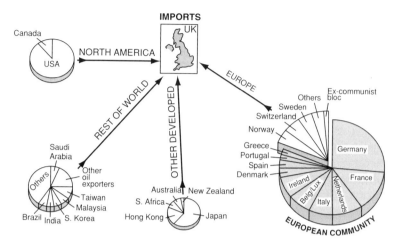

Figure 11.3 UK imports by origin 1991.

Source: Annual Abstract of Statistics

Common Market, meant that more and more British companies invested in Germany, France and, on a smaller scale, northern Europe. But France was not a top priority investment for most British companies, the spiralling labour costs being a powerful deterrent. Still, 11.5 per cent of foreign affiliates in France were British in 1991, making 9.2 per cent of turnover and 9.6 per cent of value added of all foreign affiliates. But French companies only accounted for 5.4 per cent of total foreign companies in the UK, and their share of turnover and value added was respectively 6.9 per cent and 7.2 per cent.[10]

The rise of multinationals

However, several joint ventures of importance were created in that period between the two countries. From the 1890s on, British companies

Table 11.2 Exports/imports ratio, France–UK, 1963–86

1963	54.71	1969	53.14	1975	113.18	1981	123.92
1964	56.61	1970	57.62	1976	92.37	1982	122.87
1965	62.28	1971	74.05	1977	102.61	1983	145.90
1966	59.08	1972	89.56	1978	126.66	1984	150.28
1967	67.97	1973	108.54	1979	131.80	1985	147.88
1968	63.87	1974	103.70	1980	118.96	1986	144.69

Note: Figures <100 indicate a French trade deficit; figures >100 indicate a French trade surplus.

started establishing foreign subsidiaries in France. While most were confined to distributing British products, a handful of firms, many of them in the consumer goods industry, also established production plants in Europe, mainly France and Germany, as well as the USA. In 1904, for example, biscuit maker Huntley Palmer teamed up with Rowntree to start production in France. The main motivation was to take advantage of the growing markets of continental Europe, at a time when the UK economy was slowing down. In a context of increasing tariff barriers, they needed to establish plants abroad to compete with local producers. An added factor was the political pressure put by continental governments, including the French, on foreign companies possessing new technologies to create plants on their national ground in exchange for granting patents. Dunlop was in this position.[11] On the other hand, French direct investment in the UK was scarce. Belgium, Italy, central Europe and Russia were easier markets. Foreign direct investment in the UK was overwhelmingly American. Among European firms, the Dutch were the most likely to set up plants and joint ventures in the UK (Royal Dutch Shell, Unilever), followed by the Germans (Siemens Brothers[12]), the Swiss (Nestlé[13]) or the Swedes (Ericsson[14]).

The First World War marked a watershed. The political dangers of establishing plants in an unstable European political environment, together with a growing recognition of the inadequacies of management techniques to control the finances, the production mix and quality of the foreign subsidiaries, became a serious brake on British direct investment in continental Europe. Instead, British multinationals turned to the Commonwealth markets, where it was thought there was less competition, where the language barrier did not exist and where political stability was to be found. There were a few British ventures in France. Schweppes, for example, set up a plant in France in 1928, but after only after doing so in Australia and the USA (1919), Belgium, South Africa and New Zealand[15] – a significant example of the geographical priorities set by British industrialists between the wars.

Another type of economic relationship, but more limited in scope and time, is the international cartel. Between the wars, Britain shied away from most of the international cartels, in particular the steel cartel, mainly because its industry was fragmented, which precluded international agreements. When it did, it signed deals with eastern Europe and Germany rather than France.[16] French and British companies, in fact, mostly came into contact with each other in eastern Europe. Vickers and Schneider, for example, both invested heavily there, Vickers in a succession of deals in Poland, Estonia and Czechoslovakia, where

Schneider had bought Skoda. It is most interesting to point out the high degree of support given to Schneider by the French Ministère des Affaires Etrangères, while Vickers and the Foreign Office operated at arm's length. The part played by diplomats in British and French foreign investment remains yet to be studied, just like the success rate of joint ventures: the handful of case studies available suggests that most joint ventures between partners of different nationality, whether Franco-British or not, tended not to last very long before the 1960s. These deals were undoubtedly useful in securing entry in a tariff-protected market, with a local partner providing knowledge of the country's business culture. But the interests of the two partners rarely coincided for long, and it may well be that acquiring firms or setting up from scratch was more likely to succeed. There are obvious exceptions, like Unilever and Shell, but both concern Anglo-Dutch, not Franco-British, ventures.

From the 1960s, however, exchanges of goods, people and capital started flowing again between France and Britain. France and Britain started a second wave of joint ventures, such as Concorde. This trend accelerated in the 1980s. Among the best-known cases of joint ventures are Carnaud–Metal Box, GEC–Alsthom, Eurotunnel and LVHM–Guinness. Nevertheless, France lagged behind Germany and the Netherlands as a UK investor. From the 1960s onwards, Germany became the second biggest investor in the UK after America, with, in 1988, 900 subsidiaries of German companies, mainly in chemicals and pharmaceuticals. France's investment in the UK pales by comparison, although pharmaceuticals is also well represented (Rhône-Poulenc plant in Norwich, for example). Engineering, transport, food and, in the late 1980s, water distribution, were the main sectors of French investment in the UK.

One would like to know if the cultural differences that will be studied in the following section are recent or whether they are the fruit of a historical tradition. One can advance without too much risk that such is the case with the relationship between the state and the economy, or with education. On the other hand, institutional obstacles such as company law and taxation and internal obstacles such as decision-making processes may have shifted over time.

A growing convergence of business structures, strategies and cultures since the 1950s?

This is a hotly debated topic among analysts and practitioners of business alike. It is common to oppose the American and German business culture, the first emphasizing short-term profits, market capitalization, risk-taking, individualism and confrontation between all partners (management versus workforce, individual company versus state), the second preferring long-term profitability, the use of banks and corporate partners instead of the stock exchange as a fund-raiser, and the search for consensus at all levels.

'German' versus 'Anglo-Saxon' capitalism?

Britain is often abusively described as an example of the American brand of capitalism, and France as a compromise between these two brands of capitalism, a kind of 'half way' sometimes proudly presented as a 'third way'. Indeed, France favours an individual style of management much closer to the British than to the German way, and confrontation between management and labour is much closer to what happens in Manchester than in Mannheim. On the other hand, many French companies, like German ones, give less priority to the quarterly bottom line than the British, and market capitalization, although higher than in Germany, lags behind the UK. But things are more complex. Even if these national differences in business cultures have been valid from the 1940s to the 1960s (which remains to be proven), they have been blurred between 1973 and 1998 by a growing split within both countries between several, often irreconcilable, business cultures.

Take the growing divide between small and medium-sized companies, on the one hand, and the biggest firms on the other. The latter have become, since the 1920s, and even more the 1960s, multinationals operating in several countries. The corporate structure, organizations and strategies of firms operating in global markets show more common points than differences. Let us take Usinor-Sacilor and British Steel: on paper, they are in the late 1980s a classic example of the Anglo-French divide. One, the champion of its state owner, run by *énarques* and *X-Mines*,[17] featuring a highly unionized workforce. The other, privatized by the Thatcher revolution, run by managers from the best business schools, and with domesticated unions. But a closer look shows a fascinating example of how unimportant the ownership of firms can be in the face of market forces: in the worldwide crisis of the steel industry since the late 1960s, both companies made the same strategic choices: increasing productivity to counter falling prices, they relocated production on a handful of sites on the coast (South Wales and north-east of England for British Steel, with closures in Scotland and the Midlands, Nord–Pas de Calais and the Mediterranean coast for Usinor-Sacilor, with closures in eastern France). The workforce fell in comparable proportion for both firms, and both have gained better control of stockists and retailers of steel, and developed closer relationship with the clientele, especially car manufacturers and the building trade. Similarly, there are fewer differences than common points between SmithKline Beecham or ICI, the UK pharmaceutical and chemical giants on the one hand, and Rhône-Poulenc Rorer (now Aventis) on the other. All are refocusing on their core businesses, concentrating their plants and investing heavily in biotechnologies. Even the well-advertised differences in corporate culture between Elf-Aquitaine and British Petroleum owe more to the history and individualities of these firms than to Anglo-French differences.

Another point to keep in mind is the growing circulation of people between the two countries. In the 1960s, most French managers could hope to spend the whole of their career in France; today, they are likely to spend a sizeable part of it (three years or more) abroad. And while in the 1960s, the mobility of managers (from engineers to directors and board members) mainly involved spending some time in the existing or former French colonies of Africa and occasionally Asia, it now involves travelling broadly, to North and South America, the whole of Asia, and the whole of Europe. This, of course, must be seen in this wider context of increased European mobility, rather than as a specific tightening of economic relations between the two countries.

One can therefore wonder whether national differences remain an operative concept, when national characteristics tend to crumble to leave in their place a highly diversified business structure.

'International' versus 'national' divide

One is tempted to split French and British firms into two groups. The first is characterized by firms with decreasing national differences and converging strategies and structures. This does not mean that companies do not have striking differences in identities, but that, even when they brand themselves as a 'French group', the concept of nationality is less useful to understand them than a knowledge of the segment of the market in which they operate. For example, Hôtels Méridiens may have a French menu everywhere in the world, designer furniture by Philippe Starck, their structure and strategy are nevertheless getting closer to those of other hoteliers such as Forte, in spite of their mahogany chairs and liberty counterpanes. In this 'converging group', one would find, at the top, big multinationals, in which corporate culture seeks (not always successfully) to displace national identities. Rhône-Poulenc, Saint-Gobain or Lafarge Coppée, ICI, Courtaulds and British Petroleum would be good examples of such firms. Following in their footsteps are high-tech companies of all types and sizes, specialized engineering concerns such as Valeo or GKN, computer-technology firms, catering, hotel and travel groups such as Accor or Forte. Finally, one would also find companies with national markets, but whose business is run increasingly along similar lines. The best example of these are commercial banks and big retailers. Historians should seriously consider working on Franco-British comparisons such as Carrefour/Sainsbury, Auchan/Tesco, BNP/Lloyds or Barclays/Crédit Agricole, or La Poste and Royal Mail, which should yield some interesting conclusions, both from an economic and cultural point of view.

The second group would include all firms where national identities remain an operative concept, such as some car makers (e.g. Peugeot), most building firms, some small and medium-sized food companies, many luxury goods businesses. But even this is unsure, as very little is known about the way these sectors run. Some sectoral comparisons between France and the UK, for example in the building trade, food manufacturing or leather goods would be of real interest.

An emerging 'European company'?

The existence of a 'European company', by contrast with an 'American' or 'Asian' company, could bear more relevance. Many multinationals, whatever their country of origin, are now splitting their business into three geographical zones: Europe, Asia, America. Is there any logic here, beyond geographical proximity and common legislation within the EEC? Many Britons believe that there is more in common between a British and an American company than between a French and a British one. Many case studies of mergers or alliances between French and British firms, and statistical analysis on such issues as profitability, corporate governance, geographical markets or the education and origins of managers, are needed before attempting to answer these questions. A clue is still provided by the study of IBM employees across more than 40 countries carried out by the Dutch anthropologist G. Hofstede. He selected four criteria of comparison: attitude of subordinates towards managers and company bosses, the balance between the interest of the group and those of the individual, the relative importance of masculine (high earnings, recognition, advancement and challenge) and feminine values (good relationships, co-operation, quality of life and employment security), and finally the extent to which the members of a culture feel threatened by uncertain or unknown situations (uncertainty avoidance). On these four criteria, situations differed widely between European countries. France came out of the questionnaires as a country with very large power distance, moderate individualism, moderately feminine values and high uncertainty avoidance. This may explain its taste for planning since 1945. Britain, by comparison, only shared in one of its values, individualism, although it pushed it to extremes unknown in France. On all other issues, Britain chose the opposite road: it had reasonably low power distance, similar to Germany. It had highly masculine values of challenge, money and performance and seemed to rather like difference, unpredictability and uncertainty. Hence its suspicion of *planification*, seen as too rigid to face the day-to-day uncertainties of business management. Pragmatism is often presented as an alternative to planism. All this suggested that Britain's behaviour was closest to the USA, Canada and New Zealand, and, in Europe, the Netherlands or Ireland, while France was closest to Belgium, and, to a smaller extent, Italy and Spain.

Fascinating as it is, this survey conceals, as Hofstede himself acknowledges, wide differences between social groups in each country. For example, in terms of power distance, the difference between France and Britain rested mainly in different attitudes among the middle and the higher ranks towards the boss, while at the level of the (unskilled or skilled) workers, distance was great anyway. Which may explain why Britain's score was relatively low while all accounts suggest a great distance to power, the 'them and us' attitude, and high degree of submission to authority within many industrial plants: companies with highly skilled workforce, with professionals (management consultancies, law firms, the press, computing, finance, etc.) which account for the relatively small distance perceived with the boss, translating in policies of open door, power sharing and staff consultation in major occasions. But there is less difference in management culture on the industrial shop floor and in services dealing with low-skilled workforce, such as car manufacturers, steel makers or catering. Although Hofstede's study is based on a comparison of employees in a single company, one wonders if the difference between the two countries is purely cultural, or whether it derives from the respective weight of industry (dominant in France) and high-tech services (dominant in the UK) in the two countries, the sheer weight of each lending its values to the whole of society. This can only be determined by further study. One would also like to know whether these patterns, studied for the late 1980s, are consistent in time or whether they are the product of short-term political values (such as the resurgence of values such as money, individualism and challenge, as opposed to quality of life, collective responsibility and uncertainty avoidance in the Britain of the 1990s, symbolized at the political level by the displacement of wets by Thatcherites in the Tory Party). Whatever the answer, there are some deep-seated obstacles remaining to harmonious economic co-operation between France and Britain, all of them deriving from a long historical tradition. On the three subjects of attitudes to the state, educational choices and models of corporate governance and decision-making, the two countries diverge widely.

An uneasy partnership: institutional and cultural obstacles to the 'Entente Cordiale'

Historians have to collect facts and not clichés to support their intuitions. Although business schools, management consultants and governmental organizations (including the EEC and the OECD) have been doing research in this field, much remains to be done. One of the most interesting topics is the study of mergers and acquisitions. A study of the merger and post-merger developments in such cases as Carnaud–Metal Box or GEC–Alsthom, for example, should provide interesting clues about Anglo-French differences in business cultures. Another possible study would be a survey of the expatriates who settled in both countries over the last 50 years. The hiring of European nationals has become common in most walks of life, spreading from the original core of the City, the media and the catering trade, to heavy and light industry, retailing and even agriculture – but sadly not to academia. A handful of TV programmes about the *'fuite des cerveaux'* (brain drain) cannot make a scientific basis on which to draw conclusions. Even the actual number of French people working in Britain is unknown. Some figures about sectoral and regional distribution of employment, the levels at which they are employed, and their average length of stay would be especially welcome. A collection of interviews of French managers in London and British businessmen in France would also be of interest.

Nevertheless, one can argue there are a handful of major impediments to working relationships between French and British businesses, some such as company legislation and education, both of the workforce and the business leaders, others as the way companies treat their shareholders and the way in which decisions are taken.

Attitude to the state and the law
Describing the widely diverging attitudes of France and Britain towards the role of the state sounds clichéd. In spite of their convergence in the

1945–79 period, Britain remains the land of laissez-faire as opposed to that of *colbertisme* and state intervention. Even during the heyday of statism in the Labour governments of Attlee, Wilson and Callaghan, the state always kept its intervention in the world of business to a minimum. The running of state-owned industry (the exception being coal), was left to its traditional leaders. British Steel was led throughout its two periods of nationalization in the 1950s and from the late 1960s onwards by the same managerial teams as during its periods in private hands. The management which took over from the mid-1970s onwards to carry out major restructuring throughout the Callaghan and Thatcher eras was groomed at the leading private steel firm of the 1960s (i.e. United Steel), not in the offices of the Civil Service. The latter's role of supplying industry, private or public, with leaders was minimal in the UK, while in post-1945 France it almost became the norm. One could even blame the British government for not intervening enough: it did not keep a close eye on the bottom line of its companies, failing in its role as a major shareholder to create value. It let the situation in British Leyland and British Steel reach catastrophic proportions before taking vigorous action.

In contrast, France displayed throughout the twentieth century, but mainly since 1945, the opposite tendency to meddle, with indifferent results (think of the Concorde project, or the Bull and Crédit Lyonnais fiascos). The closeness of the relationship between French business and the state is based on three pillars: mutual transfers of personnel between the civil service and business, the financing of research and investment in strategic areas (i.e. aeroplanes, or the hi-tech industry), and finally a propensity to rescue large firms going through difficult times, thereby encouraging the belief, as in the Crédit Lyonnais case, that nothing can go wrong as 'the state will never let us go bankrupt'. The French state is also much more interventionist in terms of business location and regional policies, although Britain, especially in the 1960s and the 1970s, also showed similar concerns. The disaster of the Dunkirk thermo-cracker in the chemical industry, put there in the 1970s at the intimation of the French government against any business sense, was matched by the establishment of a strip mill in Ebbw Vale, one of the most isolated Welsh valleys, or the opening of Ravenscraig in Scotland, once again against the industry's better judgement. On restructuring in heavy industry, though, one can probably say that both governments played a similar and rather positive role, in steel as in coal, in forcing major changes, which no private company could have sustained for both financial and political reasons. Beyond theory therefore, real differences between France and Britain have been exaggerated and, from widely different philosophy, both states came to play from the 1960s to the 1990s a fairly similar role in business.

Less well known but probably more important to understand the misunderstandings that are rife in Franco-British economic relations is the attitude to the law. One cannot stress enough that French business law draws its cultural heritage from Roman law while the British have been deeply influenced by the common law. In the first case, 'codification' is all-important, everything must be written down and the letter of the law is essential, and must be adhered to until the law is rewritten, while in the second the spirit of the law and jurisprudence dominate, leaving ample room for interpretation and evolution. This is a source of endless misunderstandings when drafting legal agreements between French and British corporations, the French considering it as a final document and pressing for the precise definition of the scope of the venture and the obligations and rights of the partners, while the British are happy with a simple statement of intention which, they think, may be altered with time and changing circumstances. Precision to the point of punctiliousness on one side, generalities leading to the fudging of the main issues on the other.

Education

Youssef Cassis's study of the education of French and British business leaders over the whole of the twentieth century suggests widely diverging educational choices, with a tendency to diminish from the 1960s on.

Cassis's work helped to quantify what had been felt for a long time. Table 11.3 confirms that British businessmen were throughout the twentieth century among the least educated in Europe while the French were among the best educated, ahead of the Germans, at least if one takes length of formal schooling as a benchmark. More surprisingly, this gap, although narrowing after 1945, remained large throughout the 1960s to the 1990s: in 1989, 64 per cent of British businessmen had been to university against 95 per cent of the French.

More importantly, education also differed in its content (Table 11.4). French businessmen were overwhelmingly scientific graduates, most of them engineers, while the Britons that went to university preferred a general arts education or a law degree. This reflects the fact that British businesses recruit management trainees at Oxford and Cambridge, among others, with no regard to the type of degree, be it music, Latin or PPE, while France's elite schools (Polytechnique, Centrale) are all, except two, engineering schools. This may account for the remark of a

Table 11.3 Educational level of business leaders (%)

	1907			1929			1953			1972			1989		
	GB	F	D	GB	F	D	GB	F	D	GB	F	D	GB	F	D
Apprenticeship	18	7	31	11	0	18	10	0	11	3	0	12	0	0	10
Secondary school	47	21	7	39	10	15	33	2	11	28	4	2	17	3	0
Training college	0	0	5	3	2	6	12	2	3	10	6	4	19	2	2
University	35	72	57	47	88	61	45	96	75	59	90	82	64	95	88
Total	100	100	100	100	100	100	100	100	100	100	100	100	100	100	100
No. of cases	86	46	53	104	56	73	87	77	71	63	55	51	50	57	51
No data	20	17	11	11	15	7	5	12	9	2	4	1	3	0	1

Source: Youssef Cassis et al., Management and Business in Britain and France (Oxford University Press, 1993).

Table 11.4 Fields of higher education (%)

	1907			1929			1953			1972			1989		
	GB	F	D	GB	F	D	GB	F	D	GB	F	D	GB	F	D
Dual training[a]	0	0	4	0	0	2	0	8	0	3	4	2	6	11	6
Arts	26	10	4	9	3	0	8	3	0	3	0	0	10	2	0
Economics, business studies	0	5	0	5	3	2	11	3	9	19	4	10	27	15	31
Law, politics	30	14	38	7	28	40	11	18	39	17	35	44	10	22	32
Science, engineering	9	71	50	21	63	52	19	62	48	19	57	37	20	50	25
Others, unspecified	35	0	4	58	3	4	51	6	4	39	0	7	27	0	6
Total	100	100	100	100	100	100	100	100	100	100	100	100	100	100	100
No. of cases	23	21	24	43	36	41	37	63	46	36	46	41	30	54	44

[a] Arts, economics, or law *and* science or engineering.
Source: As Table 11.3.

German businessman that the French were hopeless financiers while the British did not have a clue in technical matters. This makes co-operation at boardroom level difficult, as the points of reference are completely different. The French, in this instance, are closer to the Germans, although the German engineering schools are as practical as the French are theoretical. One must also bear in mind that an large proportion of German bosses also did art or law degrees. Germany would appear to be the middle way here between France and Britain. One added dimension of possible incomprehension is brought out by Cassis's study of the businessmen's previous careers (Table 11.5). France's unique proportion of former civil servants made for a very different frame of mind indeed, more intent on growth and market share than on profitability, the favourite word of the British.

These differences are not confined to business leaders, although much remains to be done in the study of middle management and the workforce. Everything points to a shorter length of formal education. British banks traditionally recruited clerks at the O and A level stage, while French banks preferred them to have a short period of specialization after the *baccalauréat*, in management, accountancy or marketing. Most firms in the City and in industry recruited and still recruit future middle managers at the BA level, and trained them in house, via trade-established professional exams or internal courses rather than with degrees in management or engineering which form the traditional background of French middle managers. As for the workforce, the French emphasis on a wide curriculum, as opposed to a smaller one in the UK, means most ordinary French employees have some basic notions in maths and physics unlike many of their British counterparts. That said, it is not absolutely certain which system is best adapted to the business world. A critical spirit, the ability to work in teams and flexibility may be more important than notions of maths and physics which often remain highly abstract.

But even more important than the length and the content of the curriculum is the way of thinking that education hammers into schoolchildren, teenagers and young adults. The British and French ways of thinking are on the whole diametrically opposite. The French educational system puts an enormous emphasis on logic and deductive thinking, while the British system fosters a more intuitive, haphazard but stimulating way of presenting ideas. The currently fashionable concepts of 'vertical' versus 'lateral' thinking may aptly describe both countries' tradition: what strikes foreign journalists most of all when interviewing French managers is their tendency to formulate their ideas

Table 11.5 Previous career of business leaders who joined their firm at top hierarchical level (with the exception of inheritors) (%)

	1907			1929			1953			1972			1989		
	GB	F	D	GB	F	D	GB	F	D	GB	F	D	GB	F	D
Civil service	3	38	14	5	43	6	0	55	16	14	50	14	6	57	17
Private firm	58	32	46	55	18	30	41	0	25	24	15	18	12	0	0
Senior management	8	5	31	33	14	55	38	36	50	48	25	64	58	37	78
Junior management	13	10	3	0	0	3	3	0	3	4	5	0	6	6	0
Professions	6	0	6	0	0	6	6	0	0	0	0	0	6	6	0
Other	12	15	0	7	25	0	12	9	6	10	5	4	12	0	5
Total	100	100	100	100	100	100	100	100	100	100	100	100	100	100	100
No. of cases	36	19	36	44	28	36	32	11	32	21	20	22	17	30	18

Source: As Table 11.3.

in a logical, Cartesian way. On the other hand, many, though not all, British businessmen think laterally: they foster new ideas not by deduction, but by association of apparently unconnected ideas. They also probably score higher, at least in the 1970s and 1980s, on what sociologists call emotional intelligence, i.e. on their ability to manage people, forge consensus and implement change. In other words, they are often more capable than the French of assessing the feasibility of a particular project, rather than just its desirability or its intellectual value. It is probably not a coincidence that the leading theorists of behavioural management theory, which stresses the importance of human management techniques alongside scientific management, were British: Lyndall Urwick, the Cadbury brothers and Seebohm Rowntree were leaders in this field between the wars, while one of the most influential European theorists of scientific management, Bedaux, was French.

Corporate priorities and the process of decision-making

One cliché about British and French business is its attitude towards long-term versus short-term objectives. British business leaders tend to concentrate on short-term financial objectives while French company bosses will take a longer-term view on profitability. They will, in particular, be prepared to give more time to new ventures to pay for themselves, while the British will demand short-term profitability. Some historians consider this as a cultural trait inherent to British businesses since the Industrial Revolution. I would argue that is much more recent, and dates, at the earliest, from the aftermath of the Second World War, and mainly from the 1950s. Two factors explain this focusing on the short-term bottom line. The first is the role of the stock exchange. British companies tend to be more widely capitalized on the stock exchange, and to rely less on bank loans, with their fixed terms and fixed interest rates. This means that the stock price is essential to a British company if it wants to finance further projects. The second is the composition of the shareholders. While in France and Germany the main shareholders tend to be other industrial firms and banks, in Britain it is dominated by pension and insurance funds, which require maximization of revenue year after year to attract new clients. There is also more willingness generally in the UK from all investors to switch between stocks, while stock loyalty is more developed in France. The volatility of British shareholding is both its main problem and asset: it often rules out risky or long-term investments, but forces managers to think of shareholder value and often stops them from engaging in intellectually attractive but commercially unsound ventures, unlike their French counterparts. It did not stop them from investing in Concorde however, and these differences must not be exaggerated.

More important as a source of friction between French and British partners, in my opinion, is the differences in the decision-making process. The two countries share a relatively non-collective way of decision-making within corporations, unlike Germany. The boss is usually the one who makes the final decision, rather than the board or the executive committee. But the role of meetings in the decision-making process differ. It is seen in France as the last stage in the decision-making process, while it is considered in Britain as a first step. Hence tensions and misunderstandings in many joint ventures or alliances. The same word means widely different things. Every study by international consultancy points to the fact that French participants in a meeting arrived extremely well prepared, having led widespread informal consultations 'in doorways' before the meeting and having reached conclusions and decisions, which they intend to defend at the meeting. Hence the accusation of arrogance and inflexibility often read on the British partners' lips. The British, on the other hand, like to arrive at their meetings with an open mind, unprepared, and like to listen to all sides of the arguments before reaching a decision. They also, more often than not, like to think about it before taking the decision, which irritates their French partners, leading to the accusation of temporization and wavering. Hence the judgement of a German senior manager in a multinational that the British are valuable for brokering consensus at meetings, arriving with no previous commitment to a well-defined set of decisions. This is of course a generalization and there are many exceptions, but it comes up time and time again in the judgements made by their European partners.

Notes

1. Youssef Cassis, François Crouzet and Terry Gourvish (eds), *Management and Business in Britain and France* (Oxford: University Press, 1993).
2. See in particular DTI, Parliamentary Papers, Ministère de l'Economie et des Finances. The latter compiled statistical series of payments made by French firms for patents acquired abroad (by nationality) and of royalties paid to French patentees from foreign firms.
3. Of particular interest are the personnel archives which may enable the historian, if the files are detailed enough, to compile figures of Frenchmen employed by British firms and vice versa. Note that the British authorities do not require registration of EEC nationals living in the UK, and many do not feel the need to register with the French embassy, so that figures of French

nationals working in the UK are only an educated guess. French bureaucracy ensures that figures of Britons living in France are more accurate.

4. See in particular *Courrier International, the Financial Times, The Economist, The Guardian*, the Sunday papers, *Le Point, L'Expansion, Usine Nouvelle, Capital* and *les Échos*.

5. Eurostat, *U.K. Business in Europe*, (HMSO, 1995), p. 45.

6. Including mining.

7. Eurostat, *U.K. Business in Europe*, p. 30.

8. Ibid., p. 31.

9. Ibid.

10. OECD, *Annual Report*, 1995.

11. See Geoffrey Jones, *British Multinationals: Origins, Management and Performance*, (London: Gower, 1986).

12. Siemens Brothers was the UK subsidiary of the giant German firm Siemens & Halske. Their links were severed at the outbreak of the First World War.

13. From 1905 onwards.

14. Which set up a plant in Nottinghamshire before the First World War, which operated until the late 1960s.

15. See T.A.B. Corley, 'The Nature of Multinationals', in Alice Teichova *et al.* (eds), *Historical Studies in International Corporate Business* (Cambridge: Cambridge University Press, 1989).

16. Such as the Anglo-Polish agreement signed in 1934 in coal mining, and, in the same sector, the German–British agreement of 1939, which never came into force.

17. *Polytechniciens* with an added specialization acquired at the École des Mines.

12
The 'Problem of de Gaulle', 1958–1967

Richard Davis

In January 1962 a Foreign Office paper on Anglo-French relations came to two broad conclusions: firstly, that 'French and British interests in the world of today are becoming more and more similar', that 'the Russian threat, still more than the previous German threat, *imposes Anglo-French solidarity*', and secondly, that

> the history of this country has shown that the French have never been exactly easy allies or partners in foreign affairs...in the last sixty years we have learnt that if the French are crossed or suspicious of our motives they have a positive genius for making life difficult for us out of all proportion to their real power or influence.

These two points outline the central problem facing the British in their relations with France in the 1960s: how could the recognized 'community of interests'[1] between the two countries be reconciled with the enormous difficulty they had in co-operating effectively.

The problems for Britain were aggravated by the coincidence of a particularly awkward adversary in Paris with the realignment of British foreign policy then being timidly undertaken. This redirection of policy towards a more European stance, itself based on a forced reappraisal of the links with the Commonwealth and the United States, placed Britain in an uncomfortably exposed international position, a position which de Gaulle was able to exploit fully. This, combined with their diametrically opposed views on many of the major international questions of the moment, placed Britain and de Gaulle on a collision course from which neither side would back down with the inevitable consequences. It was, therefore, hardly surprising that de Gaulle should become the *bête noire* of British diplomacy, somebody who, the Foreign Office warned, could be expected 'to create obstacles across *all* the paths down which we should like to go'.[2] The attention paid to what they summed up as the 'problem of de Gaulle'[3] quickly took on almost obsessive proportions.

Despite the recognized hostility of de Gaulle to the aims of British foreign policy sentiments towards him among British diplomats and politicians were mixed, ranging from admiration and respect in certain quarters to a growing exasperation bordering on hysteria. There were those who recognized de Gaulle's achievement in saving France from the instability of the Fourth Republic or the threat of civil war; others thought him preferable to a reformed Popular Front or military dictatorship. Equally some of those British politicians and diplomats who worked most closely with de Gaulle boasted of their excellent personal relations with him.[4]

If, however, there was an underlying admiration for de Gaulle as a great man[5] there was also a far less flattering portrayal of his character in the many reports prepared by British diplomats which were littered with condemnations of his 'outrageous behaviour',[6] 'idiosyncrasy'[7] and 'ego-centric views',[8] obstinacy and 'megalomania',[9] 'pride and vindictiveness',[10] his 'somewhat devious' methods,[11] and generally dictatorial behaviour.[12] Comparisons were drawn with Napoleon III, Richelieu and Louis XIV (de Gaulle himself complained that Macmillan had had him compared to Hitler[13]). Alexander the Great, Napoleon and Bismarck were reported to be his heroes.[14] The overall conclusion was that de Gaulle may well go down in history, but that in the mean time the policies of this 'thoroughly dangerous man'[15] were 'inimical' and 'nefarious'.[16]

If there was little trouble in identifying the 'problem of de Gaulle' how it could be overcome was far more problematic. Reflecting the almost insuperable nature of the predicament that faced it, British policy swung between often inconsistent alternatives: efforts to coax him into a more amenable posture via concrete inducements were made in parallel with often thinly veiled threats; if de Gaulle proved not to be susceptible to such pressure hopes were held out that he could be isolated, thus allowing the problem to be bypassed altogether.

The belief that de Gaulle could be isolated was frequently defended in London even during those periods of the worst reverses for Britain. Even when de Gaulle was in effect closing the door on British membership of the EEC many British diplomats argued that it was France and not Britain which was being cut off from the rest of Europe. This most Anglocentric view seemingly forgot that it was Britain, and not France, which was on the outside looking in on an ever closer European union.

Whatever sympathy the British may have enjoyed among some member states of the EEC (and there was a tendency for British diplomats to exaggerate this) the Six continued to share membership of the same club, a club from which Britain was still excluded, and to which their loyalty outweighed any support they might have had for Britain.

Nor were hopes that de Gaulle could be conveniently bypassed any more well founded even if such a policy was widely advocated in the Foreign Office: NATO, EFTA, the Western European Union and the OECD were all put forward as arenas in which Britain's exclusion could be circumvented. However, the EEC, where France continued to occupy the centre of the stage, was becoming increasingly vital in determining Europe's political and economic future. As such the 'de Gaulle problem', instead of being sidelined as British diplomats had hoped, only grew. British frustration increased accordingly.

The conclusion that de Gaulle would continue to constitute an un-avoidable obstacle led many in London to long for the day when this could be removed once and for all.[17] However, although there were some rather over-optimistic hopes that Britain could hasten this devel-opment,[18] it was generally recognized that there was little they could do in practice. Such advice was a counsel of despair, an admission that the only course of action was to wait on events until such time as de Gaulle disappeared from the scene; in the mean time, as the British ambassador in Paris admitted, 'an understanding with the French (is) impossible as long as General de Gaulle remains in power'.[19] Despite repeated predic-tions that de Gaulle would not survive long in office or that his star was waning,[20] he proved to be, much to the chagrin of the Foreign Office, a far more permanent feature of the situation that confronted them.

In so far as British policy towards de Gaulle was positive, and not merely reactive, it was based on a carrot and stick approach. At various meetings with the French leader British politicians attempted to adopt a threatening posture. Macmillan and later Wilson both took this rather unconvincing line, warning that unless he became more amenable to British demands they would adopt 'an alternative policy which would cut across his aims for France's role in the world'.[21] This grossly overesti-mated the weight of British diplomacy and its capacity to obstruct de Gaulle's policies as he had obstructed Britain's. Threats that if France was not more understanding Britain would drift away from Europe and move into an ever closer relationship with the United States[22] actively working against a French-led Europe carried little force. For de Gaulle, already convinced that Britain had sold its soul to the United States, that it was no longer itself to use a favourite Gaullist expression, such an eventuality was unlikely to arouse little more than growing contempt for the 'poor English'.

The reverse side of this policy held out greater hopes of success. Some British diplomats and politicians certainly liked to believe that there were grounds for agreement with de Gaulle: their shared suspicion of the supranational elements in European construction was indeed a possible starting-point. An enlarged Common Market would, so some argued, offer advantages for both Britain and France not only economically but also politically, allowing each to hold onto its position in a world increasingly dominated by the two superpowers. The economic and political advantages for de Gaulle, however, were meagre when placed up against the dangers that would result from the admission of such a rival into the Common Market.

There was, nevertheless, one area where the British did hold a potentially decisive advantage. De Gaulle's overriding concern for the restoration of France's international status, and the central position occupied by the question of France's nuclear capacity in this, was fully appreciated in London. Britain, which still had something of a head start in this area both in terms of the nuclear weapons and the rocket technology required for the delivery systems, even if these were becoming increasingly dependent on American rather than British technology, did, therefore, have something which might conceivably persuade de Gaulle to come to an agreement. The question was, however, a delicate one given Britain's commitments to the Americans. Some ministers recommended proposing a straight trade-off between British nuclear know-how and a settlement of the question of British membership of the Common Market. Although such a clear-cut offer was rejected, hints were made that some degree of Anglo-French nuclear co-operation might be acceptable should de Gaulle offer some corresponding concessions on the European question. At their meeting in June 1962 Macmillan, in his typically elliptical fashion, told de Gaulle that given the doubts about the credibility of the American nuclear commitment to western Europe 'some European deterrent was therefore perhaps necessary'.[23] This rather ambiguous statement was as far as he was prepared to go although the question, however, continued to come up at regular intervals both in the foreign policy debate in London and in Anglo-French diplomatic exchanges at ministerial level.[24]

This was, however, a card which the British were not at the end of the day willing to play. As Macmillan recognized, any nuclear offer was limited by the proviso that it must be acceptable to the Americans and have their active participation. Such a course of action offered only a very limited possibility of success: America's reluctance to make any substantial nuclear offer to the French was well known. It was also to misunderstand de Gaulle if Macmillan believed that he would welcome a position equivalent to that of Britain's dependence on America in the nuclear field.[25] Moreover, although as late as the summer of 1963 the British Defence Minister still regarded this nuclear offer as a 'trump card'[26] in their negotiations with de Gaulle, it had by then lost a great deal of its value. The choice of the American Skybolt system and even more so that of Polaris in December 1962 may have provided Britain with the most up-to-date delivery systems for their nuclear deterrent; these choices, however, also fatally undermined the value of any trade-off with de Gaulle. Thereafter they were less and less in a position to propose what was in fact not theirs to offer. More importantly still these agreements, as de Gaulle scathlingly noted, tied Britain hand and foot to the Americans, decisive proof that Britain would continue to look across the Atlantic rather than to the continent for its most vital needs.

Instead of resolving the problem the British saw themselves continually obstructed by de Gaulle, most famously in January 1963 when he brought to an end the long-running negotiations over Britain's eventual entry into the Common Market. The immediate reactions in London took the form of an outburst of anger at the way de Gaulle had 'deceived' Britain, of his 'bad faith' or his 'sabotage'[27] of the talks in Brussels. French claims that there had, in fact, been no 'veto' because there had been no formal British application, or that they were simply stating the obvious when they said that the talks had broken down, received little sympathy in London. In reply all that was left to Britain was to complain to their friends abroad, and directly to the French themselves, of the 'lies and misrepresentations'[28] coming out of Paris. The sense of indignation only served to even further undermine relations between London and Paris.

The trauma suffered in London as a result their diplomatic Waterloo at the hands of de Gaulle was all the greater for having been unexpected, at least in the degree of its severity, and as a result of London's frustrating incapacity to do anything about it. The previous expressions of optimism and the tendency to overestimate the strength of Britain's diplomatic hand made the fall, when it came, all the more galling.

The long-established tendency to look down on France and the French, and even more so on the Gaullists, was still clearly visible in the Foreign Office of the 1960s. One can only wonder, for example, at the supposed value of one report from the British embassy that the IQ of the Gaullists was lower than that of the average Frenchman.

The same source expressed doubts as to the ability of the Fifth Republic to overcome years of political instability given the 'naturally critical and destructive bent of the Gaul'.[29] Nor was de Gaulle himself any less prone to analysing Anglo-French relations in such a stereotyped fashion. Given the weight of these images, combined with the lingering impact of the lessons drawn from the centuries of Anglo-French confrontations that continued to pepper the debate on either side of the Channel, it is hardly surprising that Anglo-French relations remained difficult.

At the same time the Foreign Office continued to underestimate the strength of de Gaulle's international position. On the very eve of de Gaulle's 'bombshell' press conference of January 1963 which left Britain's European ambitions in ruins, he was still being represented as an 'inconvenience' but not an 'insuperable obstacle',[30] it being argued that he would not run the risk of unequivocally blocking British demands because of the storm of protest both in France and across the rest of Europe that this would unleash. Nor did the British seem to learn from experience. De Gaulle had already scuttled Britain's Free Trade Area proposals in 1958, setting a clear precedent for later British demands. After January 1963 it was still being argued in the Foreign Office that it was de Gaulle and not the British who were suffering most from his veto.[31] Again in 1967 there were predictions that de Gaulle would not, or that he could not, obstruct British policy for ever. If de Gaulle was resistant to pressure from Britain, so the argument went, surely he would not be able to fly in the face of a concerted international opposition from the Americans and the rest of western Europe and from Britain's supporters inside France. Once again the miscalculation was complete: de Gaulle was not as susceptible to such pressure as the British had liked to imagine, nor indeed was this pressure on Britain's behalf as strong as they had liked to believe. Even more improbable were the suggestions made in London throughout the decade that the EEC would collapse, that the Five would in effect ditch the French allowing a new European alignment to be created around Britain;[32] or the belief that Britain alone was in a position to provide Europe with the necessary leadership.[33]

The difficulties that de Gaulle posed for British foreign policy were certainly considerable. There is evidence, however, that these were exacerbated as much by British ineptitude and incomprehension of the problem as by de Gaulle himself. Nor did either Macmillan or Wilson show any great skill in their personal dealings with the French President although both liked to boast that it was just such personal contacts that would enable them to overcome the problem.[34]

Certainly de Gaulle was an enigmatic figure, and not only for the British,[35] and it is understandable that they had difficulties in anticipating his policies beforehand or even in deciphering them once they had been unleashed. The result was that British diplomats were often left floundering, unsure how to get to grips with the French leader and his diplomatic thunderbolts.

There were also those, including de Gaulle himself, for whom the difficulties in Anglo-French relations could be put down to a series of misunderstandings.[36] Both sides, not altogether unfairly, blamed each other for not being entirely clear during the decisive summit meetings in June and December 1962; de Gaulle was also reported as having been upset as much by what Macmillan had not said as by what he actually had said.[37] While there is perhaps some justification for the claim made by the Foreign Office that this was all part of a deliberate French smoke-screen to hide the real motives for de Gaulle's actions, it is certain that the failure to establish an effective understanding between Macmillan and de Gaulle only added to the problems faced by the British.

Over the necessarily secretive question of nuclear weapons these difficulties were even more evident. A possible transfer of nuclear technology was discussed at length in London, but it remains uncertain just how far de Gaulle was really disappointed at Macmillan's failure to make a more concrete offer. Several French ministers in the mid-1960s informed the British that it was indeed nuclear help that they wanted.[38] Earlier in 1962, however, de Gaulle was reported as saying that he was not interested in Britain and France pooling their nuclear resources.[39] Was he deliberately cultivating a certain mystery around his foreign policy so as to to beguile his adversaries or was it, as Macmillan argued, a typical case of de Gaulle's dislike of asking directly for concessions? Either way it was hardly surprisingly that the British were left more than a little perplexed as to the General's true intentions – although once again the dysfunctioning of the channels of communications was as much the result of British shortcomings as of those of de Gaulle.

The impression left by the diplomatic records is that on several occasions the British and French were quite simply not talking the same language. British emphasis on the inevitability of interdependence in the field of nuclear weapons stands in stark contrast to de Gaulle's desire for a truly independent French nuclear force without strings attaching them to the Americans. Similarly, Anglo-French discussions often went round in circles: the British promising that once inside the Common Market they would loosen their ties with the Americans while de Gaulle insisted that the American connection be downgraded as a necessary precondition for the opening of the door to Europe. This, as Macmillan helplessly complained, resembled the story of the chicken and the egg.[40] The debate had not greatly progressed by 1966 when Wilson was confronted with the same difficulties.

By the late 1960s the mood in the Foreign Office had become far more pessimistic towards the 'problem of de Gaulle'. Earlier in the decade Macmillan had outlined a catastrophic scenario of a diminished Britain, excluded from a French-dominated Europe, increasingly ignored by the Commonwealth and by the United States, existing in a sort of international limbo. By 1965 this was becoming reality: de Gaulle's widely reported prediction that he only had to bide his time for the British to be so far reduced that they would be forced to accept membership of the Common Market on French terms had become a frightening reality. French domination of the Common Market, their ability to ignore any pressure coming from its other members, and their success in fixing its rules to their advantage were, the increasingly helpless Foreign Office concluded, 'not comforting' for Britain.[41]

The 1960s marked an about-turn in the pattern of Anglo-French relations: Britain, for so long the senior partner in the relationship, found itself in the uncomfortable position of being the *demandeur*, its fate now dependent on Paris. Having been brought up with memories of a weak and indecisive France that could in effect be cajoled into acquiescence, this reversal of fortunes came as a most unwelcome shock and one which some in London were unable to recognize. Neither the carrot nor the stick proved sufficiently convincing. Nor was the belief that de Gaulle could be bypassed any more sustainable in the face of the changes that were taking place in the international environment: all roads still led to Paris where de Gaulle continued to block British diplomatic initiatives.

The years 1958–67 were hardly glorious ones for British foreign policy. For many in London the blame for this lack of progress, on major and minor issues alike, lay principally with de Gaulle[42] (although there was much in the argument of the French ambassador that, rather than being the cause of British difficulties, France was being used as a scapegoat for the accumulation of humiliations that had hurt British pride so much[43]). British susceptibilities were all the more wounded by these failures to successfully manage the Anglo-French relationship in that they were not entirely expected. Unable or unwilling to fully comprehend the full extent of the weaknesses of their position vis-à-vis France, successive Conservative and Labour governments were unduly optimistic, initially at least, that de Gaulle would be unable to block Britain if it came down to a direct confrontation, that Britain continued to hold the whip hand in the Anglo-French relationship as it had done, by and large, for the previous 60 years. The brutal revelation that this was in fact no longer the case came as a severe shock and explains the fury of British reactions to the diplomatic reverses inflicted on them by de Gaulle.

Much of the explanation for Britain's incapacity to solve the 'de Gaulle problem' can be found in the growing vulnerability of Britain's position. Certainly their hand was not a strong one. There is, however, evidence that they did not play those cards that they did hold with any great skill and that the question of de Gaulle was mishandled. Despite all the time and effort spent on attempting to fathom de Gaulle's thinking, there remained a good deal of incomprehension. Certainly de Gaulle himself cultivated an approach which left friends and foes alike unsure as to his real motives. Most importantly, however, the failure of both Macmillan and Wilson when they came up against de Gaulle was the result of their own indecision, their refusal to face up to Britain's changed international circumstances and to draw the necessary conclusions. The complaint of one French diplomat that Britain had 'more than one iron in the fire'[44] was basically justified: faced with a choice between a new approach to Europe and the continuation of its old links to the Commonwealth and the United States, both Macmillan and Wilson tried in vain to convince all concerned that the choice did not exist, that they were not incompatible. As long as they were unwilling to renounce in any meaningful way their extra-European connections the British were unable to convince de Gaulle to ease his opposition; the consequences were catastrophic for British foreign policy in its entirety. By the end of the 1960s, while some comfort was drawn from the conclusion that French foreign policy had been no more successful than their own, British diplomats were recognizing their diplomatic defeat at the hands of de Gaulle.

The balance sheet of British and French foreign policies during the years of de Gaulle's presidency is, therefore, hardly a positive one, a result which was in large part due to the failure to place Anglo-French relations on a more constructive footing. Instead London and Paris neutralized one another, setting themselves against the most fundamental foreign policy objectives of their so-called ally. In this they were not without success. Such achievements were, however, entirely negative. Perhaps both sides should have taken more heed of Macmillan's view (a view that he himself was not willing to back up with the necessary policy changes) that Britain and France were never as effective as when they worked as partners on the international stage. However, the repeated calls for such co-operation were made in vain and we are left wondering, as has so often been the case, what might have been achieved had Britain and France succeeded in working together rather than in opposition to one another.

Notes

1. FO 371 163494, CF 1022/1. 'Note on French Foreign Policy under de Gaulle', Rumbold, 9 January 1962.
2. FO 371 163494, CF 1022/43, Rumbold to Home, 23 August 1962.
3. FO 371 169115, CF 1022/25, Rumbold to Hood, 27 March 1963.
4. The British ambassador in Paris, Pierson Dixon, noted that 'the General has a long established relationship of friendship with the Prime Minister' (PREM 11/4230, Notes for Macmillan's Meeting with General de Gaulle, 14 December 1962).
5. Like many British politicians George Brown recorded that although he might disagree with him over policy 'in his presence you felt that you were in the presence of a really great man . . . I regard him as among the most outstanding human beings I have ever been privileged to meet' (Lord George Brown, *In My Way* (London: Victor Gollanez, 1971), p. 245).
6. FO 371 169107, CF1011/1, Annual Review for France, 3 January 1963.
7. PREM 11/3338, Dixon to Foreign Office, 15 November 1961.
8. FO 371 173342, WU 1074/44(A), Dixon to Foreign Office, 9 February 1963.
9. FO 371 169114, CF 1022/15/G, Report from the Bureau of Intelligence and Research, 26 January 1963.
10. FO 371 169124, CF 1051/41, Caccia Note, 6 May 1963.
11. FO 371 169116, CF 1022/42, Dixon to Foreign Office, 11 July 1963.
12. FO 371 169114, CF 1022/15/G, Shuckburgh to Hood, 20 February 1963.
13. FO 371 169114, CF 1022/10 (B), Dixon to Foreign Office, 6 February 1963.
14. FO 371 172070, F 1022/6/1022, Dixon to Home, 7 October 1963.
15. FO 371 172070, F1022/6/1022. Note by Overton, 24 October 1963.
16. FO 371 169124, CF1051/41. Note by Caccia, 6 May 1963.
17. One British diplomat concluded that 'if only the French people would send General de Gaulle back to Colombey-les-Deux-Églises this would be one of the most hopeful developments in international affairs' (FO 371 163494, CF 1022/43, Rumbold to Home, 23 August 1962). Even Couve de Murville advised the British 'to look ahead to a time when present personalities were no longer there' (FO 371 171447, M1092/89, Dixon to Foreign Office, 26 January 1963).
18. 'We can hardly be so presumptious', Dixon advised, 'as to put it among the objectives of our foreign policy to bring about the downfall of General de Gaulle. But at least we can include among those objectives the creation of conditions which will facilitate it' (FO 371169124, CF 1041/22/63, Dixon to Caccia, 2 May 1963).
19. FO 371 169124, CF 1051/47, Dixon to Home, 24 May 1963.

20. In November 1962 the British embassy in Paris reported that 'most observers thought that the Gaullists would lose seats, that the General would then have to take account of parliamentary opinion and even that within a year or so he might be out of power' (PREM 11/4230, 28 November 1962). In September 1963 Home thought there was a real liklehood of the fall of de Gaulle (FO 371 172070, F 1022/4/022, Record of a Conversation between Home and Rusk, 26 September 1963).
21. PREM 11 4230, 'Notes for the Prime Minister's Meeting with General de Gaulle' (Dixon), 14 December 1962.
22. See Harold Wilson quoted in *The Crossman Diaries: Selections from the Diaries of a Cabinet Minister, 1964–1970*, edited by Anthony Howard (London: Hamish Hamilton and Jonathan Cape, 1979), p. 308.
23. PREM 11/3775, Record of a Conversation at the Chateau de Champs, 3, June 1962.
24. The French record of British openings in the nuclear field are recorded in the Quai d'Orsay archives, Série 16, sous-série 24, dossier 1. Wapler au Quai d'Orsay, 19 January 1963.
25. One American participant in these talks recognized that the proposals were sure to 'outrage' de Gaulle. The General, he pointed out, 'was not one to wear anyone's cast off clothing' (George W. Ball, *The Past Has Another Pattern: Memoirs* (London: W. W. Norton, 1982), p. 268). Home's reaction that it was 'puzzling' why, if de Gaulle really wanted to develop France's nuclear capacity, he had refused the Polaris offer reveals an almost total lack of understanding of what made the General tick (FO 371 173513, Z8/36/G (B), CF 1192/28G, Home to Minister of Defence, 19 July 1963).
26. PREM 11 4224, Thorneycroft to Macmillan, 19 July 1963.
27. FO 371 169122, CF 1051/7, Tomkins to Hadow (News Department), 1 February 1963; FO 371 169122, CF 1051/7, Rumbold to Tomkins, 28 January 1963; FO 371 173341, WU 1074/25, Paper by Hood, 5 February 1963, 'Political Action after Brussels'.
28. FO 371 169114, CF 1022/10, Dixon to Foreign Office, 6 February 1963.
29. FO 371 169107, CF 1011/1, 3 January 1963, 'Annual Review for France, 1962'.
30. FO 371 169107, CF 1011/1, 3 January 1963 'Annual Review for France 1962'.
31. FO 371 169114, CG 1022/4, Note by Tomkins, 15 January 1963.
32. PREM 13/306 'Memorandum by the Foreign Secretary – EFTA–EEC links', 18 May 1965.
33. In 1961 Macmillan's private secretary was seriously advising that there existed an opportunity for Britain 'saving Europe by joining it' (PREM 11/ 3339 'Note for the Prime Minister', 19 May 1961). George Brown argued in his memoirs that 'Britain is destined to become the leader of Europe... I don't see where else leadership can come from other than from this country' (*In My Way*, pp. 202–5).
34. How, for example, could Wilson tell de Gaulle in 1965 that the Commonwealth and the Common Market were irreconcilable and two years later attempt to convince him of the opposite?
35. One British diplomat complained that 'it is part of General de Gaulle's method to take mysterious initiatives and then to add to the mystery by delphic utterances and ambiguous official comment' (FO 371 169114, CF 1022/13, Ledwige to Murray, 6 March 1963). Hood similarly noted 'we

cannot go into too much detail about what passed between General de Gaulle and Mr. Macmillan. Nor of course can anyone be dogmatic about what goes on in General de Gaulle's mind...this is not something on which one can present conclusive proof like a proposition of Euclid' (FO 371 173346, WU 1074/136(D), Hood to Dixon, 31 October 1963). At the Anglo-French summit meeting at Rambouillet in December 1962 Couve de Murville, when pressed by his British counterpart Lord Home for the exact meaning of one of de Gaulle's previous statements, had to admit that he himself did not know what the General had meant (PREM 11/4230, Record of a Conversation between Dixon and Couve, 16 December 1962).

36. Maurice Schumann told the British that the difficulties at the Rambouillet summit meeting in December 1962 'might have been due to a misunderstanding' (FO 371 169115, CF 1022/26, Leadbitter to Elliot, 28 March 1963). De Gaulle himself told Wilson in 1965 that 'it had to be admitted that relations between Britain and France were not clear and were not on a well-established basis at the moment. He felt that this was not merely because there were differences of outlook on world affairs, but also a number of misunderstandings which had arisen between the two countries' (PREM 13/317 'Record of a Conversation between the Prime Minister and General de Gaulle at the French Embassy, January 29, 1965').

37. Couve told Dixon that 'the General...had been disappointed by the Prime Minister's attitude. It had partly been the things that had been said but perhaps more important what had not been said. It was the psychological effect of all this on the General that mattered.' Dixon added 'I thought it would be going a little too far to suggest that the General should see a psychiatrist' (FO 371 169122, CF 1051/5, Dixon to Foreign Office, 19 January 1963). Another French official told the Foreign Office that de Gaulle 'had completely misunderstood what the Prime Minister had said to him on the nuclear defence issue at the last meeting at Rambouillet' (FO 371 169122, CF 1051/14/G, Note by Reilly, 1 April 1963).

38. Thorneycroft reported a conversation with Pierre Messmer during which the latter 'made it plain that what the French really wanted was British help over the nuclear issue. They would favour a package deal which would include a settlement of the Common Market and joint targeting of nuclear weapons ...Courcel spoke in the same sense' (PREM 11/4224, Thorneycroft to the Prime Minister, 19 July 1963). In 1966 Couve told Wilson and George Brown that 'they desired Franco-British association in the nuclear field' (PREM 13/1509, 'Record of a Conversation during the French Prime Minister's Luncheon for the Prime Minister at the French Embassy, 8 July 1966').

39. PREM 11/3775, Dixon to Foreign Office, 22 May 1962.

40. PREM 11/4230 'Record of a Meeting at Rambouillet on Sunday December 16, 1962'.

41. PREM 13/1509, Reilly to Stewart, 14 July 1966 'Pompidou's Visit to London, 6–8 July 1966'.

42. Britain's failures in Europe were obviously the most prominent examples. British difficulties in Rhodesia, Nigeria and in defending the value of sterling were also explained in London by the unreliability, and at times open hostility, of the French.

43. Quai d'Orsay, Série 16, sous-série 23, dossier 3/1. Courcel au Quai d'Orsay, 30 January 1963.
44. Quai d'Orsay. Série 16, sous-série 24, dossier 1. Wapler to Lucet, 26 March 1963. Why, the French diplomat asked, had the British never followed up earlier suggestions that Britain and France co-operate more actively in the nuclear field. This, he argued, was because 'le Premier Ministre courrait deux lièvres à la fois: Europe, États-Unis'.

13
Britain, France and Economic Planning in the 1960s: the Commissariat au Plan: Role Model or Counter-model?*

Jacques Leruez

When, in July 1961, Harold Macmillan's government decided, virtually overnight, to create planning institutions which owed a lot to the French example, neither the idea nor even the practice of 'planning' were really new to Britain. In the 1930s, there had existed, on both sides of the Channel, a debate on the pros and cons of 'planism', as it was called at the time.[1] The supporters of planning were above all Labour Party members and socialists, of course, but they also included senior civil servants, as well as some Conservative and Liberal politicians, such as future Prime Minister Harold Macmillan who had searched for a 'middle way' between capitalism and socialism and a 'socialist democracy'.[2]

Although in 1945 there existed a consensus in favour of increased state economic intervention, the Labour Party leaders, whose policies of nationalization were already arousing apprehension within the private sector, committed the error of using the term 'planning' in order to describe the controls apparatus that had been put in place during the war. This type of *dirigisme* was to be less and less tolerated in the late 1940s.[3] So, when the Conservatives returned to power in 1951, they had no difficulty in increasing their popularity by suppressing rationing (it had completely disappeared by 1953) and the 'controls'. While this was simply a matter of rejecting the *dirigiste* mechanism which had served its time, it was seen as an anti-planning crusade. The notion of economic planning was abandoned for ten years. It was to reappear under the guise of indicative planning *à la française*.

Economic planning revisited

The reasons

Resorting to economic planning under the Conservative government was the culmination of a period of national introspection on the role of Great Britain in world affairs, on the part she could still assume and on the best way of doing it.

What could then be wrong with the Conservative way of handling the economy when, in October 1959, they won their third general election in a row with 49.4 per cent of the votes cast and an overall majority of 100 seats in the Commons – a victory generally, and rightly, attributed to the current global economic prosperity? Britain, like her European neighbours, had indisputably experienced a period of economic expansion since 1951. However, it did hide a *relative* decline, even if it was not to be felt by the general public until after 1959. While the British average annual GNP growth was of 2.2 per cent between 1950 and 1960, it reached 3.5 per cent in France, 5.3 per cent in Italy and 6.5 per cent in West Germany. In 1960 the French GNP per capita overtook that of Britain for the first time since statistics had been collected, a feat that greatly shook British pride, all the more so as the relatively low proportion of productive investment (10 per cent a year at the start of the 1950s and 13 per cent in 1958–63, against respectively 14 and 16 per cent in the six countries of the Common Market) suggested an acceleration of this trend.[4] This relative decline was, be it right or wrong, attributed to the short-term economic management which prevailed at the time, and notably the famous *stop and go* cycles,[5] which were the result of the rudimentary demand regulation that formed the basis of Conservative economic policy during the 1950s.

The *stop-and-go* cycle was criticized for hindering economic growth both in the short and the long term. In fact, the companies that suffered most from the 'stop' periods were those which nurtured economic growth and sustained exports; this led to a certain apathy and reluctance to invest within British industry. It is therefore not surprising that the conversion to the idea of 'planning' developed first among British employers, but, of course, it had nothing to do with that of the postwar period, still tainted with the ideas of nationalization and intervention.

The campaign in favour of 'planning'

At the heart of this campaign was Hugh Weeks, who chaired the economic policy committee of the Federation of British Industry (FBI).[6] A trained economist who had worked as a civil servant, Weeks was the director of several companies such as the ICFC (Industrial and Commercial Finance Corporation), a semi- public organization created in 1945 in order to help small and medium-sized companies to modernize. He and his supporters, although a minority in the FBI, were to be at the root of what has been labelled as the 'Brighton revolution'.

Indeed, the FBI conference held in Brighton in November 1960 which debated on 'the next five years' marked an important turning point. Workshop number 3, one of the five it was divided into, chaired by Sir Hugh Beaver, managing director of Guinness, deemed that priority should be given to economic growth and demanded 'a more conscious attempt to assess plans and demands in particular industries for five or even ten years ahead'[7] and suggested, after having severely condemned *stop and go*, that the government should accept the idea of working with the world of industry to examine 'whether it would be possible to agree on an assessment of expectations and intentions which should be before the country for the next five years'.[8] These conclusions, although only advocated at the time by a minority in the FBI, were soon to become the quasi-official doctrine of the organization.

The institutional legacy of the 1940s and 1950s

Meanwhile, the most open-minded civil servants of the Treasury had also been converted to the virtues of long-term prospective.[9] Yet, for most of them, the country's problems were an inflated level of public expenditure, a balance of payments deficit, and inflation. In short, they thought it necessary to continue the incomes policy as broadly delineated by the Council on Prices, Productivity and Incomes – this council of three 'wise men' appointed in 1957 by Harold Macmillan and chaired by Lord Cohen, which had met regularly for the past four years and published four reports, all of which placed an emphasis on the disparity between the average rate of output growth and that of real incomes, the latter being twice as high as the former. There was also an Economic Planning Board, created by Sir Stafford Cripps in 1947, which had not produced any work since 1953. Yet the image of the EPB was too closely associated with wartime and post-war interventionism for its re-emergence to bring satisfaction to the reformers. This explains why a foreign model was adopted.

The French model

In 1961, the implementation of the Third Plan (1958–61) was coming to an end. Pierre Massé, the third *Commissaire général au Plan* after Jean

Monnet (1946–52) and Étienne Hirsch (1952–59), had taken over in February 1959 and would continue until January 1966. With the Third Plan, France came out of the reconstruction period to enter that of *Planning for Growth* (1962–75).[10] Despite political instability, economic and social crises and a change of Republic, 'indicative' planning went its way peacefully and in the late 1950s, one began to talk of a French 'economic miracle', like that of West Germany but with different methods.

The organization in London of a three-day conference on the French planning system, on 20–22 April 1961, acted as a significant turning point. The conference was at the initiative of a British senior civil servant of the OEEC and was held at the seat of the National Institute for Economic and Social Research (NIESR). The main French speakers, including the *Commissaire général*, Pierre Massé, were sent by the Plan itself and the minutes were to be published by the Political and Economic Planning (PEP) in issue 454 of its review, *Planning*. The French delegation was very skilfully composed and included a strong proportion of industrialists who regularly attended the modernizing committees of the Plan, with whom the British businessmen present could feel on equal footing. These industrialists were best placed to highlight the non-partisan character of the French planning system, something all British participants were not yet convinced of.

Pierre Massé's presentation naturally attracted the largest audience and his usual sense of rhetorics was at its best. He skilfully anticipated what he felt were to be the two major worries of the British: the risk of bureaucracy and the danger of governmental intervention. He insisted on how small the team of the Commissariat général was, on the 'uncertainty reducing' character (as he would later say), on the purely indicative nature of the sectoral programmes and on the way the Plan could be seen as 'a market study on a national scale'. Of course, he did not deny the interventionist framework within which French economic policy was operating, but he definitely understated the 'means of practical influence' (tax relief, credit facilities, low interest rates, various bonuses and subsidies) which were at the French state's disposal.[11] The aftermath of the debate showed that certain British participants were not entirely convinced by Massé's oratory. Besides he had not answered the question that concerned the British most: to what extent was the French planning system responsible for the high rate of growth in the French economy? It was difficult for Massé to give any precise answer since at the time the French leaders reaped in the benefits of expansion without really wondering about its origin.[12] The good light in which the planning system had been presented to the British perhaps explains what followed: they launched themselves into a planning experiment without the majority of the decision-makers being convinced of its necessity for Great Britain and they drew up two fine plans with little regard for the internal means and external conditions at the time of its implementation.

The government's decisions

Shortly after the FBI conference (November 1960), Selwyn Lloyd, Chancellor of the Exchequer since July, started to take a serious interest in the planning question. In no time, he submitted the idea to the Prime Minister who gave it a favourable reception. But he faced the opposition of the Treasury and of a large proportion of the Cabinet members, including the President of the Board of Trade, Reginald Maudling; all were hostile to an organization independent from the government and the administration. Another crisis of the balance of payments was needed (July 1961) for the Chancellor to take the risk of stating that he was not opposed to the creation of an organization 'certainly not [limiting] itself to the idea of some planning board within the Treasury'.[13] This statement was made during a two-day parliamentary debate (25–26 July), after he had announced a series of emergency measures including a nine- month wage freeze which, of course, was not the best way to conciliate the unions. So it was only on 25 January 1962, after six months of protracted negotiations – during which the trade unions had been given the assurance that there would be no short-term, authoritarian, incomes policy – that the General Council of the TUC decided, by 27 votes to 8, to take part in the planning council to come.

Planning under the Conservatives (March 1962–October 1964)

The National Economic Development Council

On 7 March 1962, therefore, an organization was born, which most contemporary observers only gave small hope of survival.[14] What the press took to nickname 'Neddy' was a two-tier organization: the Council itself, whose full name was the National Economic Development Council (NEDC), and a permanent office, the National Economic Development Office (NEDO). As requested by both the FBI and the TUC, it worked entirely out of the control of the government, even though it was funded on a state budget, and its staff did not have the status of civil servants. It constituted therefore what was later to be known as a 'quango' (quasi-autonomous non-governmental organization).

The 1962 list of council members was finalized only a few days before the first meeting. It comprised 20 members, 4 members serving ex officio (including 3 ministers: Finance, Trade and Labour, and the director-general of the NEDO) and 16 appointed members (6 representatives of private industry, 6 representatives of the unions affiliated to the TUC, 2 chairmen of the nationalized industries and 2 independent experts). It was to meet on a monthly basis with the Chancellor of the Exchequer in the chair. It was striking that the whole range of economic interests were not represented – agriculture was not, nor the service industries, the City, nor even the Bank of England. Obviously its main concern was industrial development, despite the fact that the tertiary sector was already the most important source of jobs in the British economy.

As for the Office, its permanent staff originally numbered 75 (around 100 between 1964 and 1970) and had three divisions. There was an administrative division (secretariat to the Council and personnel management), an economic division mainly in charge of global planning and an industrial division which took care of the problems and plans of specific industries. At its head a director-general was appointed by the government after consultation with the other partners: they were Sir Robert Shone (1962–66) and Fred Catherwood (1966–71) both of whom had previously held important positions in the private sector. The comparison with the Commissariat au Plan was naturally inevitable. The NEDO differed from the French Commissariat, however, both by its nature and by the source of its authority. In effect, the Commissariat au Plan was, and still is, of an essentially administrative nature, and derives its authority from being a branch of the executive power, and because the senior civil servants of the Plan are interchangeable with those of the Department of Finance and the INSEE (French National Institute of Statistics and Economic Studies), which play a large role in the conception and the execution of the Plan.

The Plan of the NEDC (1962)

From its second meeting (May 1962), the Council maintained as a working hypothesis a GNP rate of growth of 4 per cent a year, 'a figure of a reasonably ambitious nature to highlight the problems to overcome in order to reach an even faster growth'.[15] Why such a rate, when the average growth had hovered since the war around 2.5 per cent a year? There was no shortage of economic reasons. All the statistics showed that, good year or bad, the productive potential of British industry was growing by 3 per cent a year. Considering there existed a margin of untapped capacity for improvements in productivity, the NEDC thought an annual growth figure of 4 per cent was not unrealistic. Yet, compared with other rates of development attained by the rest of Europe, this target remained extremely modest. Moreover the Kennedy administration had just put forward the idea that the Western camp should fix themselves a target of a 50 per cent growth rate over ten years. Politically, therefore, it was the strict minimum for a government who wanted to give the impression that they did not accept the inevitability of economic decline.

Thus, when the NEDC Plan was published in February 1963,[16] after an enquiry had been made in 17 industrial branches throughout the summer of 1962, the target growth rate of 4 per cent was officially ratified by the government without anything having been done to put in place the structural reforms which would have allowed the economy to develop more healthily, although the NEDC was well aware of this necessity.[17] A comparative examination of the targets for growth of the NEDC and the results obtained (see Table 13.1) shows that the results were much below the proposed targets. Moreover, they were hardly progress compared to previous figures: the global GNP was growing by an average of 2.9 per cent per year (against 2.7 per cent per year between 1956 and 1961) and the GNP per capita grew very much at the same average as previously.

Besides, in 1962, the GNP increased by 1 per cent in volume; in 1964, a year of economic overheating, it increased by 5.73 per cent and in 1966, its growth fell to 1.4 per cent, because, in the meantime, it had

Table 13.1   NEDC's planning: main growth targets and actual outcome, 1961–66 (average annual percentage increase)

	NEDC projection	*Actual (1962–66)*
Gross domestic product	4.0	2.9
GDP per worker	3.2	2.2
Total fixed investment of which:	5.3	4.4
investment in manufacturing	3.3	0.2
public investment	7.0	6.4
Consumer expenditure	3.5	2.8
Public sector consumption	3.5	2.7
Exports	5.0	3.6
Imports	4.0	3.6

Source: Leruez, *Economic Planning*, Table 5.1, p. 118.

been necessary to take restrictive measures to cool down an overheated economy. The new economic cycle (1961–66) looked suspiciously like the previous one (1957–62).[18] In other words, the *stop-and-go* cycle continued as ever before. Equally worth noting was the direct link with the electoral cycle: the excesses of 1959 corresponded to the reflation budget of 1958, that of 1964 followed a budget in which the Chancellor used the targets of the NEDC Plan to stimulate demand. In each case, it was a question of using the 'feel good factor' at the time of an impending general election. If the campaign of 1958–59 had been successful (as it had already been in 1955), that of 1963–64 was also almost successful since Sir Alec Douglas Home's government, after having experienced a long period of extreme unpopularity, was only narrowly defeated in October 1964. This shows how the Plan was used for political purposes: it was to allow the Chancellor to embark with a perfectly clear conscience on a policy of growth at all costs, all this in perfect knowledge that this policy could not outlive the pre-election period.

Planning under the Labour government

In converting themselves to indicative planning and in creating Neddy in 1962, the Conservatives deprived Labour of one of their favourite economic proposals. The latter could no longer criticize the government's 'doctrinaire refusal to assume responsibility for planning our natural resources'.[19] Thus, when he became leader of the party in January 1963, Harold Wilson preferred to advocate a 'technological revolution'. Yet, the 'planning' slogan was not to be abandoned and in order to distinguish themselves from the Conservatives, Labour leaders were to emphasize the need for a planning system more integrated into the machinery of government, more 'purposive' (Harold Wilson), and with 'teeth in it' (George Brown). There was therefore no question of them simply being satisfied with the implementation of the Plan of the NEDC. Wilson was even to go as far as to suggest a growth rate of 8 per cent (twice that of the already optimistic NEDC target), a proposal that he quietly abandoned on becoming Prime Minister.

The Department of Economic Affairs (DEA)

The main duty of the DEA, created in October 1964 when Harold Wilson's Labour government came to office after 13 years of Conservative rule, was to co-ordinate the internal and external economic policies of the Cabinet in four ways: launching a national plan, an industrial policy, a regional planning system and an incomes policy. It was given a slight, theoretical, pre-eminence over the rest of the economic ministries, including the Treasury which traditionally ensured the co-ordination of the government's economic policies (in addition to its specific duties: management and control of public expenditure, fixing the level of tax revenue, foreign trade, etc.). Since the Treasury remained in charge of short-term budgetary and monetary policy, there was a risk that problems, or clashes, would arise between the two ministries. Of course, the Prime Minister was well aware of this, but he felt that the risk of 'creative tension' between the two bureaucracies, or even between the two ministers, was worth running.

One of the original aspects of the DEA was the presence of two men who were neither permanent civil servants nor politicians but who were nevertheless granted essential responsibilities. The director-general, both economic adviser to the minister and director of planning (Sir Donald MacDougall, an academic economist who had been the director of planning at NEDO from 1962 to 1964), and the co-ordinator of industrial policy (Fred Catherwood, a former private sector manager), headed a team of industrial advisers, also recruited from the private sector, whose role was to encourage consultation between the DEA and private firms. The DEA was the department with the most experts and specialists coming from all spheres, economists, industrial and scientific advisers, statisticians and planners. In spite of this the staff of the DEA never exceeded 600 people (544 in October 1965) compared with the 1580 of the Treasury and the 9500 of the Board of Trade.[20]

The creation of the DEA looked like a threat to Neddy's future. Yet it survived, although on a more modest scale. Instead of drawing up economic plans, the Council was expected to '[discuss] their formulation';[21] instead of recommending to the government 'measures of such a kind as to bring about expansion',[22] it could only review the measures proposed by the DEA and other ministries. Thus the social partners, especially the employers, were soon to be disappointed by the role left to the Council after the initial hopes of the years 1962–64.

As for NEDO, if it was no longer the Commissariat général du Plan, which it had never really been, it was to see its influence grow within the large industrial sectors, thanks to the creation of permanent economic development committees (EDCs) which the press would quickly call 'little Neddies'. If the creation of these committees had been decided before October 1964, it was only from the change of government that they were really to develop. Indeed, from a mere 9 at the end of 1964, they would number 21 by the time of the June 1970 general election.

The major sectors of production were to have their own development committee. These were agriculture, construction, chemicals, civil engineering, clothing, distributive trades, electrical engineering, electronics, food manufacturing, hosiery and knitwear, hotels and catering, machine tools, mechanical engineering, cars, distribution and repair of motor vehicles, paper and board, printing and publishing, rubber, wool textiles, post office and exports. Apart from the latter, these were 'vertical' committees in the manner of the French *Plan*.

The composition of these committees almost always followed the same pattern: 45 per cent of the members were business managers, mostly private, but the nationalized sector was also represented, 20 per cent trade unionists, 23 per cent independent experts (of whom almost half were NEDO representatives) and 12 per cent representatives of the departments (with the mandatory inclusion of an industrial adviser from the DEA). The years 1964–70, despite the relative decline of the NEDC, therefore constituted the golden age of what was known as 'tripartism', i.e. the collaboration of the government and the industrial partners, through a consultative process aimed at making governmental decisions more acceptable. This incited one of the industrial directors of NEDO to conclude that the creation of the committees had allowed 'a new development in relations between the government and industry'.[23]

The National Plan of 1965

The challenge for the new government was to reconcile its pledge to do better than the Conservatives, and the necessity to adapt the growth targets, which had to be lower not higher because of the short-term measures it had been forced to adopt when coming to office in order to curb demand in the face of a balance of payments deficit estimated at £800 million in October 1964. The outcome was that the National Plan was conceived for a period of six years (that of the NEDC was for a five-year period) with a growth rate of 25 per cent (around 3.8 per cent per annum) as opposed to a rate of 22 per cent for the previous plan (or 4 per cent per annum) over five years.

The method used to prepare the Plan was not very different from that used in 1962 by the economic division of the NEDO. Hence the recourse to an industrial inquiry similar to the one NEDO conducted in 1962, the only difference being that this inquest was extended to all industrial sectors (as against 17 in 1962). The major disadvantage of the chosen method was to be found in the main question put to each sector. They were not asked how they saw the future as it concerned them, but rather how they saw their development possibilities within the hypothetical framework of a growth rate of 25 per cent throughout the economy, which suggested to an observer that 'far from being directive or even incentive, [the Plan] was simply conditional'.[24] However, as the Plan itself confessed, 'the original estimates by industry gave a significantly lower increase in total output',[25] hence reservations and doubts, even in the milieus most favourable to planning, to say nothing of the more sarcastic remarks of the neo-liberal members of the Institute of Economic Affairs: 'only the credulous could believe that such a nice round figure [25 per cent] was the invention of science'.[26] As for the general public, despite the presentation of the Plan on television by George Brown, they showed a total indifference. Four days after its publication, a polling organization, Research Services Limited, discovered that more than 50 per cent of men and seven out of ten women had never heard of it![27] Yet Wilson employed a Gaullist-like oratory to describe the Plan: in the absence of *'ardente obligation'*, he spoke of a 'central strategy set out for all the nation to see'.[28] By July of the same year, however, the Plan had virtually been abandoned.

Confronted by ever-growing economic difficulties, notably a permanent balance of payments crisis, the Labour government went on taking more and more severe measures in order to curb demand, while at the same time refusing to even consider a change in the parity of the pound which most observers deemed clearly overvalued (the last devaluation dated back to 1948). These short-term difficulties explained the scepticism the Plan was generally welcomed with. The real turning point on this issue, however, only came about on 20 July 1966. After a new spectacular sterling crisis and several frantic days (rife with rumours of an imminent devaluation), the Prime Minister announced that Great Britain was to benefit from a substantial international loan (£413 million), that the pound was to be 'saved' once more but that a period of austerity was beginning. Direct and indirect taxes were raised, budget cuts announced, salaries and prices frozen for six months and the bank rate raised to 7 per cent – at that time a considerable figure. It could no longer be pretended that the announced expansion had not been abandoned. The head of the DEA admitted this before the House of Commons: 'I will be absolutely frank with the House; it means that the rate of growth we intended to set, and on the basis of which we predicted all other things for 1970, is no longer available'.[29] He offered to resign but his resignation was rejected;[30] yet, in August, he swapped places with the Foreign Secretary, Michael Stewart.

Once again, as under the Conservatives, the 'defence' of the pound had been put before the needs of expansion; consequently, the Plan was never considered 'the central strategy of the nation' the Prime Minister said it was to be. Indeed, its strategy, and notably the target for an annual increase of exports of 5.25 per cent, rested on a dramatic reorientation of foreign trade which could only be provoked by a substantial devaluation. But the Prime Minister would not hear nor talk of devaluation[31] and only resigned himself to it in November 1967 when he could find no other way out. This is not to say, of course, that if the devaluation had taken place earlier, the targets of the plan would have automatically been met. Simply, the devaluation was necessary in order for the Plan to keep a minimum credibility. Ironically, the only target of the plan (see Table 13.2) which was to be exceeded was that of exports, as the mechanical effects of the 1967 devaluation and of the recovery measures which followed.

The DEA survived the failure of planning by three years only. It disappeared in October 1969, during a ministerial reshuffle, not without having published, at the beginning of the year, a 'planning document'[32] that it was careful not to call a plan. The indicative planning experiment *à la française* was brought to an end in Britain. Of course, Neddy survived until 1992, as well as some of its committees, but it was less a question of planning than of consultation, more often than not without effect, especially during the Thatcher years. The failure of economic planning equally meant the decline of tripartite consultation which was one of the signposts of the French model. The partners of industry, however, had well adapted themselves to the type of participation required by the Plan. It is interesting to note that, thanks to these structures, the trade unionists had been brought along with the employers in discussing

Table 13.2 The National Plan: targets and achievements

	Targets for 1970 (basis 100 = 1964)	Actual economic growth in 1970
Gross national product	125	114
Household consumption	121	113
Running costs of the public sector	119	112
Investment	138	120
Exports	136	142
Imports	126	132
Production per capita:		
(i) Gross internal product	121	116
(ii) Industrial production	128	120
(iii) Manufacturing production	124	119

Source: W. Beckerman (ed.), *The Labour Government's Economic Record*, Table 4.1, p. 174.

economic issues of national importance such as the balance of trade, the consequences of devaluation and the problems of competitiveness and profitability. After 1979, however, with the unions on the defensive, the tripartite discussions no longer held any interest for the employers or the government.

Today, when the French planning system itself is in crisis, it is somewhat unfair to criticize the illusions held by the British planners. After all, their misinterpretation of the real role of the French plans was largely suggested by the French theoreticians themselves. In effect, indicative planning was too quickly labelled as an instrument of growth acceleration when it was essentially, on the one hand, a means of programming heavy investment and, on the other, a process of redistribution of the products of growth. One is more aware of this nowadays. No doubt, it is this misinterpretation which led to the belief that the coherence of these plans was more important than their implementation and which best explains the almost solely incantatory and symbolic character that British planning took on.

Notes

*Translated by Helen Robert, Emily Taylor and Philippe Chassaigne.

1. On this subject, see Jacques Leruez, 'Le Débat politique à propos de la planification économique, 1929–1939' (Paris: Faculty of Law and Economics, 1966, typewritten).
2. Harold Macmillan, *Reconstruction* (London, 1933), and *The Middle Way* (London, 1938).
3. See Jacques Leruez, *Economic Planning and Politics in Britain* (London: Martin Robertson, 1975), pp. 17–77, and also Samuel Brittan, *The Treasury under the Tories* (London: Pelican, 1964).
4. In practice, because of the deceleration of the French economy after the '30 Glorious Years' (1945–75), the discrepancy between French and British achievements, though still significant, was less impressive than had been thought during the 1970s. With regards to Italy, even if her GDP per capita overtook that of Britain only in 1987, it is now very close to that of France. In 1995, the GDP per capita of the three countries had settled at $19 955 (France), $19 536 (Italy) and $18 360 (UK). In 2000, of course, the strength of the pound and the weakness of the euro have to a large extent upset these rankings.
5. For a detailed description of the *stop-and-go* cycle, see Leruez, *Economic Planning*, pp. 83–4.

6. The FBI (Federation of British Industry) was the most representative organization of industrial employers. In 1965 it joined with the BEC (British Employers' Confederation) and the NABM (National Association of British Manufacturers) to form the Confederation of British Industries, or CBI.

7. Federation of British Industry, *The Next Five Years: Report of the Brighton Conference of November 1960*, p. 48.

8. Ibid.

9. This conversion was largely due to the Plowden Report (published in July 1961: *Control of Public Expenditure. The Plowden Report on the Machinery of Government*, Cmnd 1432). In addition to a reform of the departmental structures of the Treasury (see Leruez, *Economic Planning*, pp. 101–10), the Plowden Report recommended the planning of public expenditure over a period of several years. This recommendation quickly led to a first long-term document: *Public Expenditure in 1963–64 and 1967–68*, Cmnd 2235, December 1963.

10. According to the terminology of the pamphlet: *Cinquante ans de Planification à la Française* (Paris: Commissariat Général du Plan, 1996), p. 40.

11. For a more detailed analysis of Pierre Massé's intervention and the reactions that this provoked, see Leruez, *Economic Planning*, pp. 88–9.

12. One of the first works to try to search precisely into the causes (which turned out to be multiple and complementary) of French growth was: J. J. Carré, P. Dubois and, E. Malinvaud, *La Croissance française. Un essai d'analyse économique causale de l'après-guerre* (Paris, 1972).

13. House of Commons, 645, col. 484, 26 July 1961.

14. Still, Neddy was 30 years old when it was abolished, in November 1992, by Norman Lamont, Chancellor of the Exchequer in the second Major government. Yet it is true that it had only been a shadow of its former self since the beginning of the Thatcher era.

15. NEDC, *NEDO. History and Function*, July 1962, p. 7.

16. NEDC, *Growth of the United Kingdom Economy to 1966* (London: HMSO, February 1963).

17. *Conditions Favourable to Faster Growth* (London: HMSO, April 1963).

18. For a comparative graph of the economic cycles 1957–62 and 1961–66 see Leruez, *Economic Planning*, pp. 134–5.

19. *Signposts for the Sixties: a Declaration Adopted at the Labour Party Conference in Blackpool*, 2–6 October 1961.

20. Up to the creation of the Department of Trade and Industry in 1970, the Board of Trade was responsible for the whole of the business world.

21. Sir Robert Shone, 'The Machinery of Economic Planning: II – The National Economic Development Council', *Public Administration*, Spring (1966), 21.

22. Ibid.

23. T. C. Fraser, 'A New Development in Relations between Government and Industry', *Journal of Management Studies*, May (1967).

24. R. Opié, 'Economic Planning and Growth' in W. Beckerman (ed.), *The Labour Government's Economic Record: 1964–1970* (London: Duckworth, 1972).

25. *The National Plan*, Cmnd 2764 (London: HMSO 1965), Ch. II, p. 24.

26. J. Brunner, *The National Plan* (London: Eaton Papers, no. 4, 1965).

27. Reported by I. Gilmour, *The Body Politic* (London, 1969), p. 12.

28. Speech broadcast on the radio on 29 March 1966 during the electoral campaign. The election was held on 31 March.
29. House of Commons 732, col. 1849, 27 July 1966.
30. The Prime Minister had just accepted the resignation of the unionist Frank Cousins, Minister of Technology, who had rejected the freeze in salaries and wages.
31. So much so that in Whitehall he was given the nickname of 'Parity-Harold'. The word 'devaluation' was unmentionable in official committees. On this real mental block of the Prime Minister and the Chancellor of the Exchequer, J. Callaghan, see Leruez, *Economic Planning*, pp. 180–2; Beckerman, *The Labour Government*, pp. 59–64 and Ben Pimlott, *Harold Wilson* (London: Cape, 1992), pp. 404–92.
32. *The Task Ahead, Economic Assessment to 1972* (London: HMSO, 1969).

14
Lionel Jospin–Tony Blair: Building a Comparison

François-Charles Mougel

Can it be anything but risky, not to say presumptuous, to try one's hand at building a comparison between Lionel Jospin and Tony Blair? And indeed, it may be risky to try and assess such a contemporary stretch of time, when the main actors are still in place and their policies are still being implemented. Yet this is the stuff contemporary history is made of and its historian has no reason to shy from mapping out the similarities between the two Premiers: after all, the two of them came to power at the same time, in the spring of 1997, they do belong to the same family of democratic socialists and, last but not least, they rule two nations whose destinies have been closely intertwined for centuries. Our purpose will then be to highlight both the similarities and the dissimilarities between these two Premiers – in doctrine as well as in political practice –, trusting in time to tell whether our tentative conclusions happened to hold some elements of truth.

Differing ideological positions?

Beyond the inevitable and obvious differences in style, generation or political career between a youngish and charismatic Tony Blair, whose political career is a success story in every sense, and the austere-looking sexagenarian Lionel Jospin, whose march to power has been more chequered, most of the dissimilarities between the two men are accounted for by their differences in ideology and positions in their respective power networks.

The standard-bearers of two different brands of socialism

For Tony Blair, socialism is embodied in the Labour Party both as an ideology and as a governmental practice. On the doctrinal level, Labour has its roots firmly set in the 1918 Constitution which associates the practice of parliamentary democracy and the desire to build a society of 'collective' justice and social progress, as expressed in its Clause 4.[1] Radical, if not marxist, in principle, but pragmatist in method, this led the party to great achievements when in power, but its very ambivalence has also fuelled constant struggles between a socialist left wing and a revisionist right wing. The leadership of the party was then caught between two fires: the rather revisionist stance that prevailed up to 1979 succeeded the leftist about-turn of the 1979–85 period, until Neil Kinnock and John Smith started an ideological *aggiornamento* that proved long and difficult to achieve. Ideologically speaking, where did Labour stand in 1994? Still keen on social justice and social progress, it was devoted to the upholding of the Welfare State; if faithful to the principle of managed economy, it did not believe in its 'socializing' any longer; concerned about national identity, there was no longer any talk of unilateral disarmament and it had rallied round the Western and European flag.[2] Talking about the establishment of a 'Socialist Commonwealth of Britain' – 1945 style[3] – was no longer relevant; Labour had turned into a social democratic party without having to change its dogma, however remote from a moderate electoral programme.

Born in 1900 out of the unions and various socialist think tanks, the Labour Party inherited from the years spent in government a culture of power which in turn is a two-faceted one. The internal life of the party, a mass organization with millions of members,[4] is organized along democratic lines, and the block vote system gives the unions and the grass-roots members an overwhelming weight in the policy-making process. The control of the three key structures of the party – the annual Conference, the National Executive Committee, the leadership[5] – proved to be paramount. Up to 1979 the party had succeeded in keeping a somewhat balanced ideological and functional stance, and had been rather reformist in consequence. In 1980 the balance swung to the left. Its subservience to the unions and to its left wing gave the party a bad image in the public at large; in the clutch of the unions, demagogic and maximalist, it was widely perceived as unfit for power and had to suffer four electoral defeats in a row. Hence Neil Kinnock's and John Smith's efforts to democratize and modernize the Party: the 'Loony Left' tendency was expelled, the OMOV system (one member one vote) was made the rule, and an ambitious recruiting campaign launched, all this while the programme was given a distinctive left-of-centre content.

From an external point of view, Labour's power ethos derives from its position as the second great British political party, not only virtually the one and only political representative of the whole Left, but also, in a bipartisan political structure, the main opponent to the Conservatives. In the early 1990s, the Labour Party was eager to get rid of the unfortunate memories left by the MacDonald, Wilson or Callaghan governments, or by the contestation-ridden leaderships of Hugh Gaitskell and Michael Foot, to pose as the real heir to the Attlee government, those mythical years of 1945–51 when the grounds of a 'model democracy' were laid in Britain. But what Labour needed to restore its image and to regain political credibility, internal structural reforms and a renewed legitimacy, was far from achieved. When elected as the new leader on 21 July 1994, Tony Blair stood at the crossroads of these two traditions, as intricate, and even contradictory, as they were. There was then no other choice than to carry on with party reform. The 'Blair Revolution' was just about to start.[6]

For Lionel Jospin, conversely, socialism is a powerful ideal which has come a long way, under the guise of a host of political parties (PSF, SFIO, PS).[7] By tradition, French socialism has always relied on syncretism, has never been formally codified, theorized nor institutionalized. This dates basically back to the synthesis operated by Jean Jaurès early in the twentieth century, binding together the Republican tradition, idealistic progressivism and theoretical marxism. However, when the SFIO, the United Socialist Party, split up at the Tours Conference of December 1920, the new Communist Party (PCF) proclaimed to be the real heir to French socialism. While still posing in theory as a 'revolutionary' party, the SFIO was bound to be reformist in practice, mainly for tactical reasons. Often criticized as 'revisionist', ridden by a multitude of factions, constantly wavering between fierce opposition and support to the institutions, bitterly divided over the main diplomatic issues of the day – the Second World War, decolonization, the cold war, the 1968 'revolution' – the party finally died out of its own contradictions in 1969. Whether the birth of the new Socialist Party (PS) in 1969, taken over by François Mitterrand at the Epinay Conference two years later, did radically change the ideological content of French socialism is still a moot point. The theoretical underpinnings of the French Socialist Party are still ambiguous, combining, in a reformist perspective, marxian anticapitalism and egalitarian dirigisme on the one side, and the Republican, secularist and progressive tradition that can be traced back to the French Revolution on the other. Moreover, it did not preclude the passing of electoral alliances with the other left-wing parties, as shown at the time of the 1972 Common Platform with the Communist and the Left Radical parties. This idealistic and syncretic programme – complete with the catchy slogan 'How to change life' – allowed the party at last to come to power in 1981. Yet its original ambition to regenerate the country was to break on the hard rocks of reality. When running for the French presidency, François Mitterrand codified socialism in the guise of his '110 Propositions'; when in power, he tried to conceal the fact that his practice had turned to be social democratic at best, at worst 'centrist', as Mitterrand's 1988 'Letter to the French', or the 1988 and 1993 Socialist electoral manifestos, all testify. The French Socialist Party was unable to present itself as a model for a united Left; it was divided among many factions – call them either jacobinist, co-operativist, marxist, libertarian, idealistic or realistic – and left virtually stranded after the infamous 1990 Rennes Conference; moreover, its lack of any programmatical *aggiornamento* like that of Germany's SPD at the 1959 Bad Godesberg Conference meant that it could not even be presented as a real ideology.

Composite as it was in its doctrine, French socialism was equally complex in its power ethos. The 1906 Amiens Charter had stated that it would maintain the links with the trade unions, yet stand independent from them. Its main objective was mainly a political one, neither sociological nor cultural: the victim of its own internal divisions, it was to appear first and foremost as a classical political party, with leaders and militants – at best only 200 000–300 000 strong members, and often very much less. Its image was that of an opposition party that in the past had been deeply divided over the issue of governmental participation. The Popular Front, its major historical reference, could not even be entirely claimed as its own. The years spent in power during the Fourth Republic were certainly not beyond criticism; they were more a liability than an asset, be it in the eyes of the Right or of the other parties of the French Left. Moreover, the Mitterrand years (1981–95) did show that the Socialist Party was a viable party of government and scored noticeable achievements, but it did not enhance its prestige in a very significant way: did it not fail in 1986 and in 1993? Jean Jaurès, Léon Blum or Paul Faure may stand out as the main figureheads of its history, Guy Mollet is a reminder of its failures and François Mitterrand of its ambiguities.[8]

From 1995 on, Lionel Jospin was bound to position himself within this seminal yet often contradictory tradition. He was an heir to it, as much as a former actor of it. Yet he stood on much more uncertain ground than Tony Blair did the year before. He was a prisoner of the past history of socialism to a much higher degree than of its dogma, as there was neither a Constitution for him to amend, nor a party to recast. At most, he could claim that Mitterrand's legacy – that is, what his party stood for – had to be 'assessed'. While Tony Blair could pose as a new man – at least relatively speaking – Lionel Jospin looked much more archaic or old-fashioned.

Differing doctrinal intakes and differing political stances

As a leader, Tony Blair had to face up two formidable challenges: firstly, to adapt Labour's position to the then current Thatcher revolution, and, secondly, to make of this the most potent electoral asset possible. In order to do so, he was to implement thorough ideological and program-matical reforms, a grand strategy that would hopefully lead him to power and give him the chance to mould his 'New Britain'.

Tony Blair wanted first of all to exorcize the past, by carefully shun-ning any reference to the very notion of 'socialism' or, at the very least, only mentioning it in the light form of 'social-ism';[9] 'old Labour' (with a small o) was to embody all the negative side, while in contrast 'New Labour' (with a capital N) was to present the new, innovative, message. New Labour was the outcome of democratic socialism – seen as different from social democracy – in a way that allowed him to claim the liberal legacy and all of British civic culture as his own, but at the same time with a much more modern approach: this is what 'radical centrism' is all about. Firmly located in the left-of-centre of politics, the New Labour that Tony Blair describes at length in his book *New Britain*, has three major stances: a philosophical and spiritual dimension that is directly derived from the Protestant and the progressive idealistic tradition; a new, solidarist version of the old 'one nation' rhetoric taken from the Tories; finally, a pledge to share a common responsibility in the man-agement of public affairs and in the rights and duties of modern citizen-ship – that is, to implement the 'stakeholder society'. For Tony Blair, this is the way to rediscover 'ethical socialism', the very essence of Labour's ideology. Both a moral and political scheme, it aims at the regeneration of Britain as the 'young country' emerging out of a bleak past when both 'old Labour' and the 'New Right' had it wrong. Hence the four main reforms he advocates: to improve the standard of living thanks to eco-nomic growth; to make solidarity the cornerstone of the new social order to come; to implement the constitutional reforms that will reju-venate British democracy; to restore Britain's place in the world.

These intentions were swiftly translated into reality. Tony Blair, who had succeeded in reorganizing the Labour Party along more democratic lines,[10] could finally modernize it with the rewriting in democrat-social-ist terms of Clause 4 backed by a massive and democratic ballot. From then on, the gap between ideology and practice has been filled in a way that should reduce the old cleavages between left and right, trade unions and the leadership, grassroots members and electors. Labour was able to enjoy a degree of unity and a credibility that will prove to be indispensable in future years. In the meantime, Tony Blair was to use machiavellian devices with the Tories. On the one hand, he kept stigmatizing them for their mistakes, either in economic, social or European matters, or even for their individualist and amoral positions in order to pose as the champion of 'society' and collective civic virtues, of progressive economy and a down-to-earth approach to Europe and the wider world. Yet, on the other hand, he was eager to protect most of the Thatcher–Major legacy, that is financial orthodoxy, the law and order stance, employment flexibility, privatization and trade union legislation, even if he had to default them on its predecessors. Eager not to appear as 'Tory Blair', the Labour leader encapsulated all this in his moralistic vision of a new social order based on family, education and the 'stakeholder society' – when it was simply not on the mere notion of 'change'.[11] Thanks to all these programmatical reforms, Tony Blair took his party to victory on Labour Day, 1997.

With 419 seats out of 659, Labour had an overwhelming majority in front of a divided opposition where the Tories numbered a mere 163: it was fully secure for the whole of its term. Moreover, the ideological defeat of Thatcherism and the command that, on top of his electoral legitimacy, Tony Blair has over his party means that Labour is safer in power than at any moment in history, with the exception of the 1945 Attlee government. Having very little to fear from both left and right, New Labour is left free to stand in the centre or left-of-centre of British politics, to start renovating the country. The Tories could be pushed to the margins of the political spectrum, and the Liberal Democrats made overtly sympathetic: because of the very structure of the British political system, Tony Blair is among the most powerful heads of government of the West.

Lionel Jospin's situation is perceptibly different. When he returned to the French political scene in 1995, he was as much a potential figurehead for the whole of the Left as the leader of the Socialist Party. He did not have to redefine an ideology or to reform his party from the roots; yet he had his own aims to reach and his own convictions to assess. In his book *L'Invention du possible*[12] (1991), he explained what he stood for, as an individual if not as a party leader. He made clear what socialism meant to him: a bundle of values such as democracy, liberty, equality, solidarity, secularity or progress. In a word, these were run-from-the-mill Republican values, and Jospin, sticking to the old humanist ideal, discarded all ideology as being too constraining or even totalitarian. Such an idealism, as deep-rooted and forbearing as it was, allowed him to stand as far as he could from both the far Right and the far Left, from neo-liberalism and communism. Firmly believing in the primacy of politics, he sees the state, democratic, impartial and progressive, as the main way through which to achieve his major aims: a managed economy leading to economic growth and full employment; social change through civic education; the continuous fight for left-wing values as opposed to all kinds of extremism or exclusion. His version of socialism stands midway between Paul Brousse's 'possibilism' and Jean Jaurès's voluntarism, firmly rooted in a sense of French identity and very much akin to Blum's 'transformist' conception expressed in *A l'échelle humaine*.[13] The heir to the values of 1789, of 1848 and of the Resistance, he considers that history acts as a spur to modernity: he rejects revolutionary ideals, praises high pragmatic action, and stands critical to all the excesses of the Socialist Party in power, in the years 1981–95. He wants to make sense.

With skill and modesty he knew, from 1995 on, how to put the Socialist Party in marching order, both from an ideological point of view and as an electoral machine, and unexpectedly won the spring 1997 snap election. When he was appointed Prime Minister on 7 June 1997, his legitimacy did not stem from his role as First Secretary of the Socialist Party – constitutionally he had to resign from it – nor from his status as the standard-bearer of democratic socialism. It came from his status as the leader of the 'plural Left' (*gauche plurielle*) – which in turn explains the absence of any explicit ideological reference, even to socialism or the Left, in the governmental declaration of 20 June 1997. He may have defeated the Right whose 253 seats count little in the face of the 319 seats of his majority: the Socialists numbered only 250, the rest were Communists, Greens, Radicals or MDC, all of them upholding values and ambitions different from his own. Moreover, the presence of a right-wing President of the Republic was to set clear limits to his action: the new Premier could of course use to the full the powers implied in the 20th article of the French Constitution, but he also had to take into account the prerogatives, be they constitutional or customary, of a President who was drawn from another side of the political spectrum. France, in June 1997, had not given herself over to the Socialist Party: its programme was only a part of a wider political project that concerned the whole of the Left, and its mastering of the political system was only partial.

Even if not diametrically opposed, two distinct brands of democratic socialism did come to power on both sides of the Channel in the spring of 1997. Yet, beyond these ideological, institutional and programmatical differences, it is quite possible to see how Lionel Jospin and Tony Blair were led, or even bound, to co-operate.

What similarities?

It must be noted first that, as people, the two Premiers can indeed be compared since they both share a meritocratic and Protestant background; they are also prone to contextualize their action in a wider intellectual perspective and put it in a similar ambition; yet it is in the aims of their political action that most similarities can be found.

A similar approach

This stems from a common intention to place democratic socialism as the main source of public interest. This was clearly expressed in the Queen's Speech of 14 May 1997, written by Tony Blair: 'My government intends to govern for the benefit of the whole nation', the Prime Minister adding in the following debate: 'We are a one-nation party, our mandate to modernize what is outdated and to make fair what is unjust and to do both by the best means available, irrespective of dogma or doctrine and without fear or favour'. This echoes what Jospin wrote in his book: 'for me, creating regulations and concepts for a new democratic socialism implies the refusal of ideology and the acceptance of plain reality in order to understand and transform it. And to do this one needs ideas and values.'[14] Instead of being sectarian, ideology must appear as a factor of unity and renewal. The Labour manifesto put it clearly: 'New Labour is a party of ideas and ideals but not of outdated ideology. What counts is what works. The objectives are radical. The means will be modern'. The same theme is echoed by Jospin in his governmental declaration of 20 June 1997:

> the French people chose this new majority because they thought it was the best qualified not to make 'change' in an abstract way but to make specific changes. . . . In this respect I intend to use to the full the mandate I received from the people to give them back something precious but which has been forgotten: a purpose, i.e. to give the country a new sense of identity and a new program of action.

To fulfil this objective he proposed a dual contract: a 'Republican pact' and a programme of development and solidarity. For the sake of regeneration, there was on both sides of the Channel the same will to go beyond existing cleavages in the name of a modern conception of democratic socialism: the 'third way'. Just as Tony Blair wanted this new concept to become the fundamental basis of an international alliance bringing together the socialist democrats of Europe and the American Democrats,[15] Lionel Jospin in his July 1998 visit to Tony Blair advocated 'a third way, in the French way'. The two prime ministers agreed on the same attitude – 'volontarism, reformism, realism' – and this was to be the very basis of the democratic socialist compact, what Lionel Jospin called 'a right balance between economic efficiency and social justice', and Tony Blair 'the alliance between economic efficiency and social justice'.[16] If, as underlined by the French Minister for European Affairs Pierre Moscovici, 'Blair has an ideological approach and Jospin a pragmatic approach', their aim is the same: using politics, and thus the state, to transform society through economy in the name of progress and social justice. As the two of them put it: 'Yes to a market economy, no to a market society.'[17] This led to a consensus both on values and methods. On values, since it was a way of bringing together neo-socialism, modernity and progress for all – the stakeholder society meeting the Republican compact of development and solidarity. On methods, since it was a way of avoiding every suspicion of archaism, sectarism or ideologism (be it old Labour or Mitterrand style) – 'there are no ideological taboos, what is important is what really works' Tony Blair says.[18]

Such similar views on the aims of politics and of 'practical ideology' are based on a strong societal consensus, first of all within the respective political families of both prime ministers. Tony Blair wants the whole of Labour to rally around his flag, but also the Liberal Democrats and, if possible, the Greens and the libertarian Left. His July 1998 governmental reshuffle was to point in this direction, and he has been busy keeping the left wing of the party silent on his planned reforms of the Welfare State, making New Labour the party of all the middle classes, the very classes that are supposed to make the whole of the nation. In a similar voluntary and realistic style, Lionel Jospin wishes, if not to build a 'New France' akin to Blair's 'New Britain', to put his governmental project firmly at the heart of the 'plural Left' by synthesizing the various, not to say contrasted or contradictory, demands of his allies and partners. Furthermore, both heads of government aim at attracting those of the right-wing voters who happen to be dissatisfied with their own political family. There is no doubt that Tony Blair has a certain appeal for left-of-centre Tories and he did not shun at offering them an alliance on European matters. Lionel Jospin tries to woo the French centrists, and he has even found an unsuspected ally in Jacques Chirac, whose crusade against the 'social fracture' and in favour of a 'third way' are well known. All of this, of course, in the perspective of general elections to be held in 2001 and 2002 on both sides of the Channel, with the prospect in France of a concomitant, and highly sensitive, Presidential election. Finally, the two Prime Ministers aim at federating the European social democratic parties – from Scandinavia, Italy and, since 27 September 1998, Germany – around them in an alliance advocating a progressive programme at the scale of the European Union. The June 1999 European elections, although unfavourable to Labour, due to a new voting system, proved that a majority of European citizens share in this new ideological approach that cuts accross nations, classes and values.

A last common feature lies in the very mechanics of power. Tony Blair and Lionel Jospin both believe that politics matter first and they want to be firmly in control to implement the changes in a voluntary way. This explains the 'presidentialization' in style – even if this notion does not have the same meaning on both sides of the Channel – that has become conspicuous after several years in power. Both of them fully use their own networks to manage their parties and Cabinets as well as to seduce their electorate (see their 'spin doctors' clusters). These networks extend far beyond the state technostructure: as national leaders, Jospin and Blair alike know how to use their countries' respective elite system. As a new member of the British establishment, Blair enjoys active support from the City and a significant part of the business community, from the worlds of culture or the media, without severing the traditional links with the trade unions. Similarly, Jospin tries to reach the same spheres – business, media, intellectuals – beyond his original background of the teaching and trade unionist world. The old-fashioned cleavages between capital and labour, Left and Right, modernity and tradition, fade in the face of an emerging modernizing stance, and the two heralds of democratic socialism are just about to turn the elites of their respective countries, traditionally deemed 'conservative', into something more progressive that they will eventually use to their maximum advantage.[19]

The issues at stake

Both the Queen's Speech of 14 May 1997 and Lionel Jospin's governmental declaration of 20 June 1997 show how close the two governments are in terms of aims and stakes. Five main fields of policies can be underlined. Firstly, the restoration of a more 'real' citizenship, based on a new pact between the state and the people built on a better definition of mutual rights and duties, an institutionalized devolution, a better-defined national identity and a new conception of the role of the state. All this to avoid the dangers of overcentralization, bureaucratism, sleaze and lack of sense of responsibility: in other words, to recreate the social contract between politics and the nation, governance and governed. Secondly, the establishment of a growth economy thanks to the limitation of state intervention and the wider use of market rules and of the private sector. All this to sustain full employment, the rise of living standards, a better allocation of resources in favour of social and regional policies and, at the same time, to fight against the threats of inequality, financial bubbles and the power of money. For Blair as well as for Jospin, democratic socialism means mainly economic growth and full employment. Thirdly, the building of a new social order both in physical terms (urban policies, public services, housing) and 'ethical' ones, for instance in education – a focal point in New Labour's manifesto and a major goal for Jospin, former Minister of Education in 1988–91 – justice, health, sport, culture or social rights. Fourthly, Europe. Both Premiers intend to place their own country as a leader of the new Europe, free from eurocratism and open to new commitments on the continent as well as overseas. This leads – a fifth priority – towards a wider scope of policy, Britain and France aiming, as former world powers, at shaping new actions in the fields of peace, co-operation and human rights.

Of course, Jospin and Blair are not acting in the same way and with the same means. The former uses dirigisme and the state when the latter prefers pragmatism and partnership. The antagonism between the inherited traditions of Colbertism and liberalism is still very strong, for instance in the job market where British flexibility differs widely from French employability. The same could be said about the euro, the Civil Service, the tax system or social policies. But when effective actions are assessed and compared, similarities overcome differences. Why is it so?

Because these actions are generated out of a common volontarism: within 18 months of their accession to power, both Blair and Jospin implemented two-thirds of their programmes. A second argument is their common sense of reformism ('reform is our method to transform society', Jospin said) not excluding a sense of messianism, according to Blair's words: 'our revolution is peaceful, but it is a revolution'. On the reverse, the protest of Labour's left-wingers, or French Greens or Communists against their respective leaders, tends to prove their mutual and consensual centrism, backed, according to opinion polls, by a majority of their respective public opinion. Finally, one can emphasize the Blair and Jospin common will to place their actions in a long-term perspective: Blair has now won second mandate when Jospin awaits the same electoral year of 2002 to give him a new springboard to power.

In so far as effective policies are concerned, many similarities can be put into focus.[20] In the political field the solutions to the Northern Ireland question can be compared to those scheduled for Corsica and New Caledonia, or devolution in Scotland and Wales to the new steps in French decentralization, the launched reform of the House of Lords to that scheduled of the French Senate, the planned new British Bill of Rights to the widening of collective rights in France. The reforms of the legal and judiciary systems in France are derived from the English model whereas the British intend to reorganize the financing of their political parties along French lines.

In the economic field, the new status of the Bank of England derives from that recently tailored for the Banque de France while, at the same time, the French now favour privatization and the type of popular capitalism praised by the English. Although their economic cycles are still not synchronized, the two countries agree on the priority to be given to productive investment, public works and the opening of markets. And if Britain is not yet a part of 'Euroland', Tony Blair is preparing his country for the single currency according to the conditions fixed in the Amsterdam Treaty and the European Pact for Stability and Growth he signed in 1997 along with the Eleven. In the field of education, the same priority is awarded to meritocracy: the English would like to increase the number of their graduates up to the French level while the French would like to offer a new type of continuous curriculum on the British pattern. Meanwhile, the two governments have adopted parallel methods to deal with problems of health, social welfare and old-age pensions, in a common spirit of social justice and partnership. And if their job policies still differ, their approaches to unemployment are becoming closer, the English ' welfare to work' scheme following the same path as the French 'jobs for the young' programme. The signing by London of the Maastricht Social Chapter and the implementation of a minimum wage are akin to French policy, whereas the scheduled lowering of social contributions and the implementation of 'flexibility' at work, in the guise of an annual working timetable, decided by Paris, follow an English recipe. In the twin fields of defence and foreign policy, both governments walk in the same direction: co-operation within a European framework, professionalized armed forces, a common participation to international institutions (UN, NATO, WEU, WTO).

If, in all these fields, priorities and the rhythm of reform itself are not always the same, both Premiers insist on their similarities in their visions: 'in aims and goals we share a lot', Blair said, to which Jospin added, 'we walk together and we get closer and closer'. A new step from convergence towards co-operation?

Blair and Jospin: towards a mutual co-operation?

Although conscious of their personal differences and of the identity gap between the two countries,[21] Jospin and Blair have clearly realized they share what they call their 'common destiny': 'let's recognize our differences as it makes our wealth, let's nurture our friendship as it makes our strength', Jospin said significantly. From Barcelona where they met for the first time in 1995, both leaders have long forgotten their mutual differences, obvious at Amsterdam and Malmö in June 1997, soon after they both came to power, when the gap between the 'archaic worshipper of state' Jospin and the modern and adaptable Blair was so blatant. Soon after Blair's visit to Jospin in Ariège, France paved the way for a long series of meetings either formal or informal (see Blair's visit to the French Parliament on 24 March 1998, and Jospin's visit to Blair in London on the following 23 July) which created, besides a mutual friendship, a better political understanding and an even closer ideological approach. Spurred on by their respective left-wingers and public opinion, and determined at the same time to dwarf their own right-wing Oppositions, they work together on this new model of the Third Way which might build a new bridge between British Labourism and French socialism.[22] Now Jospin recognizes the importance of the market while trying to control it,[23] and Blair tries to use the market to frame a new vision of Britain as a national community.[24] And if Blairism is already acknowledged worldwide as the main source of the Third Way – nobody has yet talked of 'jospinism' – the Third Way appears now as the main goal of the European Union, a priority in 11 out of its 15 members, with a special focus for the new triumvirate Blair–Jospin–Schröder.[25]

One can therefore conclude that if some differences still remain, the links between Blair's and Jospin's approach and decisions are increasing, all based on a common ideal: democratic socialism.[26]

Notes

1. H. M. Drucker, *Doctrine and Ethos in the Labour Party* (London: Allen and Unwin, 1979); C. Cook and I. Taylor (eds), *The Labour Party* (London: Longman), 1980; D. E. Martin and D. Rubinstein (eds), *Ideology and the Labour Movement* (London: Croom Helm, 1979).

2. E. Shaw, *The Labour Party since 1979* (London: Routledge, 1994). See The Policy Review (1987–93), 'Meet the Challenge, Make the Change' (Report), Labour Manifesto (1992).
3. *Let's Face the Future*, Labour Electoral Manifesto, 1945.
4. In 1979, the Labour Party registered a maximum of 7.2 million members (of which 0.67 million were voluntary). In 1997, both figures receded respectively to 5.5 and 0.43 million.
5. H. B. Cole, *The British Labour Party* (Oxford: Pergamon, 1977).
6. P. Mandelson and R. Liddle, *The Blair Revolution* (London: Faber, 1996).
7. The Parti Socialiste Français (PSF) was founded by Jean Jaurès in 1902; it eventually merged with Jules Guesde's Parti Socialiste de France in the Section française de l'Internationale ouvrière (SFIO), which lasted until 1969. It was then replaced by the Parti Socialiste (PS), led first by Alain Savary (1969–71) then by François Mitterrand. J.-P. Brunet, *Histoire du socialisme en France* (Paris: PUF, 1989).
8. M. Perrot and A. Kriegel, *Le Socialisme français et le pouvoir* (Paris: EDI, 1966); J. Lacouture, *François Mitterrand. Une histoire de français* (Paris: Seuil, 1998).
9. Tony Blair, *New Britain. My Vision of a Young Country* (London: Fourth Estate, 1996), pp. 16, 30–1.
10. Blair was the first Labour leader elected directly by the members of the party.
11. Labour's Electoral Manifesto (April 1997) called: *New Labour. Because Britain Deserves Better.*
12. L. Jospin, *L'Invention du possible* (Paris: Flammarion, 1991).
13. L. Blum, *À l'échelle humaine* (Paris: Gallimard, 1945).
14. L. Jospin, *L'Invention*, p. 34 (author's translation).
15. On 21 September 1998, US President Bill Clinton, Tony Blair, Italy's Premier Romano Prodi and Bulgaria's President Stoianov met in New York City (*Le Monde*, 23 September 1998, p. 4).
16. Ibid.
17. From the talks held at Sedgefield during Jospin's visit to Blair (*Le Monde*, 26–27 July 1998, p. 22, author's translation).
18. T. Blair at the French National Assembly, 24 March 1998.
19. On British elites, see F.-C. Mougel, *Elites et système de pouvoir en Grande-Bretagne 1945–1987* (Bordeaux: PUB, 1990). On French elites see A. Wickham and S. Coignard, *La Nomenklatura française* (Paris: Belfond, 1986).
20. 'Tony Blair An II', *Le Monde*, 21 April 1998, pp. I–III; political seminar held by L. Jospin, 11 June 1998, and speech at the Summer University of the Socialist Party at La Rochelle, 30 August 1998.
21. During his visit to Tony Blair at Sedgefield, Lionel Jospin declared: 'I am not Blair's clone and he is not mine' (*Le Monde*, 26–27 July 1998, p. 22).
22. *Le Monde*, 7 November 1997, p. 2; 24 July 1998, p. 2; 27 August 1998, p. 15.
23. From Jospin's speech in London, 23 July 1998.
24. From Blair's speech at the Labour Conference in Blackpool, 27 September 1998.
25. See Anthony Gidden's thesis in *Le Monde*, 1 October 1998, p. 2, and 6 October 1998, p. I.
26. *Le Monde*, 29 September 1998, p. 28. This was confirmed after 1998 – see the conclusions of the Annual Conference of the British Political Studies Association held in London, 12 April 2000. See also, in the field of defence, the co-operation established by the St Malo Declaration of December 1998.

Index

Imperial Defence, Committee of, 95,
97, 102, 112–13, 115
Imperial Tobacco, 18
Indochina, 57, 61, 64–5
Industrial and Commercial Finance
Corporation (ICFC), 176
Industrial Intelligence Centre, British,
103–4
Industrial Revolution, 20, 158
Inskip, Sir Thomas, 97
Institute of Economic Affairs, 184
Inter-Allied Military Committee,
116
International Chamber of Commerce,
81
International Convention on the Suez
Canal (1888), 50
Ireland, 73, 150, 200
Ironside, General Edmund, 97, 118
Ismay, Major-General Hastings,
112–14, 118
Italy, 36–8, 40, 81–2, 94, 98, 100, 145,
150, 175, 198

Jamaica, 132
Jamet, General Louis-Marie, 116, 118
Japan, 8, 60, 62, 65–6, 138
Jaurès, Jean, 191–2, 195
Jews, 23
Joan of Arc, 1
Joffre, Marshal Joseph-Jacques-Césaire,
112
Johnson, Douglas, 125
Joint Stock Companies Act (1856), 12
Jones, Captain H. M., 57
Jospin, Lionel, 2, 10, 189–201

Kennedy, J. F., 180
Kent, county of, 3
Kersaudy, François, 128
Keynes, John Maynard, 90
Khartoum, 59
Kinnock, Neil, 190
Kitchener, General Herbert, 59
Kölnische Zeitung, 47–8
Kra Isthmus, 58
Kristallnacht, 101
Kruger, Jan, 47, 72
Kuropatkin, General, 50

Lafarge Coppée, 148
Lansdowne, Lord, 62
La Poste, 149
Laval, Pierre, 89, 94–5
League of Nations, 81, 88, 94, 98
Lelong, Brigadier General Albert,
115–16
Le Matin, 50
Leruez, Jacques, 3
Lescent-Giles, Isabelle, 5
Lesseps, Ferdinand de, 13, 58
Le Temps, 57
Lever, William (Lord Leverhulme), 23
L'Invention du possible, 194
Lloyd, Selwyn, 178
Lloyd-Thomas, Hugh, 96
Locarno, Treaty of (1925), 95–6
Lombard, Denys, 58
London, 3, 49–50, 58, 61–2, 74, 76,
82–3, 85–6, 88, 111, 113–14, 116,
134, 141, 151, 162–7, 169, 177,
200–1
London Stock Exchange, 12
Lorraine, 103
Loubet, President, 76
Louis XIV, 19, 126, 162
Louis XVI, 126
Lutherans, 23
LVHM-Guinness, 146
Lycée Henri-Quatre, 24

Maastricht Social Chapter, 200
MacDonald, Ramsay, 99, 191
MacDougall, Donald, 182
Macmillan, Harold, 162–3, 165–9,
174–6, 178
Madagascar, 60, 134
Maginot Line, 97, 103
Major, John, 194
Malaya, 58, 64–5
Malmö, 201
Manchester, 21, 24, 147
Mannheim, 147
Marchand, Captain, 1, 59
Marconi, Guglielmi, 28
Marine, French Ministry of, 59
Mark, 87
Marsh, Peter, 3
Masse, Pierre, 176–7

Maudling, Reginald, 178
May & Baker, 28
Mayle, Peter, 9
Mediterranean, 147
Mekong River, 57–8, 61–2
Melaka, Tan, 65
Meline tariff, 35, 38–40
Mers-el-Kébir, 2, 129–33, 136
Mévil, André, 45
Midlands, 147
Minh, Ho Chi, 65
Mitterzand, President François, 2, 138, 191–2, 197
Mollet, Guy, 192
Mond, Ludwig, 28
Monnet, Jean, 119, 177
Monson, Sir Edmund, 47, 52
Montebello, Marquis de, 50–1
Montgomery, General Bernard, 128
Moreau, Émile, 83, 85–7
Moret, Clément, 86–90
Morgan, Charles, 9
Morocco, 52, 60–1, 76
Moscovici, Pierre, 197
Mulhouse, 23, 29
Munich Conference (1938), 4, 100–1
Muraviev, Count, 46–51
Mussolini, Benito, 94, 127

Nairn, Mrs, 136
Napoleon III, 34–5, 37, 162
Napoleonic Wars, 4
National Economic Development Council (NEDC), 178–182, 185
National Economic Development Office (NEDO), 178–9, 183, 185
National Executive Committee, Labour, 190
National Government, 89
National Institute for Economic and Social Research (NIESR), 177
National Plan, 183–5
National Review, 45
Nazism, 2
Nazi-Soviet Pact (1939), 116
Nelson, Admiral Horatio, 130, 132
Nestlé, 145
Netherlands, the, 42, 102, 117, 141, 145–6, 150

New Britain,193
New Caledonia, 200
Newfoundland, 60–1
New Hebrides, 60
'New' Labour, 5, 193–4, 196, 199
New York, 28, 81, 89
New Zealand, 145, 150
Nicholas II, 46, 48–51
Nile River, 59, 71
Nive River, 136
Nonconformists, 21
Nobel, Alfred, 29
Nord–Pas de Calais, 147
Norman Conquest (1066), 1
Normandy, 24, 27, 134–5
Normandy landings (1944), 7, 134–5
Norman, Montagu, 81, 83–90
North Atlantic Treaty Organisation (NATO), 8, 163, 200
North British Rubber, 29
North Sea oil, 140
Norway, 119
Norwich, 146,
Notre Dame, 134

Observer, The, 3
Oran (Mers-ed-Kébir), 2, 129–33, 136
Organisation for European Economic Cooperation (OEEC), 177
Osten-Sacken, Count, 49
Oxford University, 25, 153

Paknam Incident, 57
Palmerston, Lord, 71
Panama Canal Company, 13
Paris, 4, 24–5, 28, 37–8, 46–7, 49, 60–1, 63, 77, 85–7, 89, 96, 100–2, 114, 116, 125, 127–8, 134, 161, 163, 165–200
Paris Bourse, 13
Paris Peace Conference (1919), 65, 80, 82, 106
Paris Universal Exhibition (1900), 47
Parsons, the Honourable Charles, 25
Paul-Boncour, Joseph, 98
'Perfide Albion', 1–2
Persia, 50, 61, 63
Peru, 57
Pétain, Marshal Philippe, 114, 128, 133